Soul Food

GIVE US THIS DAY
OUR DAILY BREAD

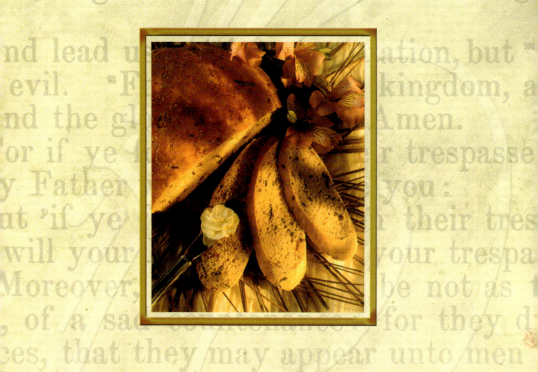

Dr. Jack Van Impe

with Rodger F. Campbell

Jack Van Impe Ministries
P.O. Box 7004, Troy, Michigan 48007
In Canada: Box 1717 Postal Station A
Windsor, Ontario N9A 6Y1

Email: jvimi@jvim.com
Website: www.jvim.com

**GIVE US THIS DAY
OUR DAILY BREAD**

Thou crownest

the year with

thy goodness.

Psalm 65:11.

THE EVERLASTING ARMS

MEMORY VERSE: *The eternal God is thy refuge, and underneath are the everlasting arms: and he shall thrust out the enemy from before thee; and shall say, Destroy them* (Deuteronomy 33:27).

When did God have His beginning?

Who was before Him?

These common questions have but one answer: God is eternal. He has always existed. Note this revelation to Isaiah: *"Ye are my witnesses, saith the LORD, and my servant whom I have chosen; that ye may know and believe me, and understand that I am he: before me there was no God formed, neither shall there be after me. I, even I, am the LORD; and beside me there is no saviour"* (Isaiah 43:10,11). Go back in time as far as you like and God is there: *"In the beginning God created the heaven and the earth"* (Genesis 1:1).

Man is tied to time. We reckon time in segments because our lives are limited to approximately threescore years and ten (see Psalm 90:10). All plans for the future must be conditioned on whether or not we will be alive.

God has no such limitation. He will always exist. His promises are forever because He will endure forever. Because He lives, we can lean on the everlasting arms and be "safe and secure from all alarms."

F. B. Meyer explained: "The Oriental shepherd was always ahead of his sheep. He was in front. Any attempt upon them had to take him into account. Now God is in front. He is in the tomorrows. It is tomorrow that fills men with dread. But God is there already, and all tomorrows of our life have to pass before Him before they can get to us."

As Fanny Crosby said, we are "safe in the arms of Jesus," the everlasting arms.

JANUARY THAW

> **MEMORY VERSE:** *I indeed baptize you with water unto repentance: but he that cometh after me is mightier than I, whose shoes I am not worthy to bear: he shall baptize you with the Holy Ghost, and with fire* (Matthew 3:11).

Now that the message of peace on earth is neatly packed away with the Christmas decorations, it is time for the yearly lapse into business as usual. Though totally inconsistent with the Bible message, that is too often our experience.

What we really need is an old-fashioned January thaw.

Let's thaw the frigid feelings that divide us from others. Icy stares and cold, meaningless greetings must go. Bitterness and strife within a church can thwart the work of God. And the world suffers.

Melting ice is no easy task. Real and imaginary wrongs have often built up such barricades that true reconciliation seems out of the question. Yet, Christ came to reconcile us to God and commanded that we forgive as we have been forgiven.

Christian leaders should abandon petty personal desires and turn their efforts toward reaching the staggering number of those who are still untouched by the gospel message. The first century church was a tiny minority in a dangerous and hostile world but they knew that the situation called for unity and they laid aside their differences in order to do the job. It was said of them: "*...they were all with one accord...*" (Acts 2:1).

Warmth can be felt in a congregation, as can the chill of low spirituality and dead formalism. What's the feel of your fellowship?

Increase your love for Christ and others. Your warmhearted action may raise the temperature enough to start the badly needed January thaw.

PEOPLE OF DESTINY

MEMORY VERSE: *And who knoweth whether thou art come to the kingdom for such a time as this?* (Esther 4:14).

God has a perfect plan for every life. Each Christian has the opportunity to become God's person for the hour. Standing at the portal of this new year, we will do well to learn from people of destiny of the past. George Burger has written: "I will, like Paul, forget those things which are behind and press forward; like David, lift up mine eyes unto the hills from whence cometh my help; like Abraham, trust implicitly in my God; like Enoch, walk in daily fellowship with my Heavenly Father; like Jehoshaphat, prepare my heart to seek God; like Moses, choose rather to suffer than to enjoy the pleasures of sin for a season; like Daniel, commune with my God at all times; like Job, be patient under all circumstances; like Caleb and Joshua, refuse to be discouraged because of superior numbers; like Joseph, turn my back on all seductive advances; like Gideon, advance even though my friends be few; like Aaron and Hur, uphold the hands of spiritual leaders; like Isaiah, consecrate myself to do God's work; like Stephen, manifest a forgiving spirit toward all who seek my hurt; like Timothy, study the Word of God; like the heavenly host, proclaim the message of peace on earth good will toward men; and like my Lord himself, overcome all earthly allurements by refusing to succumb to their enticements.

"Realizing that I cannot hope to achieve these objectives by my own strength, I will rely on Christ *for I can do all things through Christ which strengtheneth me*" (Philippians 4:13).

Esther risked her life to save her people. And God honored her faith and courage. She was ready and willing to do God's will whatever the cost. Are you?

SALT

MEMORY VERSE: *Ye are the salt of the earth: but if the salt have lost his savor, wherewith shall it be salted? It is thenceforth good for nothing, but to be cast out, and to be trodden under foot of men* (Matthew 5:13).

Jesus called His disciples "the salt of the earth." Salt preserves and purifies. Christians have the responsibility of preserving certain values and exerting a purifying influence on others. Neither of these obligations can be fulfilled through non-involvement. The quote is well known: "All that is necessary for the triumph of evil is that good men do nothing." Still, good people are often silent about issues of decency and righteousness and then wonder why evil triumphs and standards fall.

Early Christians gained a reputation for being world changers. They were known as those who turned the world upside down (Acts 17:6). Only one hundred twenty of them were present for the charge to preach the gospel to every creature. They lacked modern methods and not one church building was in existence. There were neither New Testaments nor printing presses to produce them. Even sound systems for preaching to multitudes lay nearly 2,000 years in the future. Yet, that tiny minority was so committed that within a few weeks their number had increased by thousands and in their generation they planted hundreds of churches. Their impact is still felt.

The potential for Christian outreach today is thrilling. Tools exist now that would have staggered the imaginations of our forefathers. But tools are trivial unless people are involved. E.M. Bounds wrote: "Men are God's method." The church is looking for better methods. God is looking for better men. People are the greatest potential. You are important. You are the salt of the earth.

HARD TIMES

MEMORY VERSE: *They shall not be ashamed in the evil time: and in the days of famine they shall be satisfied* (Psalm 37:19).

Difficult days come to both the righteous and the wicked. Though Christians will escape the Tribulation period, they have tribulation during their sojourn on this planet. Jesus said: *"In the world ye shall have tribulation"* (John 16:33).

Trouble is never pleasant but it may build faith. Peter speaks of the "trial of your faith." And C. H. Spurgeon wrote: "Time and trouble try the truth. Whether a man is really good or not is discovered by his perseverance in a good way. It is easy to run well just for a spurt, but to keep up the pace for years is the difficulty."

Christians experiencing hard times are assured of triumph. God directs the steps of His people. George Muller, the man of prayer and faith had made a note in his Bible beside Psalm 37:23: *"The steps of a good man are ordered by the LORD..."* Muller had written: "Yes, and the stops too!" He guides when we are marching and guards when it is necessary to stop and rest because of some affliction.

And then there is this thrilling promise: *"Though he fall, he shall not be utterly cast down..."* (Psalm 37:24). The child of God may be down but he is never out. The Lord upholds him with His hand.

Time flows continually. This year may hold some difficult days. If so, remember that our Lord is with us in the good times and the bad: *"When thou passest through the waters, I will be with thee; and through the rivers, they shall not overflow thee: when thou walkest through the fire, thou shalt not be burned; neither shall the flame kindle upon thee"* (Isaiah 43:2).

Hard times ahead? Perhaps. But the righteous will never be forsaken. Our times are in His hands. What a safe place!

HOW TO PRAY

MEMORY VERSE: *And when thou prayest, thou shalt not be as the hypocrites are: for they love to pray standing in the synagogues and in the corners of the streets, that they may be seen of men. Verily I say unto you, They have their reward* (Matthew 6:5).

A good rule is to make public prayers shorter than those we offer in private. Some seize opportunities to pray in public as a means to impress others. A minister who was asked to pray at the opening of a widely heard radio program became so eloquent that he prayed through the entire broadcast and did not finish his prayer until they had been off the air for five minutes.

The famous evangelist, D.L, Moody, did not like long public prayers. Once when a minister prayed long in one of his meetings, he rose and said: "While our brother is finishing his prayer, we will sing number 75." A medical student happened to be bored with the long prayer and just about to leave when Moody's action captured his attention. He was converted that day and became known around the world for his outstanding missionary work.

The recorded public prayers of Jesus were brief. On the other hand, when alone or in the company of His disciples, He prayed long and fervently. In the Garden of Gethsemane, He prayed so intensely that drops of blood fell from His brow and so long that the disciples who were with Him fell asleep.

Many feel that conditions in the world and the church are so serious that they constitute a call to prayer. Tense times move people to pray. But we must remember that effective prayer is not the people-pleasing variety. Prayer that moves the hand of God comes from the heart of man.

LIGHT

MEMORY VERSE: *Let your light so shine before men, that they may see your good works, and glorify your Father which is in heaven* (Matthew 5:16).

Babe Ruth once said: "Most of the people who have really counted in my life were not famous. Nobody ever heard of them, except those who knew and loved them. I knew an old minister once. His hair was white, his face shone. I have written my name on thousands of baseballs in my life. The old minister wrote his name on just a few simple hearts. How I envy him! I am listed as a famous homerunner, yet beside that obscure minister, who was so good and so wise, I never got to first base."

Ruth rightly valued the impact of his friend's influence as more important than money or applause. He saw the old minister's example being followed by others and knew that was a more lasting tribute than being in man's Hall of Fame.

Influence at its greatest flows from the unexpected. Jesus said: "*...Love your enemies, bless them that curse you, do good to them that hate you, and pray for them which despitefully use you, and persecute you*" (Matthew 5:44). Those weren't just words. Peter would later write of Him: "Who, when he was reviled, reviled not again" (I Peter 2:23).

Most of us are influenced by people whose lives reflect this admonition. People who stand out from the crowd. Even the religious crowd. Dedication and Christian discipline make them different. And they don't have to announce it. Like Ruth's friend, they write their names on the hearts of others. They are lights in a dark world.

Let your light shine. Many are walking in darkness!

ANXIETY

MEMORY VERSE: *Take therefore no thought for the morrow: for the morrow shall take thought for the things of itself. Sufficient unto the day is the evil thereof* (Matthew 6:34).

Think of the cares that would be cancelled if we could escape anxiety about tomorrow. Most feel safe about today, but the tomorrows are tough. Tomorrow the house payment is due. Tomorrow is the final day of grace on the insurance premium. Tomorrow is the day of your appointment with the doctor. Tomorrow somebody may push the button that plunges the world into another war.

But what if tomorrow does hold unknown trials? Is worry likely to change anything? Ian McClaren wrote: "What does your anxiety do? It does not empty tomorrow of its sorrow, but it empties today of its strength. It does not make you escape evil — it makes you unfit to cope with it if it comes."

The Lord's call to avoid anxiety about tomorrow followed His instruction about priorities in life today: *"But seek ye first the kingdom of God, and His righteousness; and all these things shall be added unto you"* (Matthew 6:33).

Giving God first place is an act of faith. And faith conquers anxiety. George Mueller declared: "The beginning of anxiety is the end of faith." The beginning of true faith is the end of anxiety.

There is, however, a difference between faith that is mere profession and real faith. False faith may go through all the motions and impress all the right people, but it will not hold up in the pressures of daily experience. True faith is anchored in the promises of God. And they will endure through all your tomorrows.

A WISE MAN

MEMORY VERSE: *Therefore whosoever heareth these sayings of mine, and doeth them, I will liken him unto a wise man, which built his house upon a rock* (Matthew 7:24).

General William Booth was the founder of the Salvation Army. One day his son came to tell the old general, who had struggled long with poor vision, that the doctors could do no more for his eyes.

"Do you mean that I am blind and must remain blind?" the general asked.

"I am afraid that is true," said his son.

The general moved out his hand until he felt and clasped the hand of his son. "God must know best," he said. "I have done what I could for God and the people with my eyes. Now I shall do what I can for God and the people without my eyes."

Booth's tranquility in trouble came from a life in which selfishness had surrendered. He trusted God and cared for men.

Asked one day for the secret of his success, he answered: "I will tell you the secret. God has had all there was of me to have. There have been men with greater opportunities; but from the day I got the poor of London on my heart and a vision of what Jesus Christ could do, I made up my mind that God would have all there was of William Booth. And if there is anything of power in the Salvation Army today, it is because God has all the adoration of my heart, all the power of my will, and all the influence of my life."

The old general's secret was not original. Nor did he claim it to be. His Saviour had voiced it many years before. Booth had built his life on the Rock (Christ). This Foundation stands in the storm!

SACRIFICE

MEMORY VERSE: *And Jesus saith unto him, The foxes have holes, and the birds of the air have nests; but the Son of man hath not where to lay his head* (Matthew 8:20).

Florence Nightingale, at thirty, wrote in her diary, "I am thirty years of age, the age at which Christ began His mission. Now, Lord, let me think only of thy will."

Years later, near the end of her heroic life, she was asked the secret of her life. She replied. "Well, I can only give one explanation. That is, I have kept nothing back from God."

The famous nurse had presented her life as a living sacrifice to her Saviour. She did not think it was too much to surrender all. Knowing that Christ had laid aside His heavenly riches to come to earth to save sinners, she willingly gave her all to Him.

Unless you surrender your life to Christ, you will be swept along with others in the mad race of getting. Your whole life will then revolve around what you can accumulate. Regardless of your occupation, your main purpose in life will be to gather as much money and property as possible. You will become a junk collector.

A man who had just discovered he had a terminal sickness confided his feelings to me. "It's been deceiving," he said. He had spent his whole life getting and now he had little time left to enjoy or use his wealth. There had been no time to worship God for he had felt he must work long hours every day to be successful. Now he had but a few hours left and there was no way to call back the years. The real purpose of life had eluded him. What a contrast to Florence Nightingale's surrender of her life to the will of God! In giving, she gained. The world was enriched by her sacrifice.

WISE USE OF TIME

MEMORY VERSE: *So teach us to number our days, that we may apply our hearts unto wisdom* (Psalm 90:12).

Phillips Brooks wrote: "A friend says to me, 'I have not time or room in my life for Christianity. If it were not so full! You don't know how hard I work from morning till night. When have I time, where have I room for Christianity in such a life as mine?' It is as if the engine had said it had no room for the steam. It is as if the tree said it had no room for the sap. It is as if the ocean said it had no room for the tide. It is as if the man had said he had no room for his soul. It is as if the life had said it had no time to live. It is not something added to life; it is life. A man is not living without it. And for a man to say, 'I am so full in life that I have no room for life,' you see immediately to what absurdity it reduces itself."

The first wise use of time is that moment of coming in faith to Christ that brings new birth. Jesus said: *"Verily, verily, I say unto thee, Except a man be born again, he cannot see the kingdom of God"* (John 3:3). From that point on, wisdom dictates using time to lay treasures in heaven through service for Christ.

It is *wise* to take time to pray.

It is *wise* to take time to read the Bible.

It is *wise* to take time to tell others of Jesus.

It is *wise* to take time to help those who are in need.

It is *wise* to take time to bear the burdens of those who are troubled.

It is *wise* to value spiritual things above material things.

It is *wise* to act in faith.

In view of the brevity of life, we must learn to number our days and apply our hearts to wisdom. Any other course results in a wasted life.

THE TIME OF JACOB'S TROUBLE

MEMORY VERSE: *Alas! for that day is great, so that none is like it, it is even the time of Jacob's trouble; but he shall be saved out of it* (Jeremiah 30:7).

For nearly two thousand years, Christians have been living in a parenthesis, a prophetic interval, a time "in between."

During this prophetic interval, sometimes known as the Church Age, both Jews and Gentiles who are born again through faith in Christ become part of the body of Christ or the bride of Christ. The signal that the "in between" time has ended will be the removal of the Church (the bride of Christ) from the earth. This great event is described in a number of Bible portions. One of the clearest is 1 Thessalonians 4:13-18.

The event that ends the Church Age and ushers in the seventieth week of Daniel's prophecy is the return of Christ for His Church. This coming of Christ in the air is known as the Rapture of the Church; it involves the resurrection of the Christian dead as well as the exit from earth of all believers living at that time.

With the removal of the Church, earth plunges into its most awful hour. Of this time Jesus said, *"For then shall be great tribulation, such as was not since the beginning of the world to this time, no, nor ever shall be"* (Matthew 24:21). He was speaking of the seven year period known as the Tribulation, or the Time of Jacob's trouble.

There are difficult days ahead for Israel and for the world. This unprecedented period of Tribulation is not to be confused with daily tribulations which all of God's people pass through. And those who receive Christ before He comes will escape the coming tribulation...the Time of Jacob's Trouble.

Are you ready for the Lord's return?

TIME TO PRAY

MEMORY VERSE: *Now when Daniel knew that the writing was signed, he went into his house; and his windows being open in his chamber toward Jerusalem, he kneeled upon his knees three times a day, and prayed, and gave thanks before his God, as he did aforetime* (Daniel 6:10).

When trouble came, Daniel was prayed up.

This faithful prophet was in the habit of prayer.

The fact that Daniel had a regular time for prayer reveals that he counted prayer worthy of his time. He did not consider time spent in prayer wasted. If we were to total the hours most Christians spend in prayer the sum would be woefully small.

Why?

Because too many discount the importance of prayer.

Some claim to be doers while allowing others to do the praying. The truth is that most successful Christian doers are mighty in prayer. That is the reason they accomplish so much.

Since prayer is conversation with God, our Father must be grieved that we do not spend more time praying. Would not an earthly parent's heart be broken if his children considered all other activities more important than conversing with him? How shall we answer for our lack of prayer when we appear at the Judgment Seat of Christ? (See 2 Corinthians 5:10.)

Daniel's faithful praying saved his life. God answered his prayers and the lions were unable to harm him. Even King Darius was moved by the miracle and sent a proclamation throughout the kingdom telling of Daniel's deliverance by the Lord.

A lion's den may await.

Take time to pray.

TIME TO STAND

MEMORY VERSE: *But if not, be it known unto thee, O king, that we will not serve thy gods, nor worship the golden image which thou hast set up (Daniel 3:18).*

Man's vanity has often carried him to unbelievable ends. Consider Alexander the Great, the Caesars, Napoleon, or Hitler. History has a number of examples of leaders demanding worship. In the coming Tribulation period, the final world dictator will insist on being worshipped.

King Nebuchadnezzar of Babylon also let pride become his undoing. Constructing a great image in the plain of Dura he demanded that at a certain signal all in his kingdom fall down and worship it. Three in the crowd wouldn't cooperate, Shadrach, Meshach, and Abednego, Hebrews who had been brought to Babylon in the captivity of their people. As a result of their defiance of the king's order, these three were thrown into a burning fiery furnace. God wonderfully protected them there. As the song written about their experience says: "They wouldn't bend; they wouldn't bow; they wouldn't burn."

When the king looked into the furnace he saw four men walking in the flames. His reaction is worth remembering. He said: *"Lo, I see four men loose, walking in the midst of the fire, and they have no hurt; and the form of the fourth is like the Son of God"* (Daniel 3:25). God had not forsaken His own in their time of trial. They stood for Him and He delivered them.

They were so committed to the Lord that they were determined to be true even if no deliverance came. Those three men must have been conspicuous when all the company on the plain of Dura bowed and left them standing. But they are the only ones of that crowd that we know by name today. God honored them for standing. And He will honor those who stand for Him today.

FAITHFULNESS

MEMORY VERSE: *His Lord said unto him, Well done, good and faithful servant; thou hast been faithful over a few things, I will make thee ruler over many things: enter thou into the joy of thy Lord* (Matthew 25:23).

Christians are stewards. Immediately after the return of Christ, we will all give an account of ourselves: *"For we must all appear before the judgment seat of Christ; that everyone may receive the things done in his body, according to that he hath done, whether it be good or bad"* (II Corinthians 5:10). This judgment will not determine salvation but will be to evaluate our use of time and talents in the service of our Saviour.

Looking forward to this time, Jesus stressed the importance of faithfulness. The most underestimated rewards of all time are those that will be given to the faithful from the Lord's hand. It is not surprising that there will be some tears in heaven. When we see what could have been had we been more diligent and faithful in His work it is sure to bring some regret.

> "The saddest words of tongue or pen
> Are simply these: 'It might have been.'"

Jesus set the example of being faithful. He endured the mocking, the scorn and the cross for us. How can we do less for Him? Our petty grievances seem small when measured in the light of His great sacrifice.

Why have you stopped serving? What made you resign your office? What trifle touched off your temper? What changes are necessary to have "FAITHFULNESS" describe your life? Remember, there's a "WELL DONE" waiting for the faithful.

LEAVING ALL

MEMORY VERSE: *Then Peter began to say unto him, Lo, we have left all, and have followed thee* (Mark 10:28).

When Jesus called His disciples, they left their temporal work and invested their lives with Him. They must have appeared to be fanatics and fools to their neighbors and associates. But how many of their friends' names do you know on this date nearly two thousand years later? Time has demonstrated the wisdom of their dedication.

Few who reach for fame in this world attain it, but those who choose eternal values will never regret their decisions. Of course, not all who surrender completely to Christ are called to leave their jobs and careers to give full time to preaching the gospel. But all are called to be full time Christians. And many more are called to full time Christian work than respond.

Surrender always involves struggle. The flesh does not give up easily. The love of money and ease afflicts the race of Adam and eternal rewards often go begging while attention and energy are given to the toys of this life.

Enough of this talking in generalities! What about you? What are you doing about the will of God? Are you sure you are serving God as you ought? Is there a struggle for surrender within? Are you missing God's best? Will you regret your present course? Do you fear public reaction if you yield to God's will? Do you think you will lose too much by leaving all to follow Christ?

Continuing as you are you may reach the top. But don't forget: *"...many that are first shall be last; and the last first."*

SAVING AND LOSING

MEMORY VERSE: *For whosoever will save his life shall lose it; but whosoever shall lose his life for my sake and the gospel's, the same shall save it* (Mark 8:35).

There were two sons in the Taylor family in England. The older said that he intended to spend his life making a name for his family and so set as his goal an office in Parliament. The younger, Hudson Taylor, decided to invest his life in missionary work in China. By the time of his death, Hudson Taylor was known around the world for his effective missionary work and as an outstanding Christian. He is still the subject of books and is often quoted by writers and speakers. His older brother, who sought fame, is listed in one English encyclopedia only as "The Brother of Hudson Taylor."

The Taylor sons illustrate an unaltering Biblical principle that stands out in the ministry of Jesus: We save by losing and lose by saving. When we try to draw all things to ourselves and are afraid to surrender to the will of God, we lose. The person who spends his life gathering trophies to impress others is a loser. Focusing on wealth and property to the exclusion of spiritual values produces poverty in the real areas of life. It is the giver who gains; the investor who draws interest; the man of faith who moves mountains.

What then shall we do? There is but one answer: GIVE CHRIST FIRST PLACE! When we do that, in losing our lives, we save them.

And our savings will last for eternity!

LIMITING GOD

> **MEMORY VERSE:** *And he did not many mighty works there because of their unbelief* (Matthew 13:58).

No hero's welcome awaited Jesus when He returned to Nazareth. Though His wisdom astonished His countrymen when He taught in their synagogue, they questioned His authority. Isaiah had written: *"He is despised and rejected of men; a man of sorrows, and acquainted with grief..."* (Isaiah 53:3). The Saviour's home neighborhood was the first to have a part in fulfilling that prophecy.

Familiarity sometimes brings contempt. We are often slow to recognize the gifts and abilities of those nearest to us. Even familiarity with the Bible can cause one to overlook its treasures. I once advised a discouraged minister to begin reading the Gospel of John just as if he were a new convert. He took my advice and found rich blessing in doing so.

The people of Nazareth missed the opportunity of the ages. Here in their midst was the Promised One and they rejected Him. Millions, through coming millennia, would find life in Jesus, but Nazareth would not believe. Because of their unbelief they saw few miracles and missed many blessings. Eternity will haunt them.

Many limit God by lack of faith. Talk is cheap and it is easy to extol the truths of the power of God, but it is another matter to trust God for His working in daily life. As long as unbelief determines our decisions, we will remain strangers to His bounty. Do not let familiarity rob you of faith.

Believe God with the expectancy of a little child and experience His mighty power in your life!

THE TIME OF THE END

MEMORY VERSE: *But thou, O Daniel, shut up the words, and seal the book, even to the time of the end: many shall run to and fro, and knowledge shall be increased* (Daniel 12:4).

Time is winding down. No one knows the day nor the hour of the Lord's coming, but many sense that something is in the wind and students of Bible prophecy are aware of the many signs of our day that point to the return of our Saviour.

Writing on our text, Dr. H. A. Ironside commented: "Daniel was told to shut up the words and seal the book, even to the Time of the End. This is in marked contrast with the message of the angel to the Apostle John at the close of the Book of Revelation. "*And he saith unto me, Seal not the sayings of the prophecy of this book: for the time is at hand*" (Revelation 22:10). The present age or church period is looked at as being but a moment, so to speak, in the ways of God. Messiah having come and been rejected by Israel, the next thing in prophetic order is the Time of the End. If this dispensation is made a little longer, it is but an evidence of God's long-suffering to sinners, being not willing that any should perish; but that all should turn to Him and live.

"John says that all Christians who really believe in the return of the Lord take steps to get their lives in order. That is, they do more than sit around and speculate over the identity of the Antichrist. They forsake sin and seek the will of God in every area of life. Here are John's words: "*Beloved, now are we the sons of God, and it doth not yet appear what we shall be: but we know that, when he shall appear, we shall be like him; for we shall see him as he is. And every man that hath this hope in him purifieth himself, even as he is pure*" (1 John 3:2,3). Expect His return every day.

THE MIGHTY AND THE MINISTER

MEMORY VERSE: *For even the Son of man came not to be ministered unto, but to minister, and to give his life a ransom for many* (Mark 10:45).

James and John, like many of us, longed for places of power: *"They said unto him, Grant unto us that we may sit, one on thy right hand, and the other on thy left hand, in thy glory."* Jesus rebuked them for their carnal craving and taught them the value of ministering. That, He said, was His purpose in coming to earth.

And what a minister He was. As a boy in the temple, at the age of twelve, He ministered to the religious leaders, answering their questions. He ministered to the sick. They came to Him with all manner of diseases and He healed them all. He ministered to the grieving, weeping with them, and often He went to the heart of their grief, restoring their loved ones who had been lost in death. He ministered to children and parents. Though He was here on heaven's most important mission, He had time to lay His hands on little children and pray for them. He ministered to His disciples, taking a towel and basin and washing their feet. He ministered to lost sinners, explaining the way of eternal life. He ministered to a multi-married woman at the well of Samaria and gave her living water to quench her thirst of soul. He ministered to a dying thief who longed to be forgiven for a life of sin and to be remembered in the Kingdom. He ministered to His crucifiers as He prayed for their forgiveness.

What lessons there are in the life of Jesus to show us the sin of self exaltation! He humbled Himself and gave His life a ransom. We will do well to follow His steps by ministering to others today.

WHAT TIME IS IT?

MEMORY VERSE: *But of that day and hour knoweth no man, no, not the angels of heaven, but my Father only* (Matthew 24:36).

Somewhere in time there is a sacred date known only to the Lord, the date of Christ's return for His Bride...the Church. No one on earth can tell the day or pinpoint the hour of this long promised event. We know only that it is sure to come and that wise ones get ready for it.

In his book, *Pepper 'N Salt*, Dr. Vance Havner tells of a wild duck that came down on migration into a barnyard and liked it so well that he stayed there. In the fall his former companions passed overhead and his first impulse was to rise and join them, but he had fed so well that he could rise no higher than the eaves of the barn. As time passed, the day finally came when his old fellow travelers could pass overhead without his even hearing their call. Many Christians have become content in this world and scarcely hear the call of God concerning the needs in their lives. Preaching doesn't touch them. They have settled down in the barnyard and have forgotten they belong to the Lord.

On that special day to come, they will hear the call of the Lord and will rise to meet Him. All who have been born again will be taken in the Rapture of the Church...but many will be ashamed. The weight of worldly trinkets had overloaded them. John warned: *"And now, Little children, abide in him; that, when he shall appear, we may have confidence, and not be ashamed before him at his coming"* (1 John 2:28). The coming of Christ is imminent...an event to be expected at all times. He will return right on time. PERHAPS TODAY!

Remember who you are.

The time of His coming draws nigh.

Get out of the barnyard.

HIGH TIME

MEMORY VERSE: *And that, knowing the time, that now it is high time to awake out of sleep: for now is our salvation nearer than when we believed (Romans 13:11).*

We live in a strategic period of history. This is not time for lazy, lethargic Christianity. There is too much at stake, too much to do.

Vance Havner hit the target when he wrote: "We have too many casual Christians who dabble in everything but are not committed to anything. They have a nodding acquaintance with a score of subjects but are sold on nothing." Evaluating the conditions in many churches he said, "Most church members live so far below the standard, you'd have to backslide to be in fellowship. We are so *subnormal* that if we were to become normal, people would think we were abnormal!"

And all this when closing time seems to be upon us! The prospect of the Lord's soon return ought to awaken us to the need of total involvement in taking the gospel to the world. D. L. Moody said, "I have felt like working three times as hard since I came to understand that my Lord is coming again." How has that truth affected your life?

In what areas of Christian responsibility are you lethargic? What would a genuine awakening do to your lifestyle? Which of your present activities would cease? How would your involvement in your church change? What would happen to your giving?

Time is counting down.

Days of opportunity are slipping away.

Christ is coming.

It is high time to awake out of sleep.

ACCOUNTABLE

MEMORY VERSE: *For it is written, As I live, saith the Lord, every knee shall bow to me, and every tongue shall confess to God* (Romans 14:11).

We're accountable for our words.

The Judgment Seat of Christ will test our words as well as our works.

Dr. Wilber Penfield, director of the Montreal Neurological Institute, in a report to the Smithsonian Institute, said: "Your brain contains a permanent record of your past that is like a single continuous strip of movie film, complete with sound tract. This 'film library' records your whole waking life from childhood on. You can live again those scenes from your past, one at a time, when a surgeon applies a gentle electrical current to a certain point on the temporal cortex of your brain." The report goes on to say that as you relive the scene from the past, you feel exactly the same emotions that you did during the original experience.

Could it be that the human race will be confronted with this irrefutable record in judgment when God *"shall judge the secrets of men by Jesus Christ"* (Romans 2:16)?

Signs of the times indicate the return of Christ for His Church is very near. Remember — the Christian's first appointment at the Rapture is the Judgment Seat of Christ. We will give an account of all our words and works as they affected our service since we were born again.

On that great day we will gladly own Him as Lord.

Let us prepare for that day by speaking for Him at every opportunity.

At the Judgment Seat of Christ, we'll be glad we were faithful.

ETERNAL THINGS

MEMORY VERSE: *While we look not at the things which are seen, but at the things which are not seen: for the things which are seen are temporal; but the things which are not seen are eternal* (2 Corinthians 4:18).

Most spend their time working and scheming to get visible assets; money, property, stocks, bonds, etc. Yet all these things are temporal ... tied to time. And because they are temporal their value is fleeting.

Some material possessions are fleeting in value because our time on earth is limited. No matter how enduring the possession, the lifetime of the possessor determines the life of its usefulness to that person. Homes and automobiles are of no value to those who have passed from this life. The other dimension to the brevity of use of earth's trinkets is the fact that someday they will all be destroyed. In view of this truth, Peter wrote: "*Seeing then that all these things shall be dissolved, what manner of persons ought ye to be in all holy conversation and godliness*" (2 Peter 3:11).

But some things have lasting value.

Jesus said: "*Lay not up for yourselves treasures upon earth, where moth and rust doth corrupt, and where thieves break through and steal: But lay up for yourselves treasures in heaven, where neither moth nor rust doth corrupt, and where thieves do not break through nor steal*" (Matthew 6:19-20).

Faithful service for Christ may not bring earthly acclaim or material rewards, but treasures in heaven await the Christian who gives of himself in labor for his Lord. Suffering here may be difficult but it cannot be compared with the blessings awaiting those who stand true to the Saviour:

"*For our light affliction, which is but for a moment, worketh for us a far more exceeding and eternal weight of glory*" (2 Corinthians 4:17).

DANIEL

MEMORY VERSE: *But Daniel purposed in his heart that he would not defile himself with the portion of the king's meat, nor with the wine which he drank: therefore he requested of the prince of the eunuchs that he might not defile himself* (Daniel 1:8).

Daniel was given a preview of the future. He troubles skeptics because his prophecy concerning the rise and fall of the major empires of history is absolutely accurate. But what kind of man received such inside information from God? And how can we best understand his prophecies of the end time?

Dr. H. A. Ironside gives this important recommendation: "This little company, Daniel, Hananiah, Mishael, and Azariah, four devoted young men, set themselves against all the evil of the kingdom of Babylon. They said, 'We will not defile ourselves' and these were the men to whom God would communicate His mind. I believe it is important to dwell on this, because in our own day, alas, in many cases prophetic study has been taken up by very unspiritual persons. If we are going to get the mind of God in studying this book we must remember that it consists of revelations, deliverances, and visions given to a spiritually-minded man who was separated from the iniquity of his day; and if we are to understand it, we also need to be spiritually-minded, and to walk apart from all that is unholy, all that would hinder progress in divine things. We need ever to have before us the words, *Look to yourselves, that we lose not those things which we have wrought, but that we receive a full reward* (2 John 8).

So, if we are to understand Daniel's book, we must follow his example.

How is it with your heart? Have you purposed to be clean?

THE WAY UP

MEMORY VERSE: *For whosoever exalteth himself shall he abased; and he that humbleth himself shall be exalted* (Luke 14:11).

Evangelist D. L. Moody said that he had once thought that God's blessings were on shelves and that one received more as he reached higher and higher, but that he had learned later God gave His best to those who went lower and lower. Moody concluded: "Faith gets the most, love works the most, but humility keeps the most."

Jesus stated an unaltering law: *"...he that humbleth himself shall be exalted."* But humility comes hard. Even a small amount of success can bring songs of praise from some and unless we learn to give all glory to God, pride overtakes us.

Humility is elusive. The moment you know you have it, you've lost it. To parade humility is to admit you don't know what it is. Some are humble and proud of it.

The clearest evidence of humility is thankfulness. The thankful person does not boast of his accomplishments but appreciates the health and ability to achieve them. He does not view his possessions as his personal kingdom, bought and paid for, but sees whatever degree of success he has attained as the blessing of God. He does not look down on others because they are different but gives thanks for the diversity of creation. He does not number his spiritual attainments and religious recognitions in order to claim a favored place with God, but lifts his voice in praise for grace enough to care for all his sins.

Jesus is the supreme example of humility. Those who walk as He walked will be exalted.

A TIME TO REJOICE

MEMORY VERSE: *It was meet that we should make merry, and be glad: for this thy brother was dead, and is alive again; and was lost, and is found* (Luke 15:32).

The scribes and Pharisees were continually critical of the life and ministry of Jesus. They were especially bothered by His love for sinners. In the parable of the prodigal son, the older brother pictures one who, like the Pharisees and scribes, did not really care for backsliders and lost people.

The older brother was a grumbler. It was a time to rejoice and he was complaining. Sadly, there is a similar attitude among Christians today. They complain about everything from the weather to their pastor. This unpleasant spirit of negativism kills churches and destroys testimonies. It renders the greatest potential force on earth (the church) ineffective. Christians must find enough in Christ to make them rejoice or they will never win others to Him.

The older brother was bitter toward the prodigal. Because his heart was not right with his brother, he fell prey to wrong attitudes about a number of things. He began to feel sorry for himself. He exaggerated his own righteousness and his brother's sins. He forgot the blessing of his father's fellowship. He lost sight of his own inheritance. You cannot serve God unless your heart is right with your brothers and sisters in Christ.

The older brother did not care about the wandering one. He worked around the homestead and kept up the buildings but he didn't care about his backslidden brother. And because of that he was unlike his father. Christians who only keep the church buildings in repair and serve on boards but do not care for souls are unlike their Heavenly Father.

He cares and so must we, if we are to be like Him.

PRIDE

> **MEMORY VERSE:** *If I then, your Lord and Master, have washed your feet; ye also ought to wash one another's feet* (John 13:14).

A British general once entertained a number of guests. The general's assistant seated a prominent lady at the left of the host rather than at his right, the place of honor. She fumed quietly and then said indignantly: "I suppose you have great difficulty getting your aide-de-camp to seat your guests properly!" "Not at all," the general responded. "Those who matter don't mind, and those who mind don't matter."

One of the most destructive traits is super sensitivity. Those who are constantly looking for some trifle to touch off their tempers and upset their dispositions are sure to be successful in their search. People who wear their feelings on their sleeves are often in a stew. Individuals who are continually drawing invisible emotional lines over which they dare others to step, will find their energies taken in nursing their many hurts and will have little time or strength left for worthwhile tasks.

If you are easily offended, you have a simple but serious problem — PRIDE. Secretly, you expect others to treat you rather special because you think you deserve that kind of treatment. No wonder your feathers are ruffled regularly!

Consider the Saviour washing the disciples' feet. Contrast His attitude to the frame of mind that makes you so hard to live with. Meditating on His humble act that day will enable you to put away petty pride and its resultant touchiness. You will become insulated against insults. And nothing will offend you!

THE COMPLAINERS

MEMORY VERSE: *Why was not this ointment sold for three hundred pence, and given to the poor?* (John 12:5).

Judas was a complainer. Though Pilate could find no fault in Jesus, Judas did. Some are specialists at picking flaws. Life will be better if you refuse to hear them.

Refuse to hear the "daily downers." Some thrive on complaints. They enjoy ill health and spread their contagion everywhere they go. Even God cannot please them and they spend their lives blind to His blessings. Though sometimes feigning spirituality, they know nothing of the Bible command to "do all things without murmurings and disputings" (Philippians 2:14). Their cups overflow — with vinegar.

Refuse to hear criticism of others. When hypercritical people find fault and gossip in your presence, tune them out. Change the subject. Inject conversation that fits Paul's call for continual praise: *"Finally, brethren, whatsoever things are just, whatsoever things are pure, whatsoever things are of good report; if there be any virtue, and if there be any praise, think on these things"* (Philippians 4:8).

So, practice that delightful deafness that breaks the chain of criticism and complaining. If you have been the guilty one, confess this serious sin to the Lord and claim His forgiveness.

Weigh your words; they'll be weighed again in judgment.

THE TIME IS AT HAND

MEMORY VERSE: *Blessed is he that readeth, and they that hear the words of this prophecy, and keep those things which are written therein: for the time is at hand* (Revelation 1:3).

Israel is a nation.

Russia has a form of government built on atheism.

The Common Market moves toward a United States of Europe.

What does it all mean?

To most students of the Bible it means that we are living in the last days.

The weight of evidence for the truth of Bible prophecy is now so strong that any informed person would have to close his eyes to escape seeing its fulfillment.

Christ is coming!

He will come in fulfillment of His promise to the disciples: *"I will come again, and receive you unto myself"* (John 14:3).

He will come as promised by the two angels who appeared at His ascension. These heavenly messengers announced, *"This same Jesus, who is taken up from you into heaven, shall so come in like manner as ye have seen him go into heaven"* (Acts 1:11).

He will come as described by Paul, the apostle: *"For the Lord himself shall descend from heaven with a shout, with the voice of the archangel, and with the trump of God: and the dead in Christ shall rise first: Then we which are alive and remain shall be caught up together with them in the clouds to meet the Lord in the air: and so shall we ever be with the Lord"* (1 Thessalonians 4:16,17).

Yes, Jesus will return.

"Even so, come, Lord Jesus" (Revelation 22:20).

THE CHILDREN

MEMORY VERSE: *But Jesus said, Suffer the little children, and forbid them not, to come unto me: for of such is the kingdom of heaven* (Matthew 19:14).

Following a Sunday evening service, I saw a woman crying at the rear of the church. Upon questioning her about her burden, I discovered she had recently lost a child in an accident and that the minister who had conducted the funeral had told her the child was lost because he had not been baptized. *How good it was to show her from the Bible that children go to heaven when they die!*

Jesus had time for children. The disciples, thinking He was too busy, rebuked those who brought their little ones to the Saviour, but Jesus reversed the action of His disciples and revealed His great love for boys and girls. What a thrill it must have been for the parents standing there to see the Lord fulfill their desires concerning their children. He laid His hands on them and prayed for them as the parents had requested.

And wouldn't it have been great to be one of those children? Imagine the impact of this experience when it was known later that He had risen from the grave.

The One who came down from heaven had time. The Eternal One. Yet, we often get so taken with our importance that we think we do not have time for others, especially children. When we stand at the Judgment Seat of Christ, it will surprise us to find out how badly we sorted the important from the unimportant. Hours and opportunities that escape us can never be brought back. Learn a priceless lesson from Jesus.

Take time!

February

GIVE US THIS DAY
OUR DAILY BREAD

Evening and morning, and at noon, will I pray, and cry aloud: and he shall hear my voice.

Psalm 55:17.

THE THRONE

MEMORY VERSE: *The LORD is in his holy temple, the LORD'S throne is in heaven: his eyes behold, his eyelids try, the children of men* (Psalm 11:4).

Heaven is the focal point of the universe.

God's throne is in heaven.

Justice and judgment proceed from the throne of God. There are many wrongs in the world as a result of sin. Wars rage. Oppression thrives. Dishonesty is rampant. Evil people seem to prosper. But God will make everything right. There will be a day of reckoning. The Psalmist declared: *"Justice and judgment are the habitation of thy throne..."* (Psalm 89:14).

God's throne is a throne of grace. While none deserve the privilege of prayer, God deals with us in grace. Thankfully, our merit is not a factor. We come to the throne on the basis of Christ's death for us on the cross: *"Let us therefore come boldly unto the throne of grace, that we may obtain mercy, and find grace to help in time of need"* (Hebrews 4:16).

The throne of God is a place of breathtaking beauty. John described it as follows: *"And immediately I was in the spirit: and, behold, a throne was set in heaven, and one sat on the throne. And he that sat was to look upon like a jasper and a sardine stone: and there was a rainbow round about the throne, in sight like unto an emerald... And before the throne there was a sea of glass like unto crystal..."* (Revelation 4:2, 3, 6)

The throne of God is a place of praise: *"And they sung a new song, saying, Thou art worthy..."* (Revelation 5:9).

Someday we will join the heavenly choir... and sing His praise!

A FRIEND IN HEAVEN

MEMORY VERSE: *Whom have I in heaven but thee? and there is none upon earth that I desire beside thee* (Psalm 73:25).

Upon the death of Anne Sullivan, her patient, painstaking teacher, Helen Keller said, "I look forward to the world to come where all physical limitations will drop from me like shackles; I shall again find my beloved teacher, and engage joyfully in greater service than I have yet known!"

A man of God once sat at our table and reminisced about his son who had died in the service of our country. He had been an only child and had looked forward to entering the ministry upon his return from the war. The good man shared his heart with us and said that he and his wife were looking forward to heaven to see their son.

Many anticipate heaven because a friend or loved one is there whom they long to see. Heaven will be a place of glad reunions but the greatest thrill of all will be our meeting with Jesus... our most faithful friend.

Christians have a friend in heaven. Joseph Scriven said it well: "What a friend we have in Jesus!"

People often boast of having friends in high places. Let one know the President or one of his cabinet and he will announce it to the news media so that all his friends and neighbors will know of his important connection with one in power. Name dropping becomes his favorite pastime. But we have a friend in the highest place in the universe. No earthly sphere of influence compares with the throne of God.

And our friend is there.

Aren't you glad you have a friend in heaven?

SUCH AS I HAVE

MEMORY VERSE: *Then Peter said, Silver and gold have I none; but such as I have give I thee: In the name of Jesus Christ of Nazareth rise up and walk* (Acts 3:6).

Luke, the physician, wrote the Book of Acts. It is properly called The Acts of the Apostles. And it is a book of action; the story of the Early Church on the move.

The first Christians had little of this world's goods. They had no expensive church buildings, none of the things that make a church appear successful in our day.

People are easily awed by trappings that are designed to impress, but spiritual power is far more important. The church at Laodicea, described in the Book of Revelation, looked prosperous but was poor in the areas that really mattered: *"Because thou sayest, I am rich, and increased with goods, and have need of nothing; and knowest not that thou art wretched, and miserable, and poor, and blind, and naked..."* (Revelation 3:17).

As Dr. Luke recorded the experience of Peter and John in their encounter with the lame man, he must have felt the pain and frustration of this one who had been afflicted for so long. Luke knew the limitation of man in helping some who are helpless.

"Silver and gold have I none," said Peter. And the poor man's heart must have drooped. But then the blessing came...he was healed of his affliction.

Peter had neither silver nor gold and therefore was not accountable to give what he did not have. But what he did have was exactly what the blind man needed.

Let us give "such as we have" that others may be blessed.

FELLOWSHIP

MEMORY VERSE: *And they continued steadfastly in the apostles' doctrine and fellowship, and in breaking of bread, and in prayers (Acts 2:42).*

Millions have joined in singing the great song of fellowship, "Blest Be the Tie That Binds," written by John Fawcett, an English Baptist minister. The song was written to commemorate an experience in Fawcett's life.

In 1772, after only a few years in pastoral work, John Fawcett was called to a large and influential church in London. His farewell sermon had been preached in his country church in Yorkshire and the wagons loaded with his furniture and books stood ready for departure to the new home and work.

Fawcett's congregation was brokenhearted.

Men, women, and children gathered about him and his family with sad and tearful faces.

Finally, overwhelmed with the sorrow of those they were leaving, Dr. Fawcett and his wife sat down on one of the packing cases and gave way to tears.

"Oh, John!" lamented Fawcett's wife, "I cannot bear this! I know not how to go!"

"Nor I, either," returned her husband. "And we will not go. The wagons shall be unloaded, and everything put in its old place."

The congregation was filled with joy and their continued fellowship was the basis for the song by John Fawcett that has blessed so many for so long.

The Early Church was strong in fellowship.

The church that is strong in fellowship is strong in its witness in the community.

What are you doing to deepen fellowship in your church?

REWARDS IN HEAVEN

MEMORY VERSE: *Rejoice, and be exceeding glad: for great is your reward in heaven: for so persecuted they the prophets which were before you* (Matthew 5:12).

You can't take it with you.

But you *can* send it on ahead.

The Bible is clear in its teaching that no one can earn heaven through good works: *"Not by works of righteousness which we have done, but according to his mercy he saved us..."* (Titus 3:5). Neither are we saved by faith and works: *"Knowing that a man is not justified by the works of the law, but by the faith of Jesus Christ, even we have believed in Jesus Christ, that we might be justified by the faith of Christ, and not by the works of the law: for by the works of the law shall no flesh be justified"* (Galatians 2:16). Salvation is by faith alone: *"Therefore being justified by faith, we have peace with God through our Lord Jesus Christ"* (Romans 5:1).

Equally clear is the truth that the saved can lay up rewards in heaven through faithful service for Christ. And these rewards may be the most underrated possible possessions in the universe.

One of the shocks of heaven will be the revelation of what really should have counted on earth. Riches here compared to rewards there will seem unimportant. We will wonder at our folly and the lack of wisdom in our present priorities.

We must lay down riches here to lay them up in heaven.

Interest rates here will seem small compared to God's hundredfold paid in heaven.

Where are your investments?

Heaven's dividends are eternal.

SETTLED IN HEAVEN

MEMORY VERSE: *Forever, O LORD, thy word is settled in heaven* (Psalm 119:89) .

The Bible is a completed Book. No more written revelations are to be unearthed or given. All supposed added revelations must be recognized as fraudulent. Consider Revelation 22:18: *"For I testify unto every man that heareth the words of the prophecy of this book, If any man shall add unto these things, God shall add unto him the plagues that are written in this book."*

There will never be a discovery or demonstrated scientific fact that will disprove the Bible's reliability. The supposed proofs of the theory of evolution that were taught in my college experience are now outdated. I still have the major textbook that confidently laid out the links in the chain of man's evolution. Today, a number of those links are known to be in error and have been discarded. The theory has had to be revised. Yet the Bible stands! Jesus said: *"Heaven and earth shall pass away: but my words shall not pass away"* (Mark 13:31).

There will never be a judicial act from heaven to change any part of the Bible. The constitution of the United States of America is a wonderful work and is called a living document. Nevertheless it has been amended again and again as needed. The Bible is perfect and needs no amending.

God's Word is sure. Peter declared: *"We have also a more sure word of prophecy: whereunto ye do well that ye take heed, as unto a light that shineth in a dark place..."* (II Peter 1:19).

The Bible is complete... perfect... settled in heaven.

Depend on it!

WITH JESUS

MEMORY VERSE: *Now when they saw the boldness of Peter and John, and perceived that they were unlearned and ignorant men, they marveled; and they took knowledge of them that they had been with Jesus (Acts 4:13).*

An examining committee, composed of ministers, had met to look into the qualifications of Billy Sunday to be ordained as a gospel minister. Among other questions fired at the world-famous former baseball player was a request that he identify a well-known church father, describing some of his writings.

Billy was stumped.

After fumbling around for a moment, he said, "I never heard of him! He was never on my team!"

For a time, indecision characterized the distinguished preachers. Finally one of them moved that Billy Sunday be recommended for ordination, adding that Billy had already won more souls for Christ than all his examiners.

Billy had been with Jesus.

The boldness and success of the disciples bothered the theologians who opposed them. The Sadducees rejected any teaching about resurrection and were therefore completely at odds with Peter and John, the spokesmen for the disciples.

These servants of Christ were not awed by their learned opponents. They spoke with power and had more understanding than the religious leaders who had spent their lives debating theological questions.

Why?

Because they had been with Jesus.

Many lessons are best learned at the feet of Jesus.

Want to be effective for Christ?

Take time to be with Jesus.

AS IT IS IN HEAVEN

MEMORY VERSE: *After this manner therefore pray ye: Our Father which art in heaven, Hallowed be thy name. Thy kingdom come. Thy will be done in earth as it is in heaven* (Matthew 6:9-10).

Heaven is a perfect place.

Earth isn't.

Why this difference between heaven and earth since both are from the hand of our perfect Creator?

The reason for earth's woes is sin. Every evil on earth springs from sin: *"Wherefore, as by one man sin entered into the world, and death by sin; and so death passed upon all men, for that all have sinned"* (Romans 5:12).

Sin is the reason for every hospital and cemetery. It is the cause of every prison and chain. Sin enslaves while promising liberty. It offers pleasure and gives pain. Sin has caused the great chasm between heaven and earth.

Earth weeps.

Heaven sings.

Is there really any profit in praying that the Father's will be done here as it is in heaven?

Yes.

This is a prayer for the coming Kingdom of Christ... the Millennium. When the King returns, the Father's will will be carried out all over the earth *"...for the earth shall be full of the knowledge of the LORD, as the waters cover the sea"* (Isaiah 11:9).

Discouraged with world conditions?

A better day is coming. Our Lord will come again.

Perhaps today!

TREASURES IN HEAVEN

MEMORY VERSE: *But lay up for yourselves treasures in heaven, where neither moth nor rust doth corrupt, and where thieves do not break through nor steal* (Matthew 6:20).

Shortly after the death of her aged Christian father, a young lady visited his associate in business. He was not a Christian and had lived only to amass riches.

The business partner said to the grieving daughter, "Your father was a good man. He lived for God and others. His chief joy was to bring happiness to others. I have never known a man more generous with his money. Right up to the end of his beautiful life, His thoughts were of others. In death he went to his riches. In death, I will leave the riches which I could have used for God and others."

The paradox of this conversation is the realization by the surviving partner of the real issues of life and his unwillingness to do anything about them.

There are many like him.

A. J. Gordon wrote: "I warn you that it will go hard with you when the Lord comes to reckon with you if He finds your wealth hoarded up in needless accumulation instead of being carefully devoted to giving the Gospel to the lost."

The bank of heaven awaits deposits by those who have been born again. Entrusted with time, talents and material possessions, we have the opportunity to invest them for Christ and in so doing we lay up treasures in heaven. Treasures there are untouchable.

How much will you deposit today?

Heaven's deposit may require an earthly withdrawal of funds.

Are you willing to reinvest?

THE STANDING SAVIOR

MEMORY VERSE: *And said, Behold, I see the heavens opened, and the Son of man standing on the right hand of God* (Acts 7:56).

Stephen was a first. He was one of the first deacons. He was the first person other than an apostle to be given power to perform miracles. And he was the first Christian martyr.

Having been faithful in serving tables, Stephen was given a wider ministry: *"And Stephen, full of faith and power, did great wonders and miracles among the people"* (Acts 6:8). But his increased outreach brought increased opposition. When the religious leaders heard this dynamic deacon they gathered a mob to stone him.

Before the stones started flying, Stephen was given a glimpse into heaven where he saw the Lord Jesus standing on the right hand of God.

Standing?

Yes, standing.

Doesn't the Bible say that Jesus sat down at the right hand of God following His sacrifice on the cross?

Yes, but this was a special occasion. One of His servants was in serious trouble. So the Saviour was standing. He would personally welcome him into His presence in a few minutes. So He stood. He cares.

Note also that His title, "The Son of Man," is used here. As the Son of Man, He can identify with the needs of all men — all people ... their burdens, their sorrows, their fatigue, their persecutions.

Stephen was prepared for martyrdom before it took place. He was given a special blessing for a special occasion. When the stones came crushing in upon Stephen, he was able to pray for those who were attacking him unjustly. He had been given dying grace by his living Saviour.

Christians do not face trouble alone.

Their loving Saviour understands.

Jesus always rises to the occasion.

SURRENDER

MEMORY VERSE: *And he trembling and astonished said, Lord, what wilt thou have me to do? And the Lord said unto him, Arise, and go into the city, and it shall be told thee what thou must do* (Acts 9:6).

When Stephen died the Church suffered a great loss, but God cares for His work and raises up others to replace those who are promoted to heaven. The work of Christ is never dependent on the survival of one person.

Often the Lord calls the most unlikely into His service. Saul had stood guard over the coats of those who stoned Stephen. Who would have suspected that he would soon be converted to Stephen's Saviour?

Saul's conversion teaches us that the most difficult cases are not hopeless. It is unlikely that any of those early Christians expected Saul to be saved...certainly not to become the greatest missionary ever. If the believers in Damascus knew that Saul was headed their way they may have prayed for deliverance from his persecution but probably few would have dared believe he would be born again enroute to their city.

The secret of Saul's usefulness as a Christian may be found in his initial reaction to his encounter with Christ. His response: *"Lord, what wilt thou have me to do?"* indicates immediate and total surrender. He gave his life to the Saviour with no strings attached. From that point on, his desire would be to know the will of God and do it.

Every useful servant of Christ has come to the point of unconditional surrender. D. L. Moody determined to be a man who was completely yielded to the will of God and the world still reaps the benefits.

Will you surrender to the Saviour?

Unconditionally?

PERSECUTION

MEMORY VERSE: *Therefore they that were scattered abroad went every where preaching the word* (Acts 8:4).

Some of the greatest advances for Christ have been made during times of persecution. In the first century as persecution increased, believers were forced to leave their homes and flee to other areas. As they went they preached God's Word and their number increased. The pressure brought on these early Christians simply enlarged their ever widening circle of witness.

Others have also given their best when persecuted.

One day John Wesley preached to a great throng in an outdoor meeting. He pleaded with his hearers to flee from the wrath to come. Later Wesley said, "Many of the people acted like beasts and did their best to disturb the meeting. They tried to drive a herd of cows into the crowd, but without success. Then they began to throw stones — showers of them. One of them struck me between the eyes. I wiped away the blood, and went right on, declaring that God has given to them that believe, *"not the spirit of fear, but of power, and of love, and of a sound mind"* (2 Timothy 1:7). I saw what a blessing it is when it is given us, even in the lowest degree, to suffer for His name's sake!"

We know little of suffering for Christ in this good land. The heritage given America by those who laid the foundation of our government has kept our nation a place of religious freedom. Still some persecution comes to dedicated Christians by people who do not like to see a strong witness for Christ.

If persecution comes your way today...use the opportunity to tell others of Jesus. His rewards will be greater than any suffering we may endure (see Romans 8:18).

NAMES IN HEAVEN

MEMORY VERSE: *Notwithstanding in this rejoice not, that the spirits are subject unto you; but rather rejoice, because your names are written in heaven* (Luke 10:20).

The disciples were delighted. They had returned from their preaching mission having experienced blessing and power. Luke describes it: *"And the seventy returned again with joy, saying, Lord, even the devils are subject unto us through thy name"* (Luke 10:17).

But there was something better in which they could rejoice. Their names were written in heaven.

Commenting on this text, Dr. H. A. Ironside wrote: "There is something far more blessed, however, than working miracles. That is the knowledge that one is right with God! The Lord Jesus told these exuberant disciples not to rejoice simply because demons were subject to them, but rejoice rather because their names were written in heaven. This is true of all who have trusted Christ for themselves. All such have their names written in the Lamb's Book of Life, and these names will never be erased, but will remain for all eternity."

A study of heaven reveals that many things are happening there in preparation of the Christian's arrival. Heaven is a blessed place. And it is important that our names are written there! The old song is right: "There's a new name written down in glory... and its mine!"

If you are confident that your name is in the Lamb's Book of Life, you can rejoice. You've a reason to be glad. Have you longed to perform miracles? Have you longed for great power? These cannot compare with the privilege of having your name written in heaven.

When you get to heaven you'll not be a stranger.

Your name is written there!

SAVED BY GRACE

MEMORY VERSE: *But we believe that through the grace of the Lord Jesus Christ we shall be saved, even as they* (Acts 15:11).

Several young ladies were talking. "Don't use that word 'saved' when you talk to me," one said. It is strange that such a good word has come into disrepute.

If a man is drowning, he is glad to be saved. If a building is burning, the whole community rejoices over those who are saved. Why then this change of attitude about being saved from sin?

Perhaps it is because sin is not considered that serious. Yet the Bible indicts all men as sinners and pronounces death as a result. "*For all have sinned, and come short of the glory of God* (Romans 3:23). *For the wages of sin is death; but the gift of God is eternal life through Jesus Christ our Lord*" (Romans 6:23).

Another reason men dislike the word "saved" may be its inference that the sinner must be rescued from above. Our pride in accomplishment has invaded the spiritual realm. We like to think that we have become refined enough to have gained some favor with God. Surely our honesty, compassion, and reputation must carry some weight in heaven. But they don't.

Apart from God's grace (unmerited favor), there is not an ounce of hope for the best of us. "*For by grace are ye saved through faith; and that not of yourselves: it is the gift of God: Not of works, lest any man should boast*" (Ephesians 2:8,9).

The temptation to regress into law keeping has been a problem to the Church from the earliest time. That was the reason for the calling of the council of apostles and elders at Jerusalem. Some today are still trying to sidestep God's grace and earn their way to heaven.

We're saved by grace. Spread the good news.

JOY IN HEAVEN

MEMORY VERSE: *Likewise, I say unto you, there is joy in the presence of the angels of God over one sinner that repenteth* (Luke 15:10)

A humble Moravian workman asked John Wesley before his conversion this searching question: "Do you hope to be saved?"

"Yes, I do," replied Wesley.

"On what ground do you hope for salvation," asked the Moravian.

"Because of my endeavors to serve God," said Wesley.

The Moravian made no reply. He only shook his head and walked silently away. Wesley, in speaking of the incident later said, "I thought him very uncharitable, saying in my heart, 'Would he rob me of my endeavors?'"

There came a day when Wesley understood the Gospel and was saved. Then he knew why the Moravian had reacted as he had... because salvation is solely by grace, *"not by works of righteousness which we have done"* (Titus 3:5). His brother, Charles, expressed that truth in these words:

> *"Could my tears forever flow,*
> *Could my zeal no languor know.*
> *These for sin could not atone;*
> *Thou must save, and Thou alone;*
> *In my hand no price I bring,*
> *Simply to Thy cross I cling."*

Heaven is glad over every sinner who comes to Christ for salvation. And with good reason. Another will go to heaven. Another life gains meaning. Another has his record cleared, his sins forgiven. And Christ is glorified... for salvation is all of His grace.

Take Christ as your personal Saviour today. Heaven will rejoice over you!

A PREPARED PLACE

MEMORY VERSE: *In my Father's house are many mansions: if it were not so, I would have told you. I go to prepare a place for you* (John 14:2).

Dr. Charles E. Fuller received the following letter from a listener to *"The Old Fashioned Revival Hour."*

"Next Sunday you are to talk about Heaven. I am interested in that land, because I have held a clear title to a bit of property there for over fifty-five years. I did not buy it. It was given to me without money and without price. But the donor purchased it for me at tremendous sacrifice... It is not a vacant lot. For more than half a century I have been sending materials out of which the greatest architect and builder of the universe has been building a home for me, which will never need to be remodeled nor repaired because it will suit me perfectly, individually, and will never grow old.

"Termites can never undermine its foundations for they rest upon the Rock of ages. Fire cannot destroy it. Floods cannot wash it away.

"I hope to hear your sermon... but I have no assurance that I shall be able to do so. My ticket to Heaven has no date marked for the journey — no return coupon — and no permit for baggage.

"Yes, I am ready to go, and I may not be here while you are talking next Sunday evening, but I shall meet you there some day ."

Fuller's correspondent is but one of millions who have looked forward to arriving at that prepared place called heaven. The One who formed the earth, the heavens and all that are in them in six days, has been preparing places for His bride for nearly two thousand years.

Are you prepared for heaven?

If so, heaven is prepared for you!

THE THIRD HEAVEN

MEMORY VERSE: *I knew a man in Christ above fourteen years ago, (whether in the body, I cannot tell, or whether out of the body, I cannot tell: God knoweth,) such an one caught up to the third heaven* (II Corinthians 12:2).

What is the "third heaven?" It is the abode of God.

The first heaven is the atmospheric heaven that surrounds the earth. The second heaven is where the planets and stars are located. The third heaven is the focal point of the universe and the place to which Christians go when they die.

Paul was stoned at Lystra and it is generally thought that he died during this stoning and then was resurrected. See Acts 14:19-20. Approximately fourteen years later he wrote the words of our text. Most feel he was looking back to that experience. Answering a question concerning this in his book "Bible Questions Answered," Dr. William Pettingill said: *"...if we believe, as seems very probable, that Paul is discussing his Lystra Experience in II Corinthians 12:1-10 we must leave the question unanswered as to whether he actually died under the Lystra stoning, for he says he cannot tell whether or not he was in the body. Comparing the dates between Acts 14 and II Corinthians 12 you will find that just about 'fourteen years' elapsed between them. (See II Corinthians 12:2.) Whether the stoning was actually to death or not, it is certain his recovering so quickly and so fully was miraculous, and that the infirmity of the flesh resulting from the experience, was given him only that he might not be ruined in his testimony by undue exaltation."*

Reflecting on the experience, Paul said that paradise was unspeakable. He couldn't find words to describe it. Some future for Christians!

We're headed for the "third heaven!"

SEARCHING THE SCRIPTURES

MEMORY VERSE: *These were more noble than those in Thessalonica, in that they received the word with all readiness of mind, and searched the scriptures daily, whether those things were so* (Acts 17:11).

Paul commended the Bereans because they searched the Scriptures daily. The Bible deserves our daily attention because it is the verbally inspired Word of God. Some doubt this foundational fact; yet without a dependable Bible, Christianity would crumble. Thankfully, there is ample evidence of inspiration.

The unity and harmony of this divine library is miraculous. Taking over 1,600 years in the writing, it stands without flaw or contradiction. It dwarfs all other literature, and withstands the test of the ages.

Fulfilled prophecy is another strong witness. Facts about nations, empires, and moral and social conditions were foretold centuries before their occurrence. Details about the incarnation of Christ were given with pinpoint accuracy.

The Bible also contains statements of scientific truth. Revelations concerning the suspension of the earth in space (see Job 26:7) and the roundness of the earth (see Isaiah 40:22) are just a few of its teachings that awaited acceptance while men struggled with now-discarded theories about our world.

Perhaps most convincing is the Saviour's guarantee of the authority of the Scriptures. Jesus picked the most difficult portions of the Old Testament and associated himself with them. Creation, the flood, the destruction of Sodom, and the experience of Jonah, are all declared true by Jesus Christ.

Search the Scriptures every day.

FAR BETTER

MEMORY VERSE: *For I am in a strait betwixt two, having a desire to depart, and to be with Christ; which is far better* (Philippians 1:2).

An old Scotch preacher had struggled all through his ministry to help those who were facing death. He had difficulty in this part of his ministry because he had never himself conquered the fear of death.

Near the end of his life, he moved to another house. When all the furniture had been removed from the old home, he lingered there. His children had been born there. He had prepared hundreds of sermons within those walls. It was hard for him to leave. A thousand memories moved through his mind.

Finally, one of those helping in the move came to him and said, "Everything's gone; and the new house is better than this one."

It was just what he needed. The sermon in that statement was unforgettable. He understood Paul's desire to depart and be with Christ because heaven is far better. The years that remained found him capable in aiding others to prepare for heaven.

There are many wonderful sights on earth... but heaven is far better.

Fond friendships are formed on earth... but heaven is far better.

Dream homes rise out of the minds of architects and under the sound of the builder's hammer... but heaven is far better.

Sweet music is played by gifted people and it echoes in great auditoriums produced by famous orchestras... but heaven is far better.

And for the Christian, heaven is home!

PRESENT WITH THE LORD

MEMORY VERSE: *We are confident, I say, and willing rather to be absent from the body, and to be present with the Lord* (II Corinthians 5:8).

Some doubt that Christians go to heaven when they die. They are unlike Paul. He was confident.

Some think that only 144,000 will make that blessed shore. Paul knew of no such limits on God's grace.

Some think that the soul and body are one and that both will perish in the grave. Paul looked forward to a day when he would no longer be limited by the flesh. He anticipated being "absent from the body."

Some think the saints will sleep in the earth until the coming of the Lord and that they will not see Him until the resurrection. Paul never entertained such thoughts. He knew that the moment he was absent from the body he would be present with the Lord. He was confident.

Some think that Christians will bypass heaven altogether and only reign with Christ on earth. Paul rejected such conclusions, knowing that at death he would be with Jesus — and he knew that Jesus was no longer in the grave. At the end of life he was homesick for heaven.

No wonder Paul could write: *"O death, where is thy sting? O grave, where is thy victory?"* (I Corinthians 15:55). He was confident.

If you have been entertaining doubts about heaven being the home of the saved, put those doubts out of your mind and be confident.

If you are saved and have been concerned about a long stay in the grave, erase those faulty thoughts and enjoy the hope of heaven. Be confident.

Life is short at it's longest but death is not the end for one who has been born again.

I'm confident!

LORD OF ALL

MEMORY VERSE: *That at the name of Jesus every knee should bow, of things in heaven, and things in earth, and things under the earth* (Philippians 2:10).

Leonardo da Vinci took a friend to see and criticize his masterpiece, *"The Last Supper."* Upon seeing the great work, the friend remarked, "The most striking thing in the picture is the cup!" The artist immediately took his brush and wiped out the cup, saying: "Nothing in my painting shall attract more attention than the face of my Master!"

The earth has known Jesus in His humiliation. The record of His life and ministry here is one of tears and the cross. His resurrection guaranteed the truth of His words and His deity. Still millions turn Him away even today.

He has ascended to heaven to prepare places for His own and to intercede for us. We shall go to be with Him at the end of life's journey. One day He will return to take His bride to heaven. Those living at that time will not die but will be translated in a moment, caught away to heaven.

At the end of the Tribulation period, Jesus will come as King of Kings and Lord of Lords. Then his full authority will be known and recognized by all. Every knee shall bow to Him and every tongue will confess that he is Lord of all. Some allow Him to be Lord of all now. They are headed for heaven but have a taste of heaven on earth. F. B. Meyer cried, "Oh for more of heaven on the way to heaven!" Then he explained that this is a prayer we can almost answer for ourselves by seeking more of Him who is Himself the heaven of heaven — *the Lord Jesus.*

Make Him Lord of all!

CITIZENS OF HEAVEN

MEMORY VERSE: *For our conversation is in heaven; from whence also we look for the Saviour, the Lord Jesus Christ* (Philippians 3:20)..

This world is not our home.

We're just passing through.

Strangers, Peter called us. Pilgrims. No wonder we don't always fit in. We're citizens of another country. Foreigners.

Our language is different, regardless of the mother tongue. Every earthly language has its carnal and spiritual tongue. For the vast majority of earth's citizens everything centers in materialism and is punctuated with profanity. Using that same language there is a minority who speak the language of heaven, a divine dialect centered in Jesus and punctuated with praise.

The aim of heaven's citizens should be different. While others hoard earth's trinkets and struggle to own as much as possible of this troubled planet, the citizen of heaven remembers that there is a better land in which to invest. He is driven by a statement of his Lord that contrasted the owning of the whole world to the value of one soul.

Heaven's citizens are good citizens of earth. They obey the laws, treat their neighbors with respect and kindness and work for the good of the nation in which they live. They take part in worthwhile projects and bring a positive influence in any community. Still, they are not overwhelmed by earth's problems, knowing that God is working out His purpose and that at the proper time, their Lord will come.

While traveling through this world, heaven's citizens are not immune to earth's afflictions. They catch cold, get the measles and sometimes have headaches. They even experience death because they are members of Adam's race. But they know that life's end can only take them home. *And that is where they really long to be...* heaven!

HURTING JESUS

MEMORY VERSE: *And I answered, Who art thou, Lord? And he said unto me, I am Jesus of Nazareth, whom thou persecutest* (Acts 22:8).

Paul must have told his conversion story many times. Five of these occasions are recorded for us in the Bible. He never tired of calling to mind what had happened to him on the road to Damascus. Here he is giving his testimony to a great company of people gathered in the court of the Temple in Jerusalem as he defends himself against accusations being made about him.

Most are familiar with the ingredients in Paul's conversion: there was the light from heaven and the voice of Jesus questioning him about his persecutions and then, of course, his response. Imagine how surprised the persecutor of Christians must have been when he discovered he had been persecuting Jesus...that is what the voice said, *"I am Jesus of Nazareth, whom thou persecutest."*

But how could that be?

Paul had never personally hurt Jesus...only those who professed to know Him as Saviour.

Now an important truth surfaces: Jesus feels all the hurts of His people. To persecute a Christian is to persecute Jesus.

Have you wondered just how close Jesus is? Consider this revelation given to Saul (Paul) on the road to Damascus. He not only knows every wound you experience but He feels it as well...even the one you are grieving over today.

Is your heart heavy? He feels the ache...the lump in your throat. You do not carry your burdens alone. And you do not need to seek revenge. Those who have injured you have inflicted pain on Jesus and they must face Him one day in judgment.

Be kind to other Christians. Don't be guilty of hurting Jesus.

WHICH DAY?

MEMORY VERSE: *And upon the first day of the week, when the disciples came together to break bread, Paul preached unto them, ready to depart on the morrow; and continued his speech until midnight (Acts 20:7).*

Most Christians worship on Sunday. Some look upon this practice as sin. Charges are often hurled at earnest believers, labeling them as "sun worshippers" or even the recipients of the "mark of the beast." Some who worship on Sunday are insecure as to the proper day and are easy prey for Sabbath-keeping groups whose Saturday worship may be but a tiny part of a whole system of legalism.

The honest Bible student must face the fact that Saturday is the Sabbath. But sabbath-keeping was part of the Law that was nailed to the cross: *"Blotting out the handwriting of ordinances that was against us, which was contrary to us, and took it out of the way, nailing it to his cross; And having spoiled principalities and powers, he made a shew of them openly, triumphing over them in it. Let no man therefore judge you in meat, or in drink, or in respect of any holy day, or of the new moon, or of the sabbath days: which are a shadow of things to come; but the body is of Christ"* (Colossians 2:14-17).

The first day of the week then became the day or worship for the New Testament Church. NO WONDER! This was the day of our Lord's resurrection (see John 20:1) signaling complete victory.

Perhaps the spiritual meaning of the first day of the week is the most important reason for observing it as the day of worship. The Sabbath pictures the Law perfectly. Under law, one worked and then rested. The first day of the week pictures grace. Under grace, we enter into our rest in Christ and then we work to serve Him.

THE HOPE

MEMORY VERSE: *For the hope which is laid up for you in heaven, whereof ye heard before in the word of the truth of the gospel* (Colossians 1:5).

There was good evidence that the faith of the Colossian Christians was genuine. It was demonstrated in their love for all the saints. Watching the lives of these Christians one concluded they were real. Their earthly walk gave testimony that they were headed for heaven.

People who are going to heaven ought to love one another while on earth. Some expect to love others in heaven but they don't seem to be practicing here below.

To live above with saints in love
Will be eternal glory;
To live below with saints we know
Is quite another story.

But love for one another is the identifying mark of those who are citizens of heaven: *"We know that we have passed from death unto life, because we love the brethren. He that loveth not his brother abideth in death...And this is his commandment, That we should believe on the name of his Son Jesus Christ, and love one another, as he gave us commandment"* (I John 3:14, 23).

If love for others identifies those who are born again and are going to heaven, will others know your destination by your present attitude?

If not, it's time for a change!

THE RETURN

MEMORY VERSE: *For if we believe that Jesus died and rose again, even so them also which sleep in Jesus will God bring with him* (I Thessalonians 4:14).

"If people go to heaven when they die, what is the use of the resurrection?" I was asked today.

The answer is simple.

Christians are coming back with Jesus to get their bodies.

Notice the text calls for God to bring with Him those who have died and are in heaven. Then follows an explanation of the resurrection. This great picture of the Rapture is a scene of reunion. Christians are being reunited with their bodies that have been in the graves.

And calling forth bodies from dust will be no problem for the One who formed the first man from the dust of the ground.

But what about those who have not been buried. Their bodies have been burned or lost at sea — perhaps destroyed in explosions. No matter. Our Lord knows where every atom resides. At that day, He will call them together and form again the bodies of those who have died.

And these new bodies will be superior.

No more sickness. No falling hair. No infirmities of any kind. Those who died with bodies afflicted with any of earth's diseases or deformities will be perfect in the resurrection. There are things we do not know about the resurrection body but we can be confident that it will surpass our expectations. John ended all speculation with these words: *"Beloved, now are we the sons of God, and it doth not yet appear what we shall be: but we know that, when he, shall appear, we shall be like him; for we shall see him as he is"* (I John 3:2).

Great day!

ANOTHER BEATITUDE

MEMORY VERSE: *And I heard a voice from heaven saying unto me, Write, Blessed are the dead which die in the Lord from henceforth: Yea, saith the Spirit, that they may rest from their labours; and their works do follow them* (Revelation 14:13).

Dr. George Truett asked a widow who was left with the care of several small children, "As you think of heaven, what about it appeals most to you?"

The toil worn woman put aside her sewing and said, "O, sir, that I will rest when I get over there. I am so tired. These children must have my care at all hours of the night. Their father is gone, and I have to be the breadwinner. When I am out of work, I have to go from place to place seeking work. I get so tired in body, mind and spirit. The most appealing thing to me is that I will rest in heaven!"

You may sigh a quiet "Amen."

The load you carry often seems unbearable. The bills keep coming and you must keep going. You may be working more than one job, or at least beyond your strength. The days seem long and the nights fly by. Your life seems a grind. Vacations are scarce or do not exist. Sometimes you are so tense and tired that you do not sleep well.

For now, rest in Christ. Give Him your burdens: *"There remaineth therefore a rest to the people of God"* (Hebrews 4:9).

When you reach heaven there will be another resting time.

This is not to say that heaven is full of sleepers. The invigorating atmosphere of heaven will furnish both rest and refreshment. We will be both busy and blessed.

Walk closely with Jesus. He will see that you get your rest!

ONLY THE SHIP

MEMORY VERSE: *And now I exhort you to be of good cheer; for there shall be no loss of any man's life among you, but of the ship* (Acts 27:22).

Life is all that counts.

Never mourn over the loss of money. Who can tell what good things God will do in your life because you have less. When D. L. Moody's father died, a creditor came and took the wood that had been cut for the winter. Think of entering a cold New England winter without fuel and heavy of heart because of grief. The situation sounds almost unbearable. Yet God must have done a deep work in young Moody. See what he became in later years.

Never mourn the loss of a house. It is but brick, mortar, and wood. Jesus had no permanent dwelling and said that He was more homeless than the foxes and the birds. Do you have less than He?

Never mourn the loss of an automobile. It is but metal, plastic, and rubber. Did your loved one survive the accident? That is all that matters. The car can be replaced. Don't be guilty of being upset over bent fenders and broken glass. Waste no tears over stained upholstery. Thank the Lord for survivors.

Paul encouraged his captors who were caught in a storm at sea by telling them that all of them would live through the ordeal. *"Be of good cheer,"* he exhorted them. And why not? They would only lose the ship.

Have you been distraught over the loss of some earthly possession? Or even the fear of such loss?

Rearrange your priorities. Look around you and see those living loved ones. Lift your heart in praise to God that you have only lost the ship.

March

GIVE US THIS DAY
OUR DAILY BREAD

Casting all your care upon him; for he careth for you.

I Peter 5:7.

THE PROMISE

MEMORY VERSE: *And if I go and prepare a place for you, I will come again, and receive you onto myself; that where I am, there ye may be also* (John 14:3).

Jesus is coming again.

He promised.

Two ministers, long friends, met one day after being apart for a time. They discussed their churches; then began to talk on present-day events. One said, "I don't preach on the Lord's return at all. My congregation doesn't like it. I hear you have many against you for preaching it. There's no use in setting people against you."

"My friend," said the other pastor, "by God's grace, I preach His whole Word, and if the Lord Jesus comes in my lifetime no one who is left behind will be able to say that I did not give out the truth. How about you?"

Nothing could be more sure than the return of Christ because He gave His promise that He would come again. That promise was given to encourage the disciples because of His coming crucifixion. They would soon be separated from Him and reunited only for the brief time following the resurrection. These men had left all to follow Him. He had their dedication and devotion. They needed to know about His plans for the future.

But what does the return of Christ mean to you and me?

It means there is a coming resurrection of all Christians. It means that all Christians will be caught up to meet Him when He returns, never experiencing death. It means that all should prepare for His coming.

Are you ready?

WAITING

MEMORY VERSE: *And to wait for his Son from heaven, whom he raised from the dead, even Jesus, which delivered us from the wrath to come* (I Thessalonians 1:10).

In 1860 the French scientist, Pierre Berchelt, said, "Within a hundred years of physical and chemical science, man will know what the atom is. It is my belief that when science reaches this stage, God will come down to earth with His big ring of keys and will say to humanity: 'Gentlemen, it is closing time.'"

The first part of Berchelt's prediction has come true. We live in the age of the atom. Signs on every side indicate the last part of his prediction may be near. That is, God may soon intervene, closing this present age. The prophetic event to signal that miracle will be the Rapture of the church — the personal return of Jesus Christ. Christians have been waiting for that event through the centuries. Now it seems imminent.

How should we then live? We must live waiting for the Lord's return. But we must not wait idly. D.L. Moody said, "I have felt like working three times as hard since I came to understand that my Lord is coming again."

The Thessalonian Christians gave themselves to labor, love and service while awaiting Christ's return. They were known far and wide for dedicated Christian living. They turned from idols and served God with all their heart. Had the Lord returned at that time He would have found them faithful. Ready.

Are you waiting for His return?

THIS SAME JESUS

MEMORY VERSE: *Which also said, Ye men of Galilee, why stand ye gazing up into heaven? This same Jesus, which is taken up from you into heaven, shall so come in like manner as ye have seen him go into heaven* (Acts 1:11).

What will Jesus be like when He returns? Will we see Him? Recognize Him? Take His hand?

Angels announced the answer. He will be the same as when He went away. The disciples saw Him, viewed the scars from the cross and ate with Him. And all this after the resurrection.

Some expect Christ to return as an invisible spirit. Anticipating that coming error, He refuted it, saying: *"Behold my hands and my feet, that it is I myself: handle me and see; for a spirit hath not flesh and bones, as ye see me have"* (Luke 24:39). Following this revelation, He ate broiled fish and honeycomb before them.

Writing of His return, John said: *"Behold, he cometh with clouds; and every eye shall see him, and they also who pierced him: and all kindreds of the earth shall wail because of him. Even so, Amen"* (Revelation 1:7).

The Bible calls the return of Christ the blessed hope: *"Looking for that blessed hope, and the glorious appearing of the great God and our Saviour Jesus Christ"* (Titus 2:13).

Are the skies dark today? There is a better day coming.

Does the future seem hopeless? Remember the blessed hope.

Do you feel like giving up? Look up. Jesus is coming.

Are you burdened? Depressed? It will be worth it all when we see Christ.

THE CROWN OF REJOICING

> MEMORY VERSE: *For what is our hope, or joy, or crown of rejoicing? Are not even ye in the presence of our Lord Jesus Christ at his coming?* (I Thessalonians 2-19).

An aged farmer visited his son, a popular senator in Washington D. C. The farmer was a zealous Christian. During his stay in the nation's capital, his son introduced him to the ambassador from Belgium. As soon as they had exchanged greetings, the farmer earnestly asked, "Sir, are you a Christian?" The senator was greatly embarrassed by his father's question and before the ambassador could reply, changed the subject of conversation.

Shortly thereafter the senator's father became ill and died. Hearing of his death, the ambassador sent flowers. A note was attached to them that brought tears to the eyes of the popular senator. The note said: "He was the only man in America who asked me if I was a Christian."

In the Bible's final chapter, there is a message from Jesus about rewards that will be given to Christians at His return: *"And, behold, I come quickly; and my reward is with me, to give every man according as his work shall be"* (Revelation 22:12). If we knew the real value of those coming rewards, we would surely be more diligent in our service for Him.

Paul wrote of another reward that he anticipated at the Lord's coming — that of seeing people whom he had led to Christ. He called them his "Crown of Rejoicing," and added that these converts were his glory and joy.

Many Christians miss the joy of leading others to the Saviour. Opportunities abound. And taking advantage of them is the only way to have the Crown of Rejoicing at the Lord's return.

ABOUNDING IN LOVE

MEMORY VERSE: *And the Lord make you to increase and abound in love one toward another, and toward all men, even as we do toward you* (I Thessalonians 3:12).

In ascending to the Father, after His resurrection, Jesus left his disciples all of one accord. Humanly speaking they would have had good reasons for being divided. Their personalities were very different. One of them had denied his Lord before the crucifixion and another had doubted the resurrection until he saw the risen Saviour. Nevertheless, those personal problems were laid aside and they were united in love for one another. A few days later, on the day of Pentecost, the city of Jerusalem felt the impact of a group of Christians who were of one accord and three thousand were saved in a day.

Through the centuries, there have been periods of revival in the church when carnality was conquered and the church moved forward in power. These have been times when love among Christians was evident. Love for Christ and one another has been counted more important than personal gain.

In awaiting the return of Christ, it is important that Christians abound in love. Too often churches are bogged down in personality clashes, struggles for power in the local group, petty grudges and carnal gossip. How sad to have the Lord return and find any local church in that condition!

What steps would you have to take to make love abound in your church? What would you have to forget? Who would you have to forgive?

Are you willing?

SOURCE OF COMFORT

MEMORY VERSE: *Then we which are alive and remain shall be caught up together with them in the clouds, to meet the Lord in the air: and so shall we ever be with the Lord* (I Thessalonians 4:17).

Death is an enemy. The Bible calls it the last one that shall be destroyed. For Christians, however, the sting of death is removed.

Heaven awaits the soul.

Resurrection awaits the body.

Rapture awaits all Christians living at the time of the Lord's return, at which time they will be caught up to meet Christ and will be taken to heaven. That fortunate generation will not experience physical death but will be changed in a moment: *"Behold, I show you a mystery; We shall not all sleep, but we shall all be changed, in a moment. in the twinkling of an eye, at the last trump; for the trumpet shall sound, and the dead shall be raised incorruptible, and we shall be changed"* (I Corinthians 15:51, 52).

Rivers of tears have been shed because of losing loved ones in death. This is not wrong — it is normal. God has wisely equipped us with the capacity for weeping when we sorrow. Jesus wept at a grave. Still, Christians need not sorrow in the same way as those who are without hope.

Though grief is to be expected because of separation, we have the assurance that our loved ones are in heaven. Beyond this, at the return of Jesus, the resurrection will take place and there will be a glad reunion.

If your heart is heavy because you have recently been touched by sorrow, comfort one another with these words.

DISSOLVED

MEMORY VERSE: *Seeing then, that all these things shall be dissolved, what manner of persons ought ye to be in all holy living and godliness* (II Peter 3:11).

Most people spend their lives gathering trinkets, all of which will someday be dissolved. The God who formed every visible thing out of atoms will one day release them from their responsibility for a time and allow all things to be dissolved. This is not going to happen soon for the Rapture of the church, the Tribulation and the one thousand year reign of Christ on earth precede the event. Nevertheless, it is good to be reminded that everything we see about us is temporary.

In view of this, wise people look for better investments than can be found on planet earth. Jesus said: *"Lay not up for yourselves treasures upon earth, where moth and rust doth corrupt, and where thieves break through and steal: but lay up for yourselves treasures in heaven, where neither moth nor rust doth corrupt, and where thieves do not break through nor steal"* (Matthew 6:19-20).

Peter said that the coming dissolution of all things calls for holy living. What an object lesson! Every sign of decay is to remind us of our Holy God and our responsibility to live in His will. Every sign of rust on our automobiles is a message to live holily. Every building that is falling apart and returning to the soil is a reminder that we should be holy in our conduct.

Someone said it well long ago: "There's only one life; It will soon be past; Only what's done for Christ will last."

What do you possess that cannot be dissolved?

ASHAMED

MEMORY VERSE: *And now, little children, abide in him; that, when he shall appear, we may have confidence, and not be ashamed before him at his coming* (I John 2:28).

When Shackleton was driven back in his attempt to reach the South Pole, he was forced to leave some men on Elephant Island, promising to come back for them. Time and again he tried, but was unable to reach them.

At last, although it was the wrong time of the year, he made another great attempt. An open channel formed between the sea and where he had left his men. He rushed in with his boat at the risk of being caught by the moving ice, got his men, and rushed out again before the ice crashed together. It only took half an hour.

Afterward, he turned to one of the rescued men and said, "How was it you were able to come so quickly?" The man answered, "Sir, Mr. Wild (Shackleton's second-in-command) never let a chance slip. You had promised to come and we were waiting for you. Whenever there was a chance of your coming, Mr. Wild said, 'Boys, roll up your sleeping bags, the boss may be here today,' and, Sir, our sleeping bags were all rolled up; we were ready!"

When Christ returns, some will not be ready. Lost people who are not ready because they have not been born again through faith in Christ will be left for the awful time of tribulation. Christians who are not living as they ought will be ashamed when they are caught up into the presence of their Saviour.

If Christ had come last week would you have been ashamed? Last night? Abide in Him, that, when He shall appear, you may have confidence, and not be ashamed before Him at His coming.

LIKE HIM

MEMORY VERSE: *Beloved, now are we the sons of God, and it doth not yet appear what we shall be: but we know that, when he shall appear, we shall be like him; for we shall see him as he is* (I John 3:2).

The child of God is accepted in the beloved, but may be rejected by his associates. He has come into earth's greatest fellowship, but in doing so has become a riddle to his friends. He has become a citizen of heaven, but is now a pilgrim and a stranger in this world.

This turn of events should not surprise us. Jesus said: *"If the world hate you, ye know that it hated me before it hated you. If ye were of the world, the world would love his own: but because ye are not of the world, but I have chosen you out of the world, therefore the world hateth you. Remember the word that I said unto you, The servant is not greater than his Lord. If they have persecuted me, they will also persecute you; if they have kept my saying, they will keep yours also"* (John 15:18-20).

The Christian may not be popular on planet earth.

Never mind. A better day is coming. And on that good day, we shall be like Jesus.

What will it mean to be like Him? We cannot fully understand. But we know that we will have perfect bodies that will never be affected by sickness or infirmities and that death will be no more. This anticipation should fill our hearts with joy!

If we are alive when Christ returns, we shall escape death. If death has overtaken us, our bodies will be resurrected in that perfect form. David, the Psalmist, said it well: *"As for me, I will behold thy face in righteousness: I shall be satisfied, when I awake with thy likeness"* (Psalm 17:15).

TAKE WRONG

MEMORY VERSE: *Now therefore there is utterly a fault among you, because ye go to law one with another. Why do ye not rather take wrong? why do ye not rather suffer yourselves to be defrauded* (1 Corinthians 6:7).

Here is a forgotten verse. Few obey its teaching. But think of the conflicts that would be settled if a revival would bring this verse into daily experience. Lawsuits would be dropped. Feuds would be ended. Church quarrels would be forgotten.

Meditate on these life changing questions: *"Why do ye not rather take wrong? why do ye not rather suffer yourselves to be defrauded?"*

Most professing Christians react just like the world reacts: demanding their rights. No wonder so few are moved to salvation by observing Christians in action.

How will your life change if you decide to take wrong and allow yourself to be defrauded?

Will you drop a lawsuit?

Will you forget an old debt?

Will you forego sending a blistering letter?

Will you be reconciled to one who has wronged you?

Will you stop fighting over an inheritance?

Will you stop telling your sob story about being cheated by others?

Notice Paul's interesting advice. He says certain Christians at Corinth are defrauding others by not allowing themselves to be defrauded.

How so?

When we react in the flesh...demanding our rights...we defraud those who are watching our lives and hoping to find an example of genuine Christian living.

Stop defrauding those who your witness need....take wrong... thankfully.

THE PURIFYING HOPE

MEMORY VERSE: *And every man that hath this hope in him purifieth himself, even as he is pure* (I John 3:3).

"What difference does it make if Jesus is going to return?" a minister asked. Sadly, he had missed one of the greatest incentives for holy living given in the Bible. The constant expectation of the Lord's return is a purifying hope.

Did you expect the Lord to come last week? How did it change your life? What did you leave out of your conversation, not wanting to stand in His presence with wicked words? What thoughts did you dismiss from your mind? What temptations did you conquer?

Or were there no changes due to His expected return? Perhaps the second coming of Christ is but a doctrine to which you say you subscribe, a part of your church statement of faith. To some, the rapture is only a point to argue, a good bumper-sticker topic or slogan producer. Like the Pharisees, they have all their prophetic events properly placed in their minds but their lives are not affected by these tremendous truths. How about you?

If you are not living differently because Christ may return at any moment, you have missed the point of the Lord's command: *"Watch therefore: for ye know not what hour your Lord doth come"* (Matthew 24:42).

Try this tough question. If the prospect of Christ's imminent return has not changed your way of living, do you really believe He's coming again?

What adjustments need to be made in your life today, in view of His promised return? In making them you will demonstrate the power of the purifying hope.

INCREASED KNOWLEDGE

MEMORY VERSE: *But thou, O Daniel, shut up the words, and seal the book, even to the time of the end: many shall run to and fro, and knowledge shall be increased* (Daniel 12:4).

For centuries it seemed as if the world slumbered. Thousands of years passed without major changes in most areas of life. Paul and Columbus sailed in similar ships though their voyages were nearly fifteen hundred years apart. Medical know-how moved at a snail's pace. Men watched the birds fly but all efforts to copy them were in vain.

Then, in the lifetime of many alive today, there came an explosion in knowledge and travel. People who went about in buggies and other horse-drawn vehicles lived to see the skies filled with jet planes and watched men walk on the moon. The atom was split, ushering in the nuclear age with all its perils and possibilities. Miracle drugs were discovered that conquered old killers and vaccines were developed that eliminated former plague producers.

Now we are in the age of the computer. This mind boggling invention is entering every area of life. Old methods of office procedures have been made obsolete. Records on millions of people are available at the push of the proper buttons, a scary fact if wicked men come into power.

Each day, some new invention seems to outdo another. What does it all mean? It means that we are living in what the Bible calls *"the time of the end."* One who is in possession of the Biblical facts would have to close his eyes to the truth not to recognize the signs of the times.

What are you doing about it?

STUMBLING BLOCKS

MEMORY VERSE: *But take heed lest by any means this liberty of yours become a stumbling block to them that are weak* (1 Corinthians 8:9).

This chapter raises an interesting question of conduct. The Christians in Corinth were facing the issue of whether or not to eat meat that had been offered to heathen idols. There was nothing wrong with the meat and it was often priced very reasonably. What was the proper attitude for the church?

In his book, *Studies in First Corinthians*, Dr. M. R. DeHaan sums up Paul's answer as follows: "The question then is never, Have I a right to do this or that, or is this or that in itself a sin? But the question is, Does my conduct glorify God, and does it help or hinder my testimony, and is it a help or a stumbling block to my weaker brethren? This, then, would at once settle the question of amusements, dress, business practices, and games, and all our Christian privileges. The Lord lays down the rule specifically: "*And whatsoever ye do in word or deed, do all in the name of the Lord Jesus*" (Colossians 3:17).

"That is the test by which we are to evaluate everything which is of a questionable nature. It is not a matter of legality, but a matter of honestly facing the question, Is this thing which we are doing to the glory of God, and is it a help or hindrance to those round about us?"

Not one of us will have to deal with the question of eating meat that has been offered to idols in heathen temples. That was a question pertaining especially to Paul's day and to a particular area. But every decision concerning Christian con- duct requires the same basic question. Is this thing to the glory of God, and is it a help or hindrance to others?

Facing a decision about conduct? Give it the "stumbling block" test.

ABOUNDING INIQUITY

MEMORY VERSE: *And because iniquity shall abound, the love of many shall wax cold* (Matthew 24:12).

Some expect the world to get better and better until the Kingdom of God is proclaimed on earth. Since this theory is without Biblical foundation, it will never see fulfillment. Instead, the world will continue to witness falling moral codes, increased violence and rising cultic activity. As Paul wrote: *"...the mystery of iniquity doth already work."*

Though the immediate future is cloudy, the Christian who understands His Bible is filled with optimism. He is the only person who knows that hope will not be disappointed. While the dreams of world planners crumble in the persistent pressure of the last days, he sees beyond the travail of this hour to the triumph of the Lord's return.

The question may rise, however, about what we are to do in the face of evil. Shall we close our eyes to world needs and allow iniquity to run rampant because we intend to eventually exit planet earth? Not at all. Our responsibility is to restrain evil and to let the light of the Gospel shine through us. We are to hold forth the word of life as lights that shine in a dark place. Jesus said, *"Let your light so shine before men, that they may see your good works, and glorify your Father, which is in heaven"* (Matthew 5:16).

Have you been discouraged about accomplishing any good in such dark days? Remember, the darker the day, the more visible the light.

It's a good day for shining!

THEREFORE

MEMORY VERSE: *Therefore, my beloved brethren, be ye steadfast, unmovable, always abounding in the work of the Lord, forasmuch as ye know that your labour is not in vain in the Lord* (I Corinthians 15:58).

When you find the word "therefore" in the Bible, it is a good idea to read the preceding verses and find out what it is there for. In the text above, this linking word reaches back to the message of the Lord's return and calls for the kind of life described in our memory verse in view of that return.

Because the Lord is coming, we are to be steadfast, unmovable, always abounding in the work of the Lord. Like soldiers assigned to duty in wartime, we have been charged to serve God faithfully. Distractions must be resisted. Laziness overcome. Compromise with evil is out of the question.

In Chicago, One Sunday morning, a minister pointed to a young woman who had been converted about a year and a half, and said, "What are you doing for God? Why don't you do something for God?"

To give emphasis to his words, the minister stepped down from the pulpit, went to where the young woman was sitting, took her hand, conducted her out to the middle aisle, made her turn toward the door, and giving her a push, said, "I want you to start doing something for God."

That push sent the young woman to the other side of the globe. She became a missionary to Africa and led many to Christ, including General Allenby of Britain. Her name was Miss Malla Moe. The pastor who gave her the push was D. L. Moody.

Christ is coming! That should be all the push we need.

PERILOUS TIMES

MEMORY VERSE: *This know also that in the last days perilous times shall come* (II Timothy 3:1).

Most students of the Bible do not have to be convinced that we are living in perilous times. The splitting of the atom has given man the power to bring about total destruction. In addition, we have learned to live twenty four hours a day in the rocket sights of our enemies who are bent on world domination.

Nevertheless, Christians need not panic. Not one recent event has taken God by surprise. He is in control and is allowing man to work out His program. The words of the Psalmist are relevant today: *"Be still, and know that I am God"* (Psalm 46:10).

Though times are perilous, we never walk alone: *"Fear thou not; for I am with thee: be not dismayed; for I am thy God: I will strengthen thee; yea, I will help thee; yea, I will uphold thee with the right hand of my righteousness. For I the LORD thy God will hold thy right hand, saying unto thee, Fear not; I will help thee"* (Isaiah 41:10 & 13).

Though times are perilous, we can never be separated from His love: *"For I am persuaded that neither death, nor life, nor angels, nor principalities, nor powers, nor things present, nor things to come, nor height, nor depth nor any other creature, shall be able to separate us from the love of God, which is in Christ Jesus our Lord"* (Romans 8:38-39).

Though times are perilous, these conditions are but reminders of better days ahead: *"And then these things begin to come to pass, then look up, and lift up your heads; for your redemption draweth nigh"* (Luke 21:28).

DISCIPLINE

MEMORY VERSE: *But I keep under my body, and bring it into subjection: lest that by any means, when I have preached to others, I myself should be a castaway* (1 Corinthians 9:27).

Paul was like a man in training...ever prepared to give his best in the race. He understood that this demanded discipline...self-control. But he wanted the prize and counted all sacrifices worthwhile. Eternal rewards meant more to him than momentary gratification. Until we come to this same conviction, we are poor candidates for victory in the race of life.

In his letter to the Philippians, Paul again alludes to his effort in the race: "*Brethren, I count not myself to have apprehended: but this one thing I do, forgetting those things which are behind, and reaching forth unto those things which are before, I press toward the mark for the prize of the high calling of God in Christ Jesus*" (Philippians 3:13,14).

Discipline holds an important place in the successful Christian life. It is essential in maintaining daily Bible reading. There will be times when one does not feel like reading; times when some relaxing pastime appeals right at the time for personal devotions. But no one can have victory over sin without a regular intake of God's Word. Discipline takes the tempted one to his Bible where he can receive the life-giving milk and meat that provides spiritual health.

Consistency in prayer comes through discipline. How glibly we recite our learned prayers and then wonder why answers do not come!

Discipline demands regular attendance at the services of the church where fellowship and Bible teaching combine to develop the abundant life.

We all need discipline to guarantee spiritual growth.

TEMPTATION'S LIMIT

MEMORY VERSE: *There hath no temptation taken you but such as is common to man: but God is faithful, who will not suffer you to be tempted above that ye are able; but will with the temptation also make a way to escape, that ye may be able to bear it* (1 Corinthians 10:13).

Two alcoholics were converted. One testified, "From the moment I trusted Christ to save me, and deliver me from the enslaving habit of strong drink, I have never had the slightest desire to drink anything of alcoholic content. I would have to learn all over again to love the evil which, for more than thirty years, was the greatest love of my life." The second said, "How I wish my experience corresponded with the experience of the brother who has just testified. Every day I have a terrific struggle not to partake of the evil which for years all but wrecked my life. I am depending solely upon the mighty Saviour to keep me from temptation. Pray for me!"

God may deal differently with His children concerning temptation but He has promised that all temptation is limited. Every Christian can overcome any temptation. Our Lord guarantees our ability to conquer is greater than temptation's power. He allows no temptation to come to us that is too strong for us to defeat. And He always provides an escape.

So, your excuse for yielding doesn't stand.

The power of the Holy Spirit within and the Word of God at your disposal equips you to conquer. Prayer taps the resources of God making you invincible.

Others have faced the same temptation.

And you are equipped to win.

FOOLISHNESS

MEMORY VERSE: *For the preaching of the cross is to them that perish foolishness; but unto us which are saved it is the power of God* (1 Corinthians 1:18).

In the second century, Justin Martyr wrote: "Many spirits are abroad in the world, and the credentials they display are splendid gifts of mind, learning, and of talent. Christian, look carefully. Ask for the print of the nails."

The conflicts in the church at Corinth were beyond the reach of tact or psychology, the message of the cross was the only answer. Lost people need to hear this message to be saved and Christians never outgrow their need of the preaching of the cross for daily growth.

The cross is the cure for divisions. Churches that are torn by gossip and backbiting need to be reminded of the Lord's sacrifice on the cross. Those who nurse hurt feelings need to stand at the cross and see their Saviour enduring the shame and pain of that awful hour. Who has the right to be offended in the light of His sufferings there?

Have you been wronged? Consider the cross.

Do you wonder about full forgiveness? Consider the cross.

Do you doubt God's love? Consider the cross.

The message of the cross is not popular today. Many prefer religion that is not so stern...so demanding. The preaching of the cross reveals all people as sinners and Christ as the only Saviour. Man's sinful nature and his pride object to that kind of teaching. Beautiful sanctuaries are fine but the cross seems out of date...foolishness.

But the way of the cross leads home...there is no other way but this.

Let this old and true message change your life. And God's way will not seem foolish anymore.

THE OLD LEAVEN

MEMORY VERSE: *Purge out therefore the old leaven, that ye may be a new lump, as ye are unleavened. For even Christ our passover is sacrificed for us* (1 Corinthians 5:7).

In the Bible, leaven symbolizes sin.

Christians are new creatures in Christ and ought to demonstrate this by righteous living: *"Therefore if any man be in Christ, he is a new creature: old things are passed away; behold, all things are become new"* (2 Corinthians 5:17).

One cannot sin and win.

When Chrysostom was arrested by the Roman Emperor, the powerful ruler tried to make Chrysostom recant, but without success. Frustrated, the Emperor questioned his advisors about what could be done with the prisoner.

"Shall I put him in a dungeon?" the Emperor asked.

"No," one of his counselors replied, "for he will be glad to go. He longs for quietness wherein he can delight in the mercies of his God."

"Then he shall be executed!" said the Emperor.

"No," was the answer, "for he will also be glad to die. He declares that in the event of death he will be in the presence of his Lord."

"What shall we do then?" the ruler asked.

"There is only one thing that will give Chrysostom pain," the counselor said. "To cause Chrysostom to suffer, make him sin. He is afraid of nothing except sin."

Sin brings suffering.

Christians are equipped for daily victory over sin.

Purge out the old leaven.

You've been defeated long enough.

666

MEMORY VERSE: *Here is wisdom, Let him that hath understanding count the number of the beast: for it is the number of a man; and his number is six hundred threescore and six* (Revelation 13:18).

Who is the coming world ruler known as the "beast?"

Speculation abounds.

Actually no one can know who the beast is until after the Rapture of the church: *"And then shall that wicked be revealed, whom the Lord shall consume with the spirit of his mouth, and shall destroy with the brightness of his coming* (II Thessalonians 2:8).

While we cannot know who the beast will be, it is clear that the world is getting ready for his appearance. Peace efforts continually fail. Economic conditions become increasingly complex and it is not difficult to understand how buying and selling will ultimately be totally controlled by a super-powerful government. Commerce is already moving on a system of numbers and proposals to make money as we know it obsolete are now on the drawing boards. Computers that speak are common and it no longer seems out of the question to have an image erected during the Tribulation period that will be able to do so. The stage is set for the coming of the man of sin whose number is 666.

It must be emphasized that Christ returns for His church *before* these things spoken of in Revelation 13 come to pass. With the world now ready for the fulfillment of this prophecy, all Christians must get ready for the coming of their Lord and Saviour. We are to be occupied with Him. We are to look for the coming of Christ — nor the Antichrist.

When will Christ Return? Perhaps Today!

THE LAMB'S WRATH

MEMORY VERSE: *For the great day of his wrath is come; and who shall be able to stand* (Revelation 6:17).

Who ever heard of an angry lamb? It is hard to imagine. Jesus is called the Lamb of God, John the Baptist said: *"...Behold the Lamb of God, which taketh away the sin of the world"* (John 1:29). Christ came as the Lamb of God to pay for our sins on the cross.

The Lamb of God is a fitting title for the gentle Saviour. His tender heart was broken over the needs of people. He had time for the children, for beggars, for lepers and others who were hurting.

As the Lamb of God, he stood silent before his persecutors. Isaiah described Him as follows: *"He was oppressed, and he was afflicted, yet he opened not his mouth: he is brought as a lamb to the slaughter, and as a sheep before her shearers is dumb, so he openeth not his mouth"* (Isaiah 53:7).

Few in this world anticipate a coming day when the Lamb will display wrath. Yet that day is coming. And those who have not been saved and therefore miss the Rapture of the church will be here for the Tribulation — the wrath of the Lamb.

A Christian who was being ridiculed for going to a prayer meeting, said, "It is better to go to prayer meeting now than to wait for the largest prayer meeting the world will ever know. In that one, men will pray for the rocks and the mountains to fall on them to hide them from the wrath of The Lamb."

Our God is a God of love — and justice.

Respond to His love today so you will not be here for the day of His wrath.

THE KING IS COMING

MEMORY VERSE: *And he hath on his vesture and on his thigh a name written, KING OF KINGS, AND LORD OF LORDS* (Revelation 19:16).

World conditions could make us despair if we did not have the Bible. Though men have been seeking peace among the nations for generations, wars continue.

PEACE, What a word it is for men to hear;
With peace within there is no room for fear;
Yet peace escapes the fervent search of man;
He cannot find it, though he thinks he can.

William Howard Taft once wrote, "The battlefield as a place of settlement of disputes is gradually yielding to arbitral courts of justice. The interests of great masses are not being sacrificed as in former times to the selfishness, ambitions, and aggrandizement of the sovereigns." But Mr. Taft wrote those words in 1911 and the world's most deadly conflicts have been fought since then.

The Bible speaks of continuing wars and rumors of wars. Old Testament prophets wrote of the last days as being a time of unparalleled weaponry. Small nations as well as the great are pictured in preparation for war. And what a war it will be!

Thankfully, Christ will come and end the final war, known as The Battle of Armageddon. He will return in power and great glory, bringing His church with Him. Man's evil nature will finally have run its course. The Lord will set up His Kingdom and the earth will know real peace.

Through faith, we know His peace within today.

THE MARRIAGE SUPPER

MEMORY VERSE: *Let us be glad and rejoice, and give honour to him; for the marriage of the Lamb is come, and his wife hath made herself ready* (Revelation 19:7).

God has chosen to the closest of all human relationships, marriage, to illustrate the Christian life. A bride and groom are drawn together by love. God's love draws lost people to salvation. A wedding is a time of exchanging promises and of joining together. Salvation occurs when a sinner responds to the promise of eternal life and takes the Lord Jesus Christ as his personal Saviour. Marriage is the beginning of a life that will be experienced by two who have been made one. After the new birth, the believer and his Saviour go through life together. The Lord never forsakes His own.

There is, however, another great wedding day coming. This will be the fulfilling of the type that we now see in the Christian life. Christ is the bridegroom. The church is His bride. The marriage takes place in heaven after the Rapture of the church and while the Tribulation is raging on earth. It will be a great occasion.

The revelation of the coming marriage of the Lamb makes it absolutely certain that the church will not go through the Tribulation. We'll miss the Tribulation because we have a date in heaven. We have to attend a wedding. *Our wedding.*

One of the finest Christians I have ever met said that he was confident the church would not go through the Tribulation because he knew the Lord was sure to care for His bride. Good thinking. And Biblically sound! Though we may go through much trouble, we shall escape the world's most difficult time.

Better get ready for the wedding!

ENOCH SAW IT ALL

MEMORY VERSE: And Enoch also, the seventh from Adam, prophesied of these, saying, Behold, the Lord cometh with ten thousands of his saints (Jude 14).

Fulfilled prophecy and the ability of men of God to see events thousands of years in advance is one of the most convincing proofs of the inspiration and accuracy of the Bible. Here is one of the most remarkable prophecies in the Bible. Enoch, whose life is recorded in Genesis 5:21-24, saw beyond the Rapture of the church to the second coming of Christ in power and great glory. God gave him a glimpse of the return of Christ with His saints.

This is especially significant when one considers that Enoch is one of only two men in history who did not die. The Bible says of him: *"By faith Enoch was translated that he should not see death; and was not found, because God had translated him: for before his translation he had this testimony, that he pleased God"* (Hebrews 11:5).

Enoch was then a type or picture of the church. He was taken to heaven without physical death. God then revealed to him that there would be a coming miracle greater than the one he had experienced, when all living Christians would be translated — taken up without physical death — and that this great company would then return with Christ when He comes to set up His Kingdom. What a thrill it must have been to this man of God who lived so long ago when God gave him that wonderful preview of things to come.

It will be an even greater thrill to be a part of that great company returning with Christ someday in the future. Aren't you glad you belong to Him?

SATAN CHAINED

MEMORY VERSE: *And he laid hold on the dragon, that old serpent, which is the Devil, and Satan, and bound him a thousand years* (Revelation 20:2).

You may not believe in the reality of Satan. If you do not, try resisting him! The Bible is clear in its description of this evil personality and it is a delusion to deny his existence.

Walter Brown Knight wrote: "God's children are engaged in an incessant warfare. Our adversary, the devil, is an implacable foe. In our warfare, no armistice can be declared. Some are lulled to sleep by the suavity and graciousness of false religionists who deny the existence of our adversary. It is hazardous for God's children to cease to be watchful and wakeful."

Satan's trail is traceable from the Garden of Eden to this present day. Sin and death are his trademarks, temptation his tool. Many become weary in the battle of resisting temptation. Perhaps you are one of those tired soldiers. If so, I have good news for you. There is a day coming when the devil will be unable to tempt anyone.

During the Kingdom of Christ on this earth, Satanic influence will be forbidden. This act reminds us that Satan's power is limited. We are not to be defeated and downcast. John put it well: *"Ye are of God, little children, and have overcome them: because greater is he that is in you, than he that is in the world"* (I John 4:4).

Whatever temptation is troubling you can be overcome: *"There hath no temptation taken you but such as is common to man: but God is faithful, who will not suffer you to be tempted above that ye are able; but will with the temptation make a tray to escape, that ye may be able to bear it"* (I Corinthians 10:13).

Satan will be chained later. But even now, in Christ, we're free!

GROANING TILL GLORY

MEMORY VERSE: *For the earnest expectation of the   creature waiteth for the manifestation of the sons of God* (Romans 8:19).

We live in a world where suffering is a part of life. Every hospital reminds us of human suffering. A thousand screaming sirens in the night shriek their message of the reality of suffering. Until the Lord returns, suffering will continue. It is the result of sin.

Even nature suffers. The fall of man affected all of creation. Earthquakes, violent storms, intemperate weather and other convulsions of nature remind us of the effect of sin on creation.

But suffering will end someday. Interestingly, the Bible says that all of creation awaits that day. When Jesus listed the signs of His return, He spoke of increased natural upheavals. Paul compares that to the travail of giving birth; *"For we know that the whole creation groaneth and travaileth in pain together until now"* (Romans 8:22). Nature is eager for the Lord's return.

Glory later is as sure as suffering now: *"For I reckon that the sufferings of this present time are not worthy to be compared with the glory which shall be revealed in us"* (Romans 8:18). Knowing that we would understand degrees of suffering, the Holy Spirit moved Paul to compare suffering and glory. His comparison simply demonstrates there is no comparison. And that is quite a commentary on the coming glory. We have all seen intense suffering even if we have not experienced it. Still, the Bible says, the most heart-moving examples of suffering cannot compare in degree with the glory that awaits us.

While traveling through this world, even Christians may expect some suffering and trouble. Don't fret. The glory ahead will make it all worthwhile!

REIGNING WITH CHRIST

MEMORY VERSE: *Blessed and holy is he that hath part in the first resurrection: on such the second death hath no power, but they shall be priests of God and of Christ, and shall reign with him a thousand years* (Revelation 20:6).

Though you may never hold public office in this life, you have a future in government. When Jesus comes to establish His Kingdom on this earth, those who have received Him as Saviour will rule and reign with Him.

That government will be without earthly flaws. There will be no corrupt officials, no crooked politicians and no unjust practices. Political justice and international peace will prevail. Isaiah wrote: *"And it shall come to pass in the last days, that the mountain of the LORD's house shall be established in the top of the mountains, and shall be exalted above the hills; and all nations shall flow unto it. And many people shall go and say, Come ye, and let us go up to the mountain of the LORD, to the house of the God of Jacob; and he will teach us of his ways, and we will walk in his paths: for out of Zion shall go forth the law, and the word of the LORD from Jerusalem. And he shall judge among the nations, and shall rebuke many people: and they shall beat their swords into plowshares, and their spears into pruning hooks: nation shall not lift up sword against nation, neither shall they learn war any more"* (Isaiah 2:2-4).

Just what will be our responsibilities in that Kingdom? We cannot say precisely but we know that we will have part in carrying out God's will on earth.

Meanwhile, we now have an opportunity to share in doing His will by taking the Gospel message to others. Doing His bidding now is good training for the future!

BE STEADFAST

MEMORY VERSE: *Therefore, my beloved brethren, be ye steadfast, unmovable, always abounding in the work of the Lord, forasmuch as ye know that your labour is not in vain in the Lord* (1 Corinthians 15:58).

It has been said that when the word "therefore" appears in the Bible one should always consider what it is there for. Here, this word looks back to all the truths just presented and in view of them calls for faithful service for Christ.

Because Christ is risen, be *"steadfast, unmovable, always abounding in the work of the Lord."*

Because Christ is coming to raise the Christian dead and catch away His bride, be *"steadfast, unmovable, always abounding in the work of the Lord."*

To be steadfast is "to be firm in your own convictions." To be unmovable is "to be firm against the influences of others." The Pulpit Commentary says: "There are some works of the Lord in which we cannot engage. We cannot help to control the ocean, guide the stars, or even create a blade of grass, but here we are 'labourers together with Him.'"

What a privilege!

Let us stand firm against evil and abound in service for Christ.

He lives.

And He is coming again.

Our work for Jesus will not be in vain. When He comes He will reward all who have been *"steadfast, unmovable, and always abounding in the work of the Lord. And, behold, I come quickly; and my reward is with me, to give every man according as his work shall be"* (Revelation 22:12).

THE COMING KINGDOM

MEMORY VERSE: *The wilderness and the solitary place shall be glad for them; and the desert shall rejoice, and blossom as the rose* (Isaiah 35:1).

The coming Kingdom of Christ is known as the Millennium because it will last for one thousand years. And what years they will be!

Man's struggle to conquer the environment will be over. Though a stubborn earth has resisted cultivation and produced only at the continual effort of its inhabitants, people have survived. Think how wonderful it will be when man and nature are again in harmony. Bumper crops will be the rule rather than the exception. All the earth will become productive. Even the deserts will become watered gardens.

The enmity between men and animals will be put away. Hear the prophet describe this millennial scene: *"The wolf also shall dwell with the lamb, and the leopard shall lie down with the kid; and the calf and the young lion and the fatling together; and a little child shall lead them. And the cow and the bear shall feed; their young ones shall lie down together: and the lion shall eat straw like the ox"* (Isaiah 11:6-7).

Cults and all false teachers will be non-existent. True worship of the Lord will cover the earth: *"They shall not hurt nor destroy in all my holy mountain: for the earth shall be full of the knowledge of the LORD, as the waters cover the sea"* (Isaiah 11:9).

When you are discouraged by world conditions or personal problems, remember the coming Kingdom of Christ. This earth has a great future. And so do you, if you belong to Him!

EVERYWHERE

MEMORY VERSE: *Therefore they that were scattered abroad went everywhere preaching the word* (Acts 8:4).

Following the death of Stephen, the first Christian martyr, persecution fell upon all the Christians at Jerusalem. Those were difficult days for the church, bringing imprisonment and even death for the crime of trusting in Christ and telling others about Him. As a result of this persecution, the believers were scattered... but everywhere they went they carried the message of Christ. Even the enemies of the Gospel cooperated in its propagation for as they scattered God's people they also scattered their message throughout that whole area.

In America today we know little about persecution. Though we live in the century that has probably produced more Christian martyrs than any other in history, we are virtually untouched. Still we are lax in telling the old old story of Jesus and His love. And that raises a frightening question; Will it be necessary for God to allow persecution to come to us to awaken us to the blessings we have had and taken for granted?

We hope not.

Those early Christians have set an example for us that will be well to follow. They were so determined to obey the great commission that inconveniences and even severe problems could not deter them from carrying out that responsibility.

How does that compare to our concern? Where are our weak excuses for not witnessing? How will they stand up at the Judgment Seat of Christ?

We've a message to share.

Tell it wherever you go!

April

Surely he hath borne our griefs, and carried our sorrows: yet we did esteem him stricken, smitten of God, and afflicted. But he was wounded for our transgressions, he was bruised for our iniquities: the chastisement of our peace was upon him; and with his stripes we are healed. All we like sheep have gone astray; we have turned every one to his own way; and the Lord hath laid on him the iniquity of us all.

Isaiah 53:4-6.

WELL DONE

MEMORY VERSE: *When Jesus understood it, he said unto them, Why trouble ye the woman? for she hath wrought a good work upon me* (Matthew 26:10).

Oliver Wendell Holmes said, "The human race is divided into two classes — those who go ahead and do something and those who sit still and inquire, 'Why wasn't it done the other way?'"

Mary of Bethany had undoubtedly wanted to do something for Jesus ever since the raising of her brother Lazarus. He had intervened in her hour of grief and despair. She had sat at His feet and learned valuable spiritual lessons. Finally, she settled on a way to show her dedication and appreciation for all He had done for her. She would use her alabaster box of precious ointment to refresh Him after one of His journeys.

Reaction to Mary's sacrifice was probably predictable. Regardless of what you do for Christ, some will complain! And how righteous they may sound! "This ointment might have been sold for much and given to the poor," said those who watched and criticized. They sounded pious. But Jesus knew their hearts and rebuked them.

Have others been critical of you after some act of sacrificial service? Don't let it get you down. It is easier to grumble than to give. It is easier to be part of the faction than to get into the action.

Never mind. Jesus understands. His "well done" is all that matters. He will care for the critics and will reward those who serve Him with their best (see Luke 14:14).

WHAT'S YOUR PRICE?

MEMORY VERSE: *And said unto them, What will ye give me, and I will deliver him unto you? And they covenanted with him for thirty pieces of silver* (Matthew 26:15).

The betrayal of Jesus was foretold in the Old Testament: *"Yea, mine own familiar friend, in whom I trusted, which did eat of my bread, hath lifted up his heel against me"* (Psalm 41:9).

Even the price of betrayal was prophesied: *"And I said unto them, If ye think good, give me my price; and if not, forbear. So they weighed for my price thirty pieces of silver"* (Zechariah 11:12). It is revolting to think of Judas selling the Lord. Dr. Harry Rimmer wrote of him: "Judas. A name that has become a byword in all civilized nations. A man who has become an object of abhorrence. The outstanding example of greed, the climax of treachery; and the apogee of all that is despicable." It is hard to imagine putting a price on loyalty to Jesus.

But some still have their price!

Some are loyal to Jesus unless it costs too much. The price may be reckoned to money, popularity, prestige, or pleasure. At what point does your dedication die? How much temptation is required to topple you? What's your price?

Christ deserves our loyalty and dedication at all costs. He paid the supreme price to redeem us. Loyalty to Him should be priceless.

Let it be known! YOU'RE NOT FOR SALE!

SPEAK UP

MEMORY VERSE: *Let the redeemed of the LORD say so, whom he hath redeemed from the hand of the enemy* (Psalm 107:2).

Do we honor the Lord more by righteous living or by speaking of His love and salvation?

It's a bad question.

No such choice should be considered.

The raising of this issue infers that one cannot be consistent in both life and conversation. And that just isn't so.

Certainly our lives are to be above reproach. Hypocrisy is condemned in the Bible and was often exposed by Jesus. The Pharisees despised Him for revealing their lack of faith and love while going through the motions of being religious. They were examples of those who speak well but live poorly. But their hypocrisy or that of others is no excuse for opting to be a so-called "silent witness."

The Psalmist was determined to praise God with his lips as well as his life. He declared: *"I will sing of the mercies of the LORD for ever: with my mouth will I make known thy faithfulness to all generations"* (Psalm 89:1).

A song says, "I'd rather see a sermon than hear one any day." And it contains an element of truth. Still, most of us have been influenced toward God by someone who cared enough to talk to us about our deepest needs, making application of the Gospel.

Some have difficulty speaking to others or are confined and have few contacts with those in need. I have known a few who wrote letters to share the love of Christ, especially to people passing through severe problems. They let their fingers do the talking.

Christians have something to say.

Speak up. Today!

TO MINISTER

MEMORY VERSE: *Even as the Son of man came not to be ministered unto, but to minister, and to give his life a ransom for many* (Matthew 20:28).

Millions are ministered to.

Few minister.

And in our lack of ministering, we are unlike Jesus.

Today's pattern of taking in weekly without giving out is unknown in the Bible. Even when persecution of the early church scattered its members, they were faithful ministers while fleeing: *"Therefore they that were scattered abroad went every where preaching the word"* (Acts 8:4).

Truth is given to pass on to others. Blessings are given to share. Financial prosperity is given so that one can give to those in need... and not just at the end of life to beneficiaries of a will. Health is given so that vigor and strength can be used to lift the burdens of others. Years are given so that we can have time to influence people through our lives and words and point them to God.

Receivers who do not give are losers. They lose the thrill of giving. Of seeing the sparkle in the eyes of one who has been helped. Of watching one go on to success who had been counted out. Of witnessing faith grow as a result of sharing the love of Christ.

So, we must minister.

But where shall we start?

Let us begin where we are. What have we received this week that can be given to others? What was there about the pastor's sermon that made it special to you? Tell a friend. His need is likely to be the same as yours. And in passing on the blessing you will be ministering.

It's the only way to be like Jesus!

NOT ASHAMED

MEMORY VERSE: *Whosoever therefore shall be ashamed of me and of my words in this adulterous and sinful generation; of him also shall the Son of man be ashamed, when he cometh in the glory of his Father with the holy angels* (Mark 8:38).

An old song asks:
"Jesus, and shall it ever be,
A mortal man ashamed of Thee?
Ashamed of Thee Whom angels praise
Whose glories shine through endless days'"

Unbelievable as it may seem, some Christians appear to be ashamed of their Saviour. They are ill at ease when given an opportunity to speak for Him. Other subjects flow from their lips freely: sports, fashions, the economy, the weather. But let the name of Jesus enter the conversation and they clam up — or change the subject.

How the angels must wonder at our values!

And why should we be ashamed? Even the enemies of Jesus could find no fault in Him. At the trial of Jesus, Pilate returned Him to His accusers announcing that he could find no fault in Him. Since that time, skeptics have attacked the Bible and doubted the Gospel — but not one honest person has ever found a fault in Jesus.

We have many faults. But He is not ashamed to be identified with us: *"For it became him for whom are all things, and by whom are all things, in bringing many sons unto glory, to make the captain of their salvation perfect through sufferings. For both he that sanctifieth and they who are sanctified are all of one: for which cause he is not ashamed to call them brethren"* (Hebrews 2:10, 11).

Don't be ashamed!

TO EVERY CREATURE

MEMORY VERSE: *And he said onto them, Go ye into all the world, and preach the gospel to every creature* (Mark 16:15).

The Pacific Garden Mission in Chicago has been the scene of salvation for many through the years. Billy Sunday, the evangelist, was one of their famous converts. The mission once published the following in the *"Pacific Garden Mission News:"*

"Remember, the man on Skid Row is not different in kind from the rest of us. He is merely worse in degree. On Skid Row we see fallen man at his dismal worst. In the better neighborhoods we see him at his polished best, but he is the same man for all his disguise. In the gutter we find him chained by dope and drink and dirt. On the avenue we find him bound by pride and greed and lust. To God there is no difference. He sees beyond appearances and he knows what is in every man. His remedy for every man is the same, a new birth and the impartation of a new kind of life.

"The Gospel is the power of God operating toward the moral and spiritual transformation of man. And it works! Thousands will testify that it does. No man who wants to climb up out of his past and find a new and better life should overlook the Gospel. It is God's way out, and there is no other."

God is no respecter of persons. That is, all have the same need and must come the same way: *"Jesus saith unto him, I am the way, the truth, and the life: no man cometh unto the Father, but by me"* (John 14:6).

But we often evaluate people by their position, their wealth or the color of their skin. And that is sinful. The Gospel is for everyone. It's time to see every person as one in need of salvation. Christ died for all. Go tell someone today!

Praise the Lord! 2,000,000 have come to Christ through Jack Van Impe Ministries.

OUR HIGH PRIEST

MEMORY VERSE: *Seeing then that we have a great high priest, that is passed into the heavens, Jesus the Son of God, let us hold fast our profession* (Hebrews 4:14).

We have one in heaven who understands.

His name is Jesus.

Here is the miracle of His love. He who is the Bread of Life began His ministry hungering. He who is the Water of Life ended His ministry thirsting. Christ hungered as a man, and fed the hungry as God. He was weary, and yet He is our rest. He paid tribute, and yet He is the King of Kings. He was called a devil, yet He cast out devils. He prayed, and yet He hears prayer. He wept, and He is the One who dries our tears. He was sold for thirty pieces of silver, and yet He redeemed the world with His precious blood. He was led as a lamb to the slaughter, and yet He is the Good Shepherd.

Does heaven seem distant and unreachable?

Jesus is there and awaits your cry.

Do you think you are passing through trials and tests unknown by any other "...*but was in all points tempted like as we are...*" (Hebrews 4:15).

Have you been hurt by another?

He endured the cross with all its shame.

Do you have less than others?

He had no place to lay His head.

Do some leave you out of their gatherings?

He was despised and rejected.

Our great High priest in heaven knows every burden. Take all your needs to Him and leave them there!

WHITE TO HARVEST

MEMORY VERSE: *Say not ye, There are yet four months, and then cometh harvest? behold, I say unto you, Lift up your eyes, and look on the fields: for they are white already to harvest* (John 4:35).

Procrastination robs many of success.

C. H, Spurgeon said, "...procrastination is the kidnapper of souls, and the recruiting officer of hell."

Jesus urged His hearers to look on the fields and see that they were white unto harvest. Today, Christians often lift up their eyes to the Sunday School register and say, "We're doing quite well." The conclusion is based on comparison to other Sunday Schools or to progress compared to previous weeks or years rather than on the need of the harvest. Such faulty reasoning slows the work of reaping.

The harvest is always white. People are troubled because sin brings heartache and despair. Someone near you is waiting to hear the Gospel. And here you are hesitating. You mean well. You intend to witness — someday. You plan to show up for visitation at the church — someday. You see yourself distributing tracts throughout the neighborhood — someday. Meanwhile every tick of the clock ushers more people into eternity. The harvest is white.

If the harvest was white when Jesus called for reapers, consider its condition now. Unfolding events both in nature and in the nations indicate that time is running out for the world. Earthquakes increase. Signs in the heavens are daily occurrences. Israel is a nation. Russia is a militaristic power with designs on the Middle East. Europe is uniting... reviving the old Roman Empire. Morals are sliding. Cults are legion. The time to reap in God's great harvest is now.

Don't delay. Reap today!

LIVING WATER

MEMORY VERSE: *He that believeth on me, as the scripture hath said, out of his belly shall flow rivers of living water* (John 7:38).

Christians are pictured as rivers of living water.

If they do not give out the Gospel, they become stagnant pools.

When General Grant was stricken with his fatal illness, he felt his need of the Saviour and called for a minister. Simply, the man of God presented the Gospel to him and the General responded, taking Christ by faith as His Lord and Saviour. He was filled with joy and his conversion was evident to the elated preacher.

"God's kingdom has gained a great acquisition in your conversion, General," said the minister.

Grant protested, saying, "God does not need great men, but great men need God!" Then the General added, "There is just one thing that I now greatly desire since Christ's peace has come to me."

"What's that?" asked the minister.

"I would like to live one year more so that I might tell others of this wonderful gift of God's love!" replied Grant.

Sadly, when the end of life comes, we cannot add time to witness. But we have today. And God's purpose in our lives is to cause living water to flow from us to others so that thirsty souls may be refreshed in His grace. There is no other safe drinking place in all this world. All of the world's watering places leave people thirsty still.

Consider some who have refreshed their age: Paul, C. H. Spurgeon, Dwight L. Moody, Billy Sunday. And then there are those who have been instrumental in bringing about your salvation. Name some of them.

Who will drink from the river of God's grace because you have been faithful?

Be a refreshing river — not a stagnant pool!

WHERE TO BEGIN

MEMORY VERSE: *Return to thine own house, and shew how great things God hath done unto thee. And he went his way, and published throughout the whole city how great things Jesus had done unto him* (Luke 8:39).

In his autobiography, Pierre Loti tells how, as a small boy, reading stories of sainthood led him to aspire to become a saint. He resolved to imitate Simeon Stylites, who lived on top of a pillar and won a great reputation for sanctity. Pierre therefore mounted a high stool in the kitchen and announced his plan to remain there for forty years. His mother, however, would have none of his sanctity in the kitchen and at the end of an hour he was wistfully recording in his diary, "Thus I discovered that it is exceedingly difficult to be a saint while living with your own family."

Those who study the Bible know that all who are born again are saints. Nevertheless, the lesson is a good one. Testimonies that move crowds and influence strangers may be very weak at home. And it is at home that the acid test of Christianity is given. It is well and good to dream of being used of God on some far-off mission field, but if one is not faithful at home he will be of little use as a missionary. Hudson Taylor said it well: "A small circle of usefulness is not to be despised. A light that does not shine beautifully around the family table at home, is not fit to rush to a long way off to do a great service elsewhere."

How does your family regard your testimony for Christ? Are you consistent at home? Is your temper controlled by the Holy Spirit? And what about the return of Jesus? If He had come last week, would you have felt comfortable in His presence — considering your actions at home?

Begin your ministry for Christ where it's most needed — at home!

April 11   *Luke 15:3-7*

THE LOST SHEEP

MEMORY VERSE: *What man of you, having an hundred sheep, if he lose one of them, doth not leave the ninety and nine in the wilderness, and go after that which is lost, until he find it?* (Luke 15:4).

In his book, *"Addresses On Luke,"* Dr. H. A. Ironside shared an experience from a visit to a sheep ranch. He wrote:

> "Years ago I was staying with friends who had a great sheep ranch, and one evening we were awaiting supper until the husband came home. We expected him to arrive about six o'clock, but he was late. When he came into the house he said to his wife, 'My dear, I shall have to drink a cup of coffee and eat only a snack tonight, for as I came from the station I heard the bleating of a lost lamb, and I must hurry and find it before the coyotes or rattlesnakes get it.' I was amazed to see that man's interest in one lost lamb. He and a friend had more than five thousand sheep, and literally thousands of lambs; and yet that one lost lamb had such a place in his heart that he could not resist going out in the night to find it. I said, as we went along a narrow trail, 'You nave so many sheep and lambs, I wonder why you are so concerned about one.' He said, 'I would not be able to sleep tonight for thinking about that little lamb out in the wilderness, and perhaps torn into pieces by the coyotes or bitten by a rattler.' "

The concern of Jesus for lost sheep is far greater than that of any earthly shepherd. Those who doubt that may simply follow the trial of sorrows to the cross where He died to save the lost.

He cares.

Do YOU?

WHAT ARE YOU DOING ABOUT REACHING THE LOST?

FRUIT BEARING

MEMORY VERSE: *Herein is my Father glorified, that ye bear much fruit; so shall ye be my disciples* (John 15:8).

An apple tree bears apples. But the process is not complete until that apple falls and allows its seeds to penetrate the earth, finally producing another apple tree. So the final fruit of any apple tree is a new apple tree. And the fruit of any Christian is another Christian. We are born to reproduce.

The seed that produces new Christians is the Word of God. The field is the world. As we are faithful in witnessing for Christ both in daily life and with our lips, we are sure to influence others to come to the Saviour.

Jesus told His disciples that fruit bearing glorifies the Heavenly Father. We sometimes forget that and in our zeal to please the Father we do a number of things that are less important than telling others of the Saviour. These good and beneficial things can often masquerade as the most important things to be done... but nothing is more important than giving out the Gospel.

Success in the Christian life is dependent on choosing priorities correctly. And witnessing must be high on our list if we are to glorify our Heavenly Father.

Witnessing for Christ may not make one popular. In this context Jesus said: *"If the world hate you, ye know that it hated me before it hated you, If ye were of the world, the world would love his own: but because ye are not of the world, but I have chosen you out of the world, therefore the world hateth you"* (John 15:18-19).

We must bear fruit... whatever the cost!

THE OPEN DOOR

MEMORY VERSE: *For a great door and effectual is opened unto me, and there are many adversaries* (1 Corinthians 16:9).

One Sunday morning in 1856, a congregation of well-dressed people had been ushered to their rented pews in Chicago's Plymouth Congregational Church. Suddenly there was a commotion near the door. Many turned and looked. Something occurred which had never before been seen by that elite congregation. In walked a young man— a 19-year-old salesman. Following him was a poorly dressed group of people that he had gathered off the streets. The young man let them into four pews he had personally rented for the visitors. He continued to do this important work each Sunday until God called him into a world-wide ministry. His name was Dwight L. Moody.

God opens doors of service to those who are willing to serve. But there are always obstacles to overcome in the service of Christ.

Phillips Brooks said: "Oh, do not pray for easy lives. Pray to be strong men and women. Do not pray for tasks equal to your powers. Pray for powers equal to your tasks. Then the doing of your work will be no miracle; but you shall be a miracle. Every day you will wonder at yourself, at the richness of life which has come to you by the grace of God."

Has God opened a door of service for you?

What is holding you back?

Are there adversaries...problems...obstacles?

They are to be expected, but God is able.

The opportunity is brief — do not delay.

The prize is glorious — do not faint.

Walk through that open door.

PILATE BEFORE CHRIST

MEMORY VERSE: *And when they had bound him, they led him away, and delivered him to Pontius Pilate the governor* (Matthew 27:2).

The world speaks of Christ standing before Pilate for judgment. There is a sense in which that was true. But in a greater dimension, Pilate stood before Christ. Rank must be considered. On that day, the earthly judge stood before the Judge of all the earth.

Pilate was uncomfortable. There was something different about this prisoner. He marveled at the calm Christ. Somehow, he must have sensed that his prisoner was in charge of the situation. Pilate was on trial.

On a future day, we shall all stand before Christ. Christians will appear before Him at the Judgment Seat of Christ: *"For we must all appear before the judgment seat of Christ; that every one may receive the things done in his body, according to that he hath done, whether it be good or bad"* (2 Corinthians 5:10). Lost people will stand before Him at the Judgment of the Great White Throne: *"And I saw a great white throne, and him that sat on it, from whose face the earth and the heaven fled away; and there was found no place for them"* (Revelation 20:11).

But we must face the fact that we are standing before Him now! Decisions determine destiny. Christians who long to receive rewards on that great day, must serve now. Lost people who intend to be saved before it is too late should be saved now (see 2 Corinthians 6:2).

What is your answer to the call of Christ TODAY?

Your verdict today will determine His verdict in judgment.

THE CROWDS AT THE CROSS

MEMORY VERSE: *And they that passed by reviled him, wagging their heads* (Matthew 27:39).

When George Nixon Briggs was governor of Massachusetts, three of his friends visited the Holy Land. While there, they climbed Golgotha's slope and cut from the summit a small stick to be used as a cane. On their return home, they presented it to the governor, saying, "We wanted you to know that when we stood on Calvary we thought of you." Accepting the gift with all due courtesy and gratitude, the governor tenderly added: "But I am still more thankful, gentlemen, that there was Another who thought of me there."

All types of people were represented in the crowds at the cross. There were the reckless ones who gambled for the garments of Jesus. They mocked and spat upon Him, rejecting His love and sacrifice. The doubters were there, starting their taunts with their characteristic "if." Those who were familiar with Jesus but faithless were there. They remembered His promise of resurrection but thought its fulfillment impossible. The religious ones were there, talking about salvation but rejecting the Saviour: *"He saved others; himself he cannot save"* (Matthew 27:42). The "seeing is believing" crowd was there. They promised to believe if He would come down from the cross.

Jesus died for all. His salvation is offered to all, regardless of previous failure or background. He changes doubters and down-and-outers: And such were some of you: *"but ye are washed, but ye are sanctified, but ye are justified in the name of the Lord Jesus, and by the Spirit of our God"* (1 Corinthians 6:1 1).

THE SILENT SAVIOUR

MEMORY VERSE: *But Jesus held his peace. And the high priest answered and said unto him, I adjure thee by the living God, that thou tell us whether thou be the Christ, the Son of God* (Matthew 26:63).

Isaiah had prophesied the silence of Jesus before His accusers: He was oppressed, and he was afflicted, yet he opened not his mouth: *"he is brought as a lamb to the slaughter, and as a sheep before her shearers is dumb, so he openeth not his mouth"* (Isaiah 53:7).

It is never easy to be silent when we are right or feel that our rights are being ignored. But that day the innocent Saviour stood accused before the high priest and did not defend himself.

What an example!

Here was living proof of His ability to live the Sermon on the Mount: *"Ye have heard that it hath been said, Thou shalt love thy neighbour, and hate thine enemy. But I say unto you, Love your enemies, bless them that curse you, do good to them that hate you, and pray for them which despitefully use you, and persecute you"* (Matthew 5:43,44).

Jesus had not come to defend himself. He had come to die. False accusations would be heaped against Him. Perjurers would provoke a verdict of guilty against the only man on earth ever to be completely righteous. He who held His Father's name in highest reverence would be declared guilty of blasphemy by the high priest. And who can understand divine restraint in view of Matthew 26:67? *"Then did they spit in his face, and buffeted him; and others smote him with the palms of their hands."*

Still, He held His peace.

And at trifles, we are offended.

COMMUNION

MEMORY VERSE: *For this is my blood of the new testament, which is shed for many for the remission of sins* (Matthew 26:28).

Following the last passover, Jesus instituted the first Communion service. It is important to remember that salvation is not gained through taking Communion. This Christian experience is the celebration of sins forgiven through the death of Christ on the cross.

The Communion service looks both backward and forward. In sharing Communion, we look back to the cross and forward to His return: *"For as often as ye eat this bread, and drink this cup, ye do shew the Lord's death till he come"* (1 Corinthians 1 1:26).

At the Lord's table, we rejoice in the great love of God that caused Him to send His Son to die for us. We anticipate meeting our Saviour. We feel the warmth of Christian fellowship, and thank God for the tie that binds our hearts in Christian love.

Still there is a solemn note here. We are to judge ourselves (see 1 Corinthians 1 1:31). A stern warning accompanies the instructions for Communion: *"Wherefore whosoever shalt eat this bread, and drink this cup of the Lord, unworthily, shall be guilty of the body and blood of the Lord"* (1 Corinthians 11:27).

Frightening? Yes, if we must become worthy through our own good works. Thankfully, that is not the case. We become worthy through Christ: *"If we confess our sins, he is faithful and just to forgive us our sins, and to cleanse us from all unrighteousness"* (1 John 1:9).

Communion speaks of our daily walk with Jesus made possible through His shed blood.

THE LAST PASSOVER

MEMORY VERSE: *And the disciples did as Jesus had appointed them; and they made ready the passover* (Matthew 26:19).

The Children of Israel had been observing the passover since the day of their deliverance from slavery in Egypt. The record of the first passover is given in Exodus 12. Through the centuries, the choicest lambs had been brought for sacrifice at passover, symbolizing God's salvation for His people at that time and looking forward to the coming of the Saviour.

Jesus met with His disciples to eat the passover meal. It was to be the last passover. In his book, "The King of the Jews," Dr. John R. Rice wrote: "There would have been no reason for a passover lamb and the feast of unleavened bread except to picture the coming crucifixion of Jesus Christ. Therefore His disciples should have expected His Crucifixion, which had been so clearly foretold before, to occur at the time of the passover — in fact, at the very hour when the passover lamb was being slain, on the day of the preparation (John 19:14,31).

John the Baptist had announced, *"Behold the Lamb of God, which taketh away the sin of the world"* (John 1:29). Now the Lamb of whom all the Old Testament sacrifices had spoken, had come to the last passover. Not one more animal sacrifice would be required. His sacrifice would be sufficient for the sins of all: *"All we like sheep have gone astray; we have turned every one to his own way; and the LORD hath Laid on him the iniquity of us all"* (Isaiah 53:6).

Christ is enough!

PILATE'S QUESTION

MEMORY VERSE: *Pilate saith unto them, What shall I do then with Jesus which is called Christ? They all say unto him, Let him be crucified* (Matthew 27:22).

Proud Pilate asked a question that has echoed through the centuries. It reveals the agony of indecision on life's greatest question.

It is a personal question. "What shall I do with Jesus, who is called Christ?" Though he would have liked to avoid answering or delegating the decision to another, he was the only one who could make that life or death decision. There were many pressures upon Pilate that day. The crowd had rejected his offer to free Jesus and had chosen Barabbas. His wife had sent word about a strange dream that had her upset. The noisy crowd continued their chant and he wanted to please them. He would have to decide.

It is a question that demands action. "What shall I do with Jesus, who is called Christ? Pilate tried to escape making a decision by publicly washing his hands of the entire situation. But he could not get away with neutrality. He must decide.

It is a question about Jesus. "What shall I do with Jesus, who is called Christ?" Pilate had made some important decisions in his life but they were all dwarfed by this one. This question was about the Saviour. It was not about religious ceremonies or laws, but about a person. That Person was Jesus.

We are faced with a decision such as Pilate had to make, a decision about Jesus.

What will you do then with Jesus, who is called Christ?

THE CROWN OF THORNS

MEMORY VERSE: *And when they had platted a crown of thorns, they put it upon his head, and a reed in his right hand: and they bowed the knee before him, and mocked him, saying, Hail, King of the Jews!* (Matthew 27:29).

Angels must have marveled at the cruelty of man when the Son of God was prepared for crucifixion. The One whom heaven praised was rejected, humiliated, and mocked by Pilate's soldiers. As a part of their mockery, they placed a crown of thorns upon His head.

Though the wicked soldiers did not realize it, their handmade ugly crown was symbolic. Christ was made a curse for us in order to redeem us. Notice the place of thorns in the curse brought by sin: *"And unto Adam he said, Because thou hast hearkened unto the voice of thy wife, and hast eaten of the tree, of which I commanded thee, saying, Thou shalt not eat of it: cursed is the ground for thy sake; in sorrow shalt thou eat of it all the days of thy life; Thorns also and thistles shall it bring forth to thee; and thou shalt eat the herb of the field"* (Genesis 3: 17, 18).

Nature has suffered because of the sins of man. Christ died to pay for our sins. When He returns to reign, the earth will know release. All creation awaits that day: *"For we know that the whole creation groaneth and travaileth in pain together until now. And not only they, but ourselves also, which have the firstfruits of the Spirit, even we ourselves groan within ourselves, waiting for the adoption, to wit, the redemption of our body"* (Romans 8:22,23).

The work of Christ on the cross was a complete work.

And we are complete in Him!

TODAY, IN PARADISE

MEMORY VERSE: *And Jesus said unto him, Verily I say unto thee, To day shalt thou be with me in paradise* (Luke 23:43).

There were three crosses on Calvary's hill. Jesus died on the center cross with a thief on either side. Two who died that day were completely guilty. One was completely innocent. Two died there paying their debts to society. One died paying our debt of sin.

The second statement of Christ from the cross was to a dying thief who trusted in Him as his Lord and Saviour. And what great faith the dying criminal demonstrated. He believed while surrounded by a crowd of doubters. He saw Jesus in His most difficult hour and owned Him as his King. He accepted the promise of the Resurrection. He looked at a cross and saw a kingdom.

The dying thief's faith was rewarded. Jesus said, *"Today, thou shalt be with me in paradise."* What great heart questions are answered in this single statement of Jesus! Can one be saved in his dying hour? Can one be saved after a lifetime of wickedness? Can one be saved without baptism or communion? Can one be sure of heaven after death? To the one who believes Christ's word to the thief, these are questions no more.

Copernicus was a great mathematician. His studies and calculations revolutionized the thinking of mankind about the universe. At death's door, he saw himself not as a great scholar but only as a sinner in need of the Saviour. He chose the following words for his tombstone: "I do not seek a kindness equal to that given to Paul. Nor do I ask the grace granted to Peter. But that forgiveness which Thou didst grant to the robber — that, I earnestly crave!"

Jesus saves thieves, scholars, and other sinners. Trust Him today.

GREAT GUARANTEES

MEMORY VERSE: *But now is Christ risen from the dead, and become the firstfruits of them that slept* (1 Corinthians 15:20).

In the Resurrection, God has given us three great guarantees.

The Resurrection guarantees the Saviour. When the critics of Christ called for some proof of His deity, He told them there would be but one sign given: THE RESURRECTION. *"Destroy this temple, He said, and in three days I will raise it up"* (John 2:19). After the Resurrection, the disciples remembered that statement and its fulfillment fired their faith and sent them out to carry His message to the world.

The Resurrection guarantees salvation. Many years ago, two English lawyers, skeptics, set out to destroy Christianity. Their names were Gilbert West and Lord Littleton. They agreed that two Christian teachings must be disproved if they were to succeed: the resurrection of Christ and the conversion of Paul. West assumed the task of getting rid of the Resurrection and Littleton tackled the conversion of Paul. Their plan was for each to research his subject for one year. At the end of that time, they would come together and prepare to present their findings to the world. *"When they met, one year later, both were Christians, each confessing to his conversion as a result of his own research!"*

The resurrection of Christ guarantees our similar resurrection. On that first Easter, Mary wept because the tomb was empty, but that very fact signaled the emptying of the graves of all believers at the return of Christ. And that's what Easter is all about!

THE CONQUERED GRAVE

MEMORY VERSE: *But thanks be to God, which giveth us the victory through our Lord Jesus Christ* (1 Corinthians 15:57).

One hundred years ago, a very wealthy woman who had been opposed to the doctrine of the Resurrection died. Before her death she gave orders that her grave should be covered with a slab of granite; that around it should be placed square blocks of stone, and that the corners should be fastened to each other and to the granite slab by heavy iron clamps. Upon the covering, this inscription was to be placed: "THIS BURIAL PLACE PURCHASED TO ALL ETERNITY MUST NEVER BE OPENED."

The doubting lady had gone to great trouble to secure herself against an event in which she professed not to believe. However, time mocked her.

Not long after her death, a tiny birch tree seed sprouted and the root found its way between the side stone and the upper slab and grew there. Slowly, but steadily, it forced its way until the iron clamps were torn apart. Finally the granite lid was raised and made to rest upon the trunk of the large and flourishing birch tree.

Nearly two thousand years ago, another grave was sealed. The authority of the Roman Empire was enlisted to see that it should never be opened. It was the grave of Jesus.

Three days later, the stone that had been placed at the entrance of the tomb was rolled away. Christ arose! Death could not hold Him: "*Whom God hath raised up, having loosed the pains of death: because it was not possible that he should be holden of it*" (Acts 2:24).

What good news to tell to doubting people!

DOUBTING THOMAS

MEMORY VERSE: *And Thomas answered and said unto him, My Lord and my God* (John 20:28).

"Doubting Thomas," we call him. And with reason. He simply would not believe that Jesus had risen from the dead. There was no mistaking his opinion of the first Resurrection report: *"Except I shall see in his hands the print of the nails, and put my finger into the print of the nails, and thrust my hand into his side, I will not believe"* (John 20:25).

We aren't told why Thomas missed the first meeting with the disciples after the Resurrection when Jesus appeared. Perhaps he had a good excuse for not attending the gathering called by the risen Christ. One thing is sure: *missing that meeting made him a doubter and established his reputation through the centuries.* He would always be known as "Doubting Thomas."

There is, however, another side to the story. Thomas had left all to follow Christ. He went with the Lord through some pretty difficult days. To the best of our knowledge, he experienced approximately one week of doubt in his entire Christian experience. There may have been more doubting days than that for Thomas but we have no scriptural authority for saying so.

At the second appearance of Christ to the disciples, Thomas was present. When confronted with his faithless statement, he surrendered completely and cried, *"My Lord and my God."* From that time on it seems sure that Thomas was an outstanding Christian and that he died as a martyr in India where, because of preaching the Gospel, he was thrust through with a spear. We label Thomas because of one weak week.

Sadly, we often treat other Christians the same way!

AND PETER

MEMORY VERSE: *But go your way, tell his disciples and Peter that he goeth before you into Galilee: there shall ye see him, as he said unto you* (Mark 16:7).

Peter had not intended to become a backslider. Boldly he had proclaimed his loyalty, even being willing to stand alone. But there is a difference between determination and daily living. Dedication is only tested in the fire of experience. It is one thing to talk about ability to overcome temptation and quite another to prove it when doing battle with the tempter.

After his three denials of Christ, Peter went out and wept bitterly. The gospels are silent about his actions during the Crucifixion and some have thought he fled the scene, but in his first epistle he states that he was a witness of the sufferings of Christ (see 1 Peter 5: 1). What a sad picture he presents as he watches the Lord's sufferings through his tears!

Interestingly, in the instruction given to the women who came to the tomb after the Resurrection, Peter is the only disciple that is named. The message of the Resurrection must go to brokenhearted Peter. By that time, he may have doubted that he could be considered one of the disciples, so the Lord made sure that he knew that he was invited to the coming meeting with them. Though he had failed, His Lord loved him.

You may live with doubts and regrets. Perhaps you had great hopes of serving Christ but temptation came and you yielded. Now you think the Lord is through with you. Remember Peter. Like the denying disciple, you are the special object of God's love!

BURNING HEARTS

MEMORY VERSE: *And they said one to another, Did not our heart burn within us, while he talked with us by the way, and while he opened to us the scriptures?* (Luke 24:32).

Two discouraged disciples were retreating — going home. They had trusted that Christ was the One who would redeem Israel, but the Crucifixion had brought them to despair.

Emmaus was their destination and somewhere along that road the Saviour came and walked with them. Miraculously, the eyes of the Emmaus disciples were held by God so that they were unable to recognize Jesus. As might be expected, He asked them why they were sad. After they had told Him all about their burden, He opened the Scriptures to them and taught them about himself. What a Bible lesson that must have been! Remembering those moments, they said later that their hearts had burned within them as they listened to Him.

Burning hearts are needed today.

Who has not witnessed the fire of new converts or of those newly committed to the Saviour? Their love for Christ and others has sometimes ignited entire congregations that had become cool and complacent. With warmth and zeal, those newly born have often led mature but mechanical members of the body of Christ back to the experience of fervent love and power.

Dwight L. Moody prayed, "Lord, make me not only warm, but red hot!"

David Dawson wrote: "Fire warms! And who of us does not like to feel the warm glow among God's people?"

Ask God to give you a burning heart. You may set your church afire. And every community needs to witness that blessed glow!

WITNESSES

MEMORY VERSE: *But ye shall receive power, after that the Holy Ghost is come upon you: and ye shall be witnesses unto me both in Jerusalem, and in all Judaea, and in Samaria, and unto the uttermost part of the earth* (Acts 1:8).

The disciples longed to know all about the times and the seasons. They wanted the key of prophetic fulfillment. Instead, they were given a task... a responsibility... a work to do. They were to be witnesses for Christ; in Jerusalem, in Judea, in Samaria and to the uttermost parts of the earth.

There was one difference between that day and ours: they were to wait and then witness. The promise of the coming of the Holy Spirit was to be fulfilled on the day of Pentecost and they were to begin their witnessing following that great miracle. We are to wait and witness. We do not await the coming of the Holy Spirit for He indwells every believer at the moment he is born again... but we await the coming of the Saviour who will evaluate our service at the Judgment Seat of Christ.

The coming of the Holy Spirit would launch an era of witnessing. The disciples would be empowered by His presence within and Jerusalem would be shaken by their witnessing. The coming of the Saviour will end our opportunity for witnessing, for at His coming we shall be taken to heaven to be with Him.

The formula for witnessing given by Jesus has not changed. They were to begin where they were... Jerusalem ...and their area of responsibility encompassed the entire world. We are to begin where we are... in our own communities... our own cities and reach out to the world.

How are you doing in your "Jerusalem?"

THE SIMPLE GOSPEL

MEMORY VERSE: *For God so loved the world, that he gave his only begotten Son, that whosoever believeth in him should not perish, but have everlasting life* (John 3:16).

The Gospel is easy to understand. The difficult work in man's salvation was done at the cross by the Lord Jesus. Any sinner can believe and be saved. And we are all sinners (Romans 3:23).

A good example of the power of the simple Gospel was given by missionary George Green. Here is his story:

"When I first went out to my mission field in Africa, the boat carried me up a wide, beautiful river flowing through the jungle, and as the sun set and the night came on, I listened with much misgiving to the roll of the war drums. They continued far into the night. The captain of the boat was uneasy and tried to dissuade me from going ashore the next morning, and I admit I was trembling with fear, But I found that 'the Lord standeth within the shadows keeping watch above His own.' After years of delightful labor I left the jungle on the same boat. As it came down the river, thousands of these same natives gathered on the shores near their villages to say farewell. As the boat came into sight, they broke into song, but not a war song. They were singing the hymn that is a favorite of most of them, *'All Hail the Power of Jesus' Name.'"*

The Gospel that reaches the heart of one who has never heard of the Saviour can surely change those who have lived in this good land where Bible preaching is so available. Nearly anyone we meet has witnessed the power of God in some life and that is a powerful influence in preparing hearts to receive the Gospel.

Share John 3:16 with someone you meet.

The simple Gospel still changes lives today!

FINDERS KEEPERS

MEMORY VERSE: *He first findeth his own brother Simon, and saith unto him, We have found the Messiah, which is, being interpreted, the Christ* (John 1:41).

Andrew was a finder.

We have no record of any of Andrew's sermons. But we know that he found his brother Peter and brought him to Jesus. And Peter's powerful preaching brought three thousand to Christ on the day of Pentecost. Certainly Andrew will share in the rewards of that great harvest.

When five thousand were hungry, Andrew found a lad with five barley loaves and two small fishes with which the Lord fed the multitude. Faced with the problem of feeding that huge crowd, Philip began to fret and figure how they could get money enough to buy each one a crust of bread. Not Andrew. He set out to find a solution. And his search produced a boy with a lunch that Jesus could use.

Some fret about problems and others find solutions.

All churches need more finders. When the finders are at work all church problems are solved. Bringing people to Jesus turns the coldest church into a place of warmth and joy. Bringing people to Jesus puts new life in any congregation. Bringing people to Jesus encourages pastors.

Pastors often move because their people won't.

Andrew found his brother. He began looking for a convert right at home. The mission field is all about us. The field is the world. Jesus said the reapers in His harvest receive wages — rewards. You don't lose by giving time to serving Christ. Here especially, finders are keepers.

Find someone for Jesus today!

THE GREATEST OF THESE

MEMORY VERSE: *And now abideth faith, hope, charity, these three; but the greatest of these is charity* (1 Corinthians 13:13).

No one would question the importance of love in the Christian life. Love is the very heart of the gospel. The good news is that God loves us and has given His Son for our salvation.

There is, however, another side to this love story. John puts it well: *"Beloved, if God so loved us, we ought also to love one another"* (1 John 4:11).

Simple, you say?

Perhaps. Yet sometimes difficult.

> To live above with saints in love
> Will be eternal glory;
> To live below with saints we know
> Is quite another story.

What will happen to our relationships with other Christians if we allow the love of Christ to rule in our hearts?

We will be quick to forgive. We will be slow to wrath. We will be careful with our words. We will shut our ears to gossip and grumbling. We will want to share our blessings. We will find it more blessed to give than to receive.

And that's only the beginning! The Lord will continually give opportunities to show His love to others.

"By this shall all men know that ye are my disciples, if ye have love one to another" (John 13:35).

D. L. Moody said: "There are two ways of being united — frozen together, and melted together. What Christians need most is to be united in brotherly love."

Amen, Mr. Moody. Amen!

May

GIVE US THIS DAY OUR DAILY BREAD

For as the earth bringeth forth her bud, and as the garden causeth the things that are sown in it to spring forth; so the Lord God will cause righteousness and praise to spring forth before all the nations.

Isaiah 61:11

THE GREAT PROPHET

MEMORY VERSE: *I will raise them up a Prophet from among their brethren, like unto thee, and will put my words in his mouth; and he shall speak unto them all that I shall command him* (Deuteronomy 18:18).

Commenting on this text, Matthew Henry said, "It is here promised concerning Christ, that there should come a Prophet, great above all prophets; by whom God would make known himself and His will to the children of men, more fully and clearly than He had ever done before...He should be like Moses, only above him. This Prophet is come, even JESUS: and is 'He that should come, and we are to look for no other.'"

When Jesus came, His hearers marveled at His words. He spoke with authority. They said of Him, "*Never man spake Like this man*" (John 7:46).

He spoke to the wind and waves and they obeyed Him.

He spoke to the demons and they were subject to Him.

He spoke to little children when others thought He was too busy for them.

He spoke to lepers and made them clean — to the lame and made them whole.

He spoke to the dead and raised them to life again.

He spoke to the Samaritan woman at the well, breaking through the social barrier that divided the Jews from the Samaritans.

He spoke to a dying thief and guaranteed him Paradise.

He spoke words of forgiveness to the woman taken in adultery and rebuked her accusers.

He spoke to the weary and called them to rest.

Listen. Jesus is speaking today. Read the Bible to hear His voice. Obey it to experience the abundant life.

His Word will abide forever!

POWER

MEMORY VERSE: *Howbeit many of them which heard the word believed; and the number of the men was about five thousand* (Acts 4:4).

The friends of Mary Slessor, missionary in Africa, were amazed when they saw that she, a weak woman, had been able to mold savage chiefs to her will. One of the chiefs explained, "You have evidently forgotten to take into account the woman's God."

The Psalmist wrote: *"God hath spoken once; twice have I heard this; that power belongeth unto God"* (Psalm 62:11). Still, Christians often depend on weak willpower to win in the struggles of life and churches run programs that are little different than those produced by worldly organizations. It is time to tap the powerful resources of God.

When all sin is confessed and our relationships with others are right, we can expect the power of God to flow through us. Our surrendered wills will be channels for the Lord to use. But our wills do not surrender easily. Often old hurts are harbored and even pampered. Wanting our own way, we are afraid to submit to the will of God. Therefore we do not receive His best and we continue on our weak way.

Let's stop wasting time. The days of opportunity are coming to their close. Life is ebbing away. Christ is coming soon. It is not enough to read books and dream about the good old days when revivals swept the land. What about revival in our time?

Do you long for God's power in daily life? Would you like to see the aisles of your church filled with people seeking salvation and direction from the Bible? Then, be sure your heart is right with God and others. Pray for revival and expect the power of God in your life.

REVIVAL AND REJOICING

MEMORY VERSE: *Wilt thou not revive us again: that thy people may rejoice in thee?* (Psalm 85:6).

Revival brings rejoicing! And all too many of us lack this quality of life. There is an attitude of hyper-criticism abroad today that saps the strength of churches and renders Christian testimonies ineffective.

Grumbling and griping characterize many groups of Christians. David wrote of his cup running over with joy, while present-day saints often appear to have cups running over with vinegar. Husbands grumble about their wives and wives about their husbands. Parents grumble about their children and children about their parents. In the world's most affluent society, many grumble about their possessions. And this by people who claim to serve and love the Lord who had not a place to lay His head.

Churches grumble about pastors. When the servant of the Lord first arrives, there is a period of honeymoon when the members boast about their new pastor, but after the newness wears off and he steps on a few toes while preaching, groups gather after services to have roast preacher. While holding meetings in one area and preaching on revival, one couple told me they would like to have revival in their church but were afraid if it came the pastor would stay, and they wanted him to leave. Such negativism must be confessed as sin before revival can come.

Revival brings rejoicing because in revival, people stop looking at the faults of others and, instead, focus on the Saviour. He is the source of Christian joy. Three words can bring revival and rejoicing: "Looking unto Jesus."

LOVE

MEMORY VERSE: *And all that believed were together, and had all things common* (Acts 2:44).

A Columbian was converted to Christ through reading the Bible. He had no personal contact with any missionary or Bible-teaching church. Soon thereafter, he came to the United States to live. Upon arriving here, he began searching for a fellowship of believers so as to learn more about his newfound faith.

Most people converted in America have some tie to a Bible-centered church that provides them with immediate fellowship and spiritual guidance. My Columbian acquaintance did not have this advantage and the maze of multiplied churches and denominations was confusing to him. Finally he settled on a solution. He decided to search until he found a congregation where love, such as he saw described in the New Testament Church, was evident among the people. He felt confident that test would enable him to settle on the right church.

Nearly twenty years have passed since I learned of that Columbian convert's formula for finding fellowship. Yet, every time his experience crosses my mind I become a bit uncomfortable and an unwanted question surfaces: "If he had visited my church, would he have stayed and made it his own?"

When revival comes, Christian love is seen operating everywhere. Old differences are put away. People who have held grudges lay them aside and forgive as they have been forgiven. People become more important than money or property. Stinginess is stifled. The world looks on and says: "Behold, how they love one another!"

USE THE TONGUE

MEMORY VERSE: *Thou hast proved mine heart; thou hast visited me in the night; thou hast tried me, and shalt find nothing; I am purposed that my mouth shall not transgress* (Psalm 17:3).

John Wesley was preaching and wearing a new bow tie with two streamers hanging down from it. There was a sister in the meeting who didn't hear a word about Jesus, but sat with a long face and saw nothing but those two streamers.

When the service was over the critic went up to Wesley and said, "Pardon me, Mr. Wesley, will you allow me to give you a little criticism?"

"Yes," replied the preacher.

"Well," she said, "your bow tie is too long and it is an offense to me."

"Have you any shears?" asked Wesley.

Upon receiving a pair of shears from one in the gathering, Wesley handed them to the offended lady, saying that she would know best how to fix the tie.

Eagerly, she clipped off the streamers.

"Is that all right now?" asked Wesley.

"Yes," she said, "that is much better."

Then Wesley asked for the shears. "Would you mind me giving you a little criticism?" he asked. "Your tongue is a great offense to me — it is a little too long. Please stick it out while I take some off."

Many who self-righteously criticize outward things, are guilty of transgressing with their tongues. And according to the Bible, tongues are far more likely to offend the Lord than ties (see James 1:26).

Start the day with the psalmist's praiseworthy purpose: *"I am purposed that my mouth shall not transgress."*

BACKBITERS

MEMORY VERSE: *Lord...who shall dwell in thy holy hill? He that backbiteth not with his tongue, nor doeth evil to his neighbour, nor taketh up a reproach against his neighbour* (Psalm 15:1,3).

The dictionary says that backbiting means to slander an absent person or persons. The old sinful nature of man is easily lured into that trap.

When we criticize others we turn attention away from our own faults. At least we think so. However, Judge Harold Medina saw it another way. He said, "Criticizing others is a dangerous thing, not so much because you may make mistakes about them, but because you may be revealing the truth about yourself."

Oliver Wendell Holmes said, "The human race is divided into two classes — those who go ahead and do something and those who sit still and inquire why it wasn't done the other way."

If you find that someone has been criticizing you, don't ever let it defeat you. If the criticism is untrue, disregard it. If it is unfair, keep from irritation. If it is ignorant, smile. If it is justified, learn from it.

But how about those who eat away at others in your presence. What can you do about them? You will never escape them for the world is full of such little people. You must simply let them know that you disapprove of their backbiting. Refuse to listen to their tirades against others. Do not allow them to deposit their poisonous thoughts in your mind. Object to being a party to their sin.

The psalmist declares that those who are close to the Lord are not backbiters. Regardless of how righteous they may sound, backbiters need to get right with God!

May 7   Isaiah 59:9-16

AMERICA'S GREATEST REVIVAL

MEMORY VERSE: *And he saw that there was no man, and wondered that there was no intercessor: therefore his arm brought salvation unto him; and his righteousness, it sustained him* (Isaiah 59:16).

The beginning of America's greatest revival took place in New York City. A.C. Lanphier was working as a lay missionary in one of the crowded areas of the city. He often became discouraged, but drew strength from personal prayer. He thought others might be helped by joining him in prayer so he let it be known that he was starting a series of weekly noon-hour prayer meetings.

For the first half hour Mr. Lanphier prayed alone. Then, one by one, others came until a total of six were praying. The next week twenty appeared, and the third week brought forty. By Spring more than twenty daily noon prayer meetings were going on in New York City. Some of the largest churches were crowded to capacity. The police and fire departments opened their buildings for prayer services. Revival had begun! It spread across the land.

In a Boston meeting, a man said: "I am from Omaha, Nebraska. On my journey here I found a continuous chain of prayer all the way." Mr. Lanphier's prayer meeting had set his nation afire for God.

The revival caused churches to spread across the frontier and made them flourish in the cities. The moral fiber of the nation was strengthened. Old debts were paid. Honesty increased. Missionary work expanded.

Today, God must wonder that so few are interceding. We live twenty-four hours a day in the nuclear sights of an enemy bent on our destruction. Armageddon approaches. The signs of the Lord's return multiply. It's time to pray. You may start the prayer meeting that brings revival!

A PERFECT PRAYER

MEMORY VERSE: *Let the words of my mouth, and the meditation of my heart, be acceptable in thy sight, O LORD, my strength, and my redeemer* (Psalm 19:14).

The most dangerous beast in the world is the one that lives in that den behind your teeth...your tongue!

James compares the tongue to a flame of fire. He warns that it is full of wickedness and can poison every part of the body.

David prayed that the Lord would set a guard at his mouth: *"Set a watch, O LORD, before my mouth; keep the door of my lips"* (Psalm 141:3).

The tongue at its greatest potential is used to bring praise to God. The dedicated Christian sings:

> *"Take my lips and let them move,*
> *At the impulse of Thy love."*

The Bible teaches that one of life's greatest contradictions is to both praise God and curse men. In other words, it is the height of hypocrisy to be given to both godliness and gossip. Like oil and water, the two just do not mix.

Peter instructs us to lay aside all slanderings if we want to mature in the Christian life (see 1 Peter 2:1,2).

If the use of your tongue is really that important to the Lord, what guideline can you follow to be sure your words are pleasing to Him?

A number of proverbs and sayings have been put together to help us. One is:

> *"If your lips would keep from slips,*
> *Five things observe with care:*
> *Of whom you speak, to whom you speak,*
> *And how and when and where."*

But the best is given in the psalmist's perfect prayer contained in our memory verse. Let this be your prayer — today and every day!

PRAISE THE LORD

MEMORY VERSE: *I will bless the LORD at all times: his praise shall continually be in my mouth* (Psalm 34:1).

In China, a missionary was living a defeated life. Everything seemed to be touched with sadness and although he prayed and prayed for months for victory over depression and discouragement, his life remained the same.

As a result, he decided to leave his work and go to an interior mission station and pray until victory came. He reached the place and was entertained in the home of a fellow missionary. On the wall hung a motto with these words, "Try Thanksgiving."

The words gripped his heart and he thought, "Have I been praying all this time and not praising?" He began to praise God and was so uplifted that instead of hiding away to pray and agonize for days, he immediately returned to his waiting flock to tell them that praise changes things. Wonderful blessings attended his simple testimony and the chains of depression that had bound others in his congregation were broken through praise.

And why shouldn't we praise God? He deserves it. He loves us. He has provided salvation for us. He promises to always be with us.

Praise is profitable.

You cannot pout and praise at the same time.

You cannot worry and praise at the same time.

You cannot grumble and praise at the same time.

You cannot give up and praise at the same time.

But you can rejoice and praise God at the same time.

Praise changes things!

RESTITUTION

MEMORY VERSE: *And Zacchaeus stood, and said unto the Lord; Behold, Lord, the half of my goods I give to the poor; and if I have taken any thing from any man by false accusation, I restore him fourfold* (Luke 19:8).

At the conversion of Zacchaeus, he announced he would make restitution to those he had wronged. That was Scriptural and is a good sign of the work of God in our hearts. Here are some facts about restitution:

1. Restitution begins with a desire to be right with men.

2. Restitution is personal and private. Zacchaeus did not give details or names to the crowd, only an announcement that he would deal privately with those he had wronged.

3. Restitution has to do with money or property. It is impossible to make restitution for immoral acts.

4. Restitution is biblical (Exodus 22:1).

5. Restitution is different than reconciliation. Reconciliation is the putting away of differences so that enemies become friends.

Revivals always produce acts of restitution. Debts are paid that have long since been written off as lost. Items that have been stolen are returned or paid for. Damage that has been done to another's property is cared for by payment or repair. These are acts that flow from the God-given desire to be right with man.

A store clerk once asked: "What has happened to that young man from your church? He was in yesterday to pay for candy that he said he had stolen." God had moved his heart and he wanted to do right. That is a sign of revival. The 21st century finds churches full of hypocrisy. So-called Christians won't pay their debts and make amends.

If you don't want to do right...better not pray for revival!

HONESTY

MEMORY VERSE: *Recompense to no man evil for evil. Provide things honest in the sight of all men* (Romans 12:17).

There was in a certain village a very mean man who sold wood to his neighbors, and who always took advantage of them by cutting the logs a few inches under the required four feet. One day the report came that the woodchopper had been saved. Nobody believed the report, for they all declared that he was beyond being reached.

One man, however, slipped quietly out of the grocery store where the conversion was being discussed and soon came running back in excitement and shouted: "It's so! He has been converted! I have been to his house and measured the wood that he cut yesterday. It is a good four feet long!" That testimony convinced the crowd.

Some who are saved are still cutting short logs! If revival came to their hearts, the logs would lengthen. Their customers would begin to get fair measure. The government would receive honest income tax reports. Their employees would receive better wages. Their employers would get a day's work for a day's pay. The Lord would receive His due.

Words are wasted when one who is not honest tries to witness to others about Christ. Actions speak louder than words.

Some time ago, *Newsweek* revealed that cheating is so prevalent in our schools and colleges that the practice is considered to be normal. Those who assist the cheaters are considered "good neighbors."

When God is in control of a life, cheating and dishonesty in business must go. Revival makes men walk as they talk.

How long are your logs?

THE BRIDLE

MEMORY VERSE: *I said, I will take heed to my ways, that I sin not with my tongue: I will keep my mouth with a bridle, while the wicked is before me* (Psalm 39:1).

Some things are better left unsaid, especially in the presence of those who are looking for some reason to doubt the reality of your faith in Christ. A watching world is far more likely to remember your lapse than your light. Christians are continually on display and careless words can spoil a testimony that has taken years to build.

A fit of anger can be forgiven at the moment you confess your sin to the Lord, but it will never be forgotten by those who witnessed your explosion. Your demand for your rights may seem perfectly justified but it would be far better to take wrong if your witness for Christ would be damaged by some indignant outburst.

Perhaps you remember a time when you lowered your standards of speech before others. You complained when you should have been thankful. You used near profanity to punctuate and emphasize an argument. You gave someone a piece of your mind over a trifle.

What can you do about it?

Probably nothing. Even apologies may accomplish little.

But you can bridle your tongue in the future. There are more important things than getting your way. If you are a Christian, you represent your Saviour. You are the best Christian somebody knows. Don't give the enemies of the Lord cause to rejoice.

When you feel like exploding, keep that bridle handy.

Don't disappoint Jesus by what you say.

Take heed...that you sin not with your tongue!

A NEW SONG

MEMORY VERSE: *And he hath put a new song in my mouth, even praise unto our God: many shall see it, and fear, and shall trust in the LORD* (Psalm 40:3).

Do you remember the pit? The one you were in when Christ saved you? You called and He answered. You came to Him and found that He would not cast you out. Your heart was overjoyed and you began to tell others about your Saviour. There was a new song in your mouth, even praise to your God.

But something has happened to your song.

Like many others, your most fruitful time of witnessing was right after your conversion. Your feet stood firm on the solid rock after having been lifted from the miry clay. You felt secure for the first time in your life. Your sins were gone and you knew it. Heaven was ahead and you rejoiced in it. All your old friends became prospects for witnessing. A number of them were saved as a result of your radiant testimony. You thought seriously about becoming a missionary, a pastor, a youth worker, or some other full-time Christian servant.

Then you began to take the Christian life for granted. Seeing others content to just go to church and take in without giving out, you concluded that must be a normal Christianity. Somehow, you settled down into a rut. Not the pit...but a rut. Now you're tired of living this way. You want to get back to the basics... reality... revival.

What can you do?

Glance back at the pit again. Don't dive in, but just remember what it was that Christ did to save you from that awful miry clay. He died for you...gave himself on the cross...shed His blood.

Now aren't you glad you're saved? If you are, start singing!

THE WAY BACK

MEMORY VERSE: *Deliver me from bloodguiltiness, O God, thou God of my salvation: and my tongue shall sing aloud of thy righteousness* (Psalm 51:14).

Backsliders are silenced. Their testimonies are squelched. They feel unworthy to talk about the Lord to others. They ask, "Who am I?" Before they return to the Lord, their lives are barren — desert like. Hear David describe his feelings while in this condition: *"When I kept silence, my bones waxed old through my roaring all the day long. For day and night thy hand was heavy upon me: my moisture is turned into the drought of summer"* (Psalm 32:3,4).

But no one needs to dwell in that desert.

All backsliders are invited back to the open arms of Jesus.

Read David's description of his return: *"I acknowledged my sin unto thee, and mine iniquity have I not hid. I said, I will confess my transgressions unto the LORD; and thou forgavest the iniquity of my sin"* (Psalm 32:5). How blessed!

Psalm 51 is David's prayer of confession as he returns to the Lord. Note that he not only expected forgiveness but also knew that his song would return, as well as his usefulness: *"Then will I teach transgressors thy ways; and sinners shall be converted unto thee"* (Psalm 51:13).

Are you far from God? It is time now for you to rid yourself of that heavy load you have been carrying. Confess your sins to Christ and claim His forgiveness. Commit your life to Him and get busy in His service. Return to your church and let others know what has happened in your life!

Returning, your tongue will again sing aloud of His righteousness and love.

GOD'S ORDER

MEMORY VERSE: *For the perfecting of the saints, for the work of the ministry, for the edifying of the body of Christ* (Ephesians 4:12).

Today's church is often afflicted by the "spectator syndrome." The saints sit and soak while the pastor does most of the ministering. But this is not God's plan for His people. Here's the plan: *"And he gave some, apostles; and some, prophets; and some, evangelists; and some, pastors and teachers; for the perfecting of the saints, for the work of the ministry, for the edifying of the body of Christ"* (Ephesians 4:11-12).

Every Christian is to be ministering. This is God's order. And in revival, the saints are activated. They are no longer content to try to fulfill their obligations to God by giving toward the pastor's salary and being listeners. Yet this may describe your present participation in your church.

Ask God to stir your heart today and get busy for Christ! There is no excuse for inactivity. God has given you everything that is necessary to perform His will. Whether you are ministering to the needs of other Christians or busy in evangelizing your community or the world, you can do the task God intends for you to do. So, begin where you are and with what you have.

- Visit someone who is sick and pray for him.

- Take food to a needy person.

- Volunteer to teach a Sunday School class.

- Shock your pastor by showing up for visitation.

- Distribute tracts throughout your neighborhood.

Don't wait for the pastor to bring revival. Think on the teaching he has already given and put it into practice. Do the work of the ministry.

A REVIVAL

MEMORY VERSE: *Thy words were found, and I did eat them; and thy word was unto me the joy and rejoicing of mine heart: for I am called by thy name, 0 LORD God of hosts* (Jeremiah 15:16).

What does a revival do to the attitude of people toward the Bible? Listen to Jonathan Edwards: "While God was so remarkably present amongst us by His Spirit, there was no book so delightful as the Bible; especially the Book of Psalms, the Prophecy of Isaiah, and the New Testament. Some, by reason of their love to God's Word, at times, have been wonderfully delighted and affected at the sight of a Bible; and then, also, there was no time so prized as the Lord's Day, and no place so desired as God's House."

Since the Holy Spirit is the source of revival and is also the Author of the Bible, it is not surprising that the work of God and the Word of God are closely associated. The Bible is a mighty power in giving victory over sin. Neglect of the Bible brings spiritual bankruptcy to any Christian.

> *"These two hath God married*
> *And no man can part;*
> *Dust on your Bible*
> *Means drought in your heart."*

Revival, then, sends men to their Bibles for guidance, comfort and victory over sin. You have those needs right now. They are always with us. Therefore, we do not have to wait until someone declares the arrival of revival. Go to God's treasure chest — the Bible — and allow its message to change your life. Find spiritual food there for the battles of this very day!

RIGHTEOUSNESS

MEMORY VERSE: *Blessed are they which do hunger and thirst after righteousness: for they shall be filled* (Matthew 5:6).

One of history's greatest revivals took place in Wales in 1904. There was such a move of God evident that writers and ministers from several countries visited Wales to become eyewitnesses of the revival. One Chicago religious paper published the following account: "A wonderful revival is sweeping over Wales. The whole country, from the city to the colliery underground, is aflame with gospel glory. Police courts are hardly necessary, public houses are being deserted, old debts are being paid to satisfy awakened consciences, and definite and unmistakable answers to prayer are recorded."

Notice the emphasis on the changed life during the Welsh revival. Playing church goes out of style. The heart's desire is for righteousness during revival. And no wonder! The revived heart is surrendered to the Lord and the fruit of the Spirit comes through: *"But the fruit of the Spirit is love joy, peace, longsuffering, gentleness, goodness, faith, meekness, temperance: against such there is no law"* (Galatians 5: 22-23).

The world has seen enough empty profession. It is time for Christians to demonstrate the righteousness of Christ in daily life: *"He that saith he abideth in him ought himself also so to walk, even as he walked"* (I John 2:6).

Imagine the impact of the ministry of your pastor if every member of the church had righteousness as his aim. Gone would be the excuses of backsliders and sinners who have been pointing accusations at those who are inconsistent in Christian living.

What changes would you experience in life if righteousness became your goal?

A WHOLESOME TONGUE

MEMORY VERSE: *A wholesome tongue is a tree of life: but perverseness therein is a breach in the spirit* (Proverbs 15:4).

A wholesome tongue heals.

A perverse tongue wounds.

Dr. H. A. Ironside wrote: "How much more common is the tongue of perversity than the healing tongue! The one separates brother from brother, and makes breach upon breach; the other binds together, giving cheer and gladness, and is a tree of life to those who meditate upon its utterances. The healing tongue is the tongue of the peacemaker. The perverse tongue belongs to him who sows discord among brethren. May it be ours to covet the former and flee the latter."

What does a peacemaker do?

He forgets the gossip that he hears about others.

When the faults of his friends become the topic of discussion, he maneuvers the conversation to another subject.

When he hears something negative about another, he doesn't feel it his duty to report what was said.

When he is approached by two who are at odds, he refuses to allow his ear to become a dumping ground for criticism.

When he hears a complimentary comment concerning someone, he is eager to pass the good word along.

He is willing to meditate between those who are in a disagreement.

He has understanding about the weaknesses of all people, but doesn't major on them.

He would rather discuss ideas or events than people.

He is swift to hear, slow to speak, slow to wrath (James 1: 19).

A spiritual person is a peacemaker.

Blessed are the peacemakers!

FAITH

MEMORY VERSE: *But without faith it is impossible to please Him: for he that cometh to God must believe that he is, and that he is a rewarder of them that diligently seek him* (Hebrews 11:6).

Faith sometimes needs reviving.

All Christians understand that salvation comes through faith. Before that day of peace with God arrived you struggled and tried to find the answer to life, but to no avail. Neither religion nor ritual met your need. Finally faith made the difference: *"Therefore being justified by faith, we have peace with God through our Lord Jesus Christ"* (Romans 5:1).

But faith is more than the key to eternal life. It is to be the daily experience of the child of God: *"Now the just shall live by faith..."* (Hebrews 10:38). And the mighty people of the Bible trusted God in their everyday battles. *"By faith Abraham, when he was called to go out into a place which he should after receive for an inheritance, obeyed; and he went out, not knowing whither he went"* (Hebrews 11:8).

Today, however, your faith may be faltering, Like Peter who walked well on the water until he looked about and saw his precarious position, you may find yourself sinking under the circumstances. You put on a good front and others don't know about the churning within.

Faith grows as we focus on the strength of the object of faith, the Saviour Himself. Peter's cry, *"...Lord save me!"* (Matthew 14:30) may be about all you can muster today. But that was enough to lift the drowning disciple back to the surface. Your present problems may be designed to demonstrate the power of God to deliver you. Have faith in God.

WORSHIP

> **MEMORY VERSE:** *Give unto the LORD the glory due his name; worship the LORD in the beauty of holiness* (Psalm 29:2).

We struggle for the best definition or expression of all that is contained in the word "worship." *"Zondervan's Pictorial Bible Dictionary"* defines it as follows: "The honor, reverence, and homage paid to superior beings or powers, whether men, angels, or God." It continues: "When given to God, worship involves an acknowledgement of Divine perfections. It may express itself in the form of direct address, as in adoration or thanksgiving, or in service to God; and may be private or public... Worship presupposes that God is, that He can be known by man, and that His perfections set Him far above man."

If all that seems too technical, your heart will guide you in expressing your love and adoration of the Lord. As the Scotsman said: "It's better felt that telt."

Worship the Lord in song. Praise Him in some melody that tells of His love and power. You say you can't carry a tune? Then get alone and make a joyful noise to the Lord.

Worship the Lord through prayer. Tell Him how much He means to you,

Worship the Lord in thanksgiving. Count your blessings and remember that every good gift comes down from above. We have nothing other than what has been provided by our Heavenly Father.

Worship the Lord in your conversation. While others take His name in vain, exalt God at every opportunity. Others will take notice.

Worship the Lord with a righteous and holy life. God will be pleased and you will be blessed. *"Worship the Lord in the beauty of holiness."*

REAPING

MEMORY VERSE: *Say not ye, There are yet four months, and then cometh harvest? behold, I say unto you, Lift up your eyes, and look on the fields; for they are white already to harvest* (John 4:35).

Revival brings times of reaping. Those in your community who have seemed unreachable could melt as a result of seeing changed lives about them. When the church gets right... evangelism flourishes.

Describing conviction and the wonderful soul winning climate of The Great Awakening, Jonathan Edwards wrote: "There scarcely was a single person in the town, old or young, left unconcerned about the great things of the eternal world. Those who were wont to be the vainest and loosest, and those who had been most disposed to think and speak lightly of vital and experimental religion, were now generally subject to great awakenings. And the work of conversion was carried on in a most astonishing manner and increased more and more; souls did as it were come by flocks to Jesus Christ. From day to day, for many months together, might be seen evident instances of sinners brought out of darkness into marvelous light and delivered out of a horrible pit and from the miry clay, and set upon a rock, with a new song of praise to God in their mouths (Psalm 40:1-3).

"This work of God, as it was carried on, and the number of true saints multiplied, soon made a glorious alteration in the town... It was a time of joy in families on account of salvation being brought unto them; parents rejoicing over their children as new-born, and husbands over their wives and wives over their husbands." Sound good?

It can happen again!

SPEAKING TO GOD

MEMORY VERSE: *Call unto me, and I will answer thee, and shew thee great and mighty things, which thou knowest not* (Jeremiah 33:3).

Five men were entrapped in a spar and zinc mine in Salem, Kentucky. They had nothing to eat and were in utter darkness. One of the men could have escaped had he not run back to warn the others.

When the entombed men discovered that they could not escape, they began to pray and sing. Their prayer and praise service lasted for fifty-three hours. Then they were rescued.

After the ordeal, one of the men said, "We lay there from Friday morning till Sunday morning. We prayed without ceasing. When the rescuers reached us, we were still praying."

When the men were brought up out of the mine, on the caps of each one were scrawled these words: "If we are dead when you find us, we are all saved."

God answered the prayers of the desperate miners. Undoubtedly many relatives and friends were also praying for their rescue. Reflecting on their experience, they must have felt they had used their time and tongues wisely...praying and singing praises to God.

But a question rises: "What would they have been talking about had the emergency not occurred?" And that begs another, "What miracles are missed because we do not pray?"

Had those miners used the same amount of time praying on another day when not facing death, what might the results have been?

If you are faced with a crisis today, do you believe that God will answer your prayer and bring you safely through? Do you need a crisis to cause you to speak to God?

Claim His promise. Call upon Him. See what great and mighty things are wrought by earnest prayer!

MOTIVES

MEMORY VERSE: *Let nothing be done through strife or vainglory; but in lowliness of mind let each esteem other better than themselves* (Philippians 2:3).

Christian work that is done for the praise of men is worthless.

Many years ago, I read a statement that needs to be repeated in every church. It simply said: "It is surprising what can be accomplished for Christ if you don't care who gets the credit."

Church platform service that is rendered to exalt the performer is only a performance and is on a par with any other show business production. It ought not be considered the work of God. Though it is certainly proper to strive for perfection in any presentation, I suspect the Judgment Seat of Christ will find many flawless special numbers lacking while humble servants who were not so talented but had correct motives will be rewarded.

What is your area of service for the Lord? How do you feel about it? Do you have a responsibility this very week? Is your heart right?

Another pitfall is that of pushing one's way into a position. This kind of service is born of strife. You have the job in the church you wanted, but you had to fight for it. Someone was injured in the battle. Better reconsider your motives. Perhaps you need to go to the offended one and offer to step aside so that he can serve. In losing your office you may gain a brother.

Your selfless act may bring revival to your church. And that will be more rewarding than the applause of your admirers.

GRUMBLING

MEMORY VERSE: *Do all things without murmurings and disputings* (Philippians 2:14).

Grumbling is serious.

Consider the following examples:

When Israel murmured against Moses, they were in reality murmuring against God: *"...and what are we? your murmurings are not against us, but against the LORD"* (Exodus 16:8).

At the edge of the promised land, Israel grumbled in unbelief and it cost them forty more years in the wilderness: *"Your carcasses shall fall in this wilderness; and all that were numbered of you, according to your whole number, from twenty years old and upward, which have murmured against me. Doubtless ye shall not come into the land, concerning which I sware to make you dwell therein, save Caleb the son of Jephunneh, and Joshua the son of Nun"* (Numbers 14:29-30).

The onlookers murmured when Mary of Bethany anointed Jesus with precious ointment: *"And there were some that had indignation within themselves, and said, Why was this waste of the ointment made? For it might have been sold for more than three hundred pence, and have been given to the poor. And they murmured against her"* (Mark 14:4-5).

The Pharisees and scribes murmured because Jesus received sinners: *"And the Pharisees and scribes murmured, saying, This man receiveth sinners, and eateth with them"* (Luke 15:2),

Judgment is coming for grumblers: *"These are murmurers, complainers, walking after their own lusts..."* (Jude 16).

The grumblers have been around in every age. Are you comfortable among them?

THOUGHT PATTERNS

MEMORY VERSE: *Finally, brethren, whatsoever things are true, whatsoever things are honest, whatsoever things are just, whatsoever things are pure, whatsoever things are lovely, whatsoever things are of good report; if there be any virtue, and if there be any praise, think on these things* (Philippians 4:8).

What we think, we are. *"For as he thinketh in his heart, so is he...* (Proverbs 23:7).

Dwelling on negatives can destroy us. The person who constantly thinks about problems and approaching disasters courts unhappiness. He chooses to be miserable. Focusing his attention on trouble, he is always troubled. His mind becomes fixed on gloom, and it is not strange that his general mood is gloomy.

Those who prefer to meditate on misery are like Eve, occupied with one tree of fruit that was marked for death while surrounded with untold varieties of allowable life giving choices. And when one lingers at the forbidden place, the tempter is always nearby.

The Bible calls us to a life centered in God's blessings. Why choose error when truth is better? To ignore the wrongs in the world is head-in-the-sand thinking. To make those wrongs the constant meditation of our hearts is an even greater mistake.

All great revivals have produced joyful Christians. The reason? Christ has become the focal point of thought and action. He is the One who is true, honest, just, pure, lovely and of good report. He personifies virtue and is always worthy of our praise.

Think on Jesus.

TOTAL SURRENDER

MEMORY VERSE: *But what things where gain to me, those I counted loss for Christ* (Philippians 3:7).

Christ had all of Paul. From the time of that experience on the road to Damascus until he finished his earthly course, he was a totally surrendered man. He counted all things loss for Christ,

A number of things were important to Paul before that lifelong surrender. There had been his pride of ancestry, his position as a Pharisee, his respect among his people, his future as a leader among them. Now all those things were counted but loss. Eternal things had priority, Christ was Lord of his life.

There is but one area through which we gain by total surrender. On the battlefield, surrender means defeat. However, in our walk with God, surrender means victory. It speaks of complete agreement with His will. And this is the greatest choice in life.

Paul's total surrender allowed him to reach his goal in life — the prize of the high calling of God in Christ Jesus. Few reach their goals. Youthful dreams often turn to nightmares. Castles tumble. Hopes crumble. Ideals are compromised for the sake of convenience. Not many arrive at their chosen destinations in life. But here was a man who surrendered and won. He discovered the way to blessing was in giving everything over to his Lord. And he never regretted it.

It is not too late for total surrender. You can abdicate the throne of your life in favor of Christ. That is the road to personal revival and blessing. Others may not understand, as was the case with Paul, but how many of his contemporaries do you know by name?

Give Christ first place in your heart.

VAIN RELIGION

MEMORY VERSE: *If any man among you seem to be religious, and bridleth not his tongue, but deceiveth his own heart, this man's religion is vain* (James 1:26).

The ability to communicate is one of God's greatest gifts to us. We can express the deep feelings of our hearts in words and songs of praise and thanksgiving. When we hurt, we can describe our pain to another who may be able to help. Love would be frustrated without means of communication. Poets and writers have capitalized on this and a never-ending stream of books and songs flow from their pens.

Some over communicate.

A woman once said to John Wesley, "My talent is to speak my mind." He answered, "God won't object if you bury that talent."

There is no sin quite so destructive as gossip. Churches have been divided, homes broken, and reputations ruined through careless words. Washington Irving said, "A sharp tongue is the only edge tool that grows sharper with constant use."

But the Christian has been given power to control his tongue and to use it for the glory of God. When he does not do so but continues to use his tongue to slander and divide, he is on dangerous ground. James casts doubt on the salvation of such a person by saying that his religion is vain...useless.

Heaven will hold many surprises. One of them will be the absence of many who claimed to be saved but had no real walk with God through faith in Christ. A mark of such people, according to the Bible, is their inability to bridle their tongues.

Don't follow a gossip.

He may be mistaken about his destination!

GREAT DAY

MEMORY VERSE: *And that every tongue should confess that Jesus Christ is Lord, to the glory of God the Father* (Philippians 2:1l).

What does the name "Jesus" mean to you?

Mrs. Booth used to tell a beautiful story of a man whose consistent Christian life left a permanent impression on her own. He seemed continually to grow in grace and at last he could speak of nothing but the glories of his Saviour and his face was radiant with awe and affection whenever he spoke that name.

When he was dying, a document was discovered that required his signature and it was brought to him. He held the pen for one brief moment, wrote, and fell back upon the pillows, dead. On the important paper, he had not written his own name, but the name that is above every name. Within sight of heaven, the name of Jesus was all that mattered to him.

To some the name of Jesus is but a means of emphasizing a point...a word to use in a tirade of profanity. To others the mention of the name brings to mind a prophet or a good man, perhaps a martyr to a cause. But to the Christian the name of Jesus speaks of salvation, heaven, resurrection, and a kingdom that will never be destroyed.

The name Jesus may call to mind His love for the outcasts, His tenderness with children, His compassion for all people, or His outpouring of love on the cross.

There is a day coming when at the name of Jesus every knee shall bow and every tongue confess that He is Lord, to the glory of God the Father.

That day is fast approaching.

Get ready.

Let Him be Lord of your life today!

GIVING

MEMORY VERSE: *For even in Thessalonica ye sent once and again unto my necessity. You can give without loving, but you cannot love without giving* (Philippians 4:16).

Revived people are giving people — generous people.

The old nature of man majors on getting. Enough seems unattainable. Witness the constant striving of wealthy people to get more and more. Selfishness is unmasked. Money is worshipped by many.

A few learn one of life's greatest lessons: It is more blessed to give than to receive. The Christians at Philippi were givers. They sent gifts to Paul even when things were difficult for them. Their generosity has not gone unnoticed. Centuries have come and gone and Paul's commendation of their acts of love remains. We're thinking about it today.

A favorite verse of thousands is Philippians 4:19: *"But my God shall supply all your need according to his riches in glory by Christ Jesus."* Many fail to notice that this often claimed promise is premised on generous giving. In the text, Paul is assuring these Christians that God will supply their needs because they have been faithful in sending gifts to him in his time of need.

There is another dimension to giving. George Muller wrote: "God judges what we give by what we keep." The giving heart is never satisfied while the coffers remain full. He gives cheerfully and is blessed in his giving.

We ought to give because we have been given so much: *"For God so loved the world, that he gave his only begotten Son, that whosoever believeth in him should not perish, but have everlasting life"* (John 3:16).

AREA WIDE REVIVAL

MEMORY VERSE: *So the people of Nineveh believed God, and proclaimed a fast, and put on sackcloth, from the greatest of them even to the least of them* (Jonah 3:5).

Many scoff at efforts for area wide revival. They have unnumbered reasons for their unbelief: The days are too wicked. The time is too late. Hearts are too hard. People will not listen. The cost of the effort is too great. But they seldom admit the reason for their defeatist attitudes — the cost of personal revival.

Revival cannot be pumped up — advertised in — promoted through — instead, it must be prayed down. Unless individuals get right with God there will be no revival. *In Nineveh, the king was one of the first to turn from his sin.* Others then followed. Area wide revivals are simply examples of many turning from sin to the Lord.

Most great revivals are built around strong preaching. Wesley, Finney, Moody and others were key servants of God in times of revival. It is interesting that God uses preaching. Foolishness, Paul called it. Yet he declared that God had chosen preaching to save them that believe — to give the message of the Gospel so that people can hear, believe and be saved.

Prayer and preaching — what a combination. You may not be able to preach, but you can pray. Through your praying, alone and with others in your area, God may ignite the fires of revival. When that happens, He will raise up someone to preach the Word in power so the move will be blessed with multiplied conversions.

Ask God for a burden for revival in your area. Begin to pray. An area wide revival may be the answer to your prayer.

UNTAMED THOUGHTS

MEMORY VERSE: *Out of the same mouth proceedeth blessing and cursing. My brethren, these things ought not so to be* (James 3:10).

Dr. Bob Jones Sr. wrote: "If any man offend not in word, the same is a perfect man, and able also to bridle the whole body." That is what the Holy Spirit said through James in the third chapter of the book he wrote.

"This statement we should know to be true even if it were not in the Bible. All of us know, if we stop to think, that our most difficult task is to control our tongues. There is nothing today that is doing more to deaden the spiritual testimony of orthodox Christianity than the long, backbiting, mean tongues of some supposedly orthodox Christians.

"There are Christians that talk much about a separated life, and boast about what they do and do not do, and speak with great pride about their loyalty to orthodoxy, who spend their time dipping their tongues in the slime and slander and speaking the death warrant to the reputation of other orthodox Christians.

"The Bible is filled with condemnation of people that slander other people. It condemns with great severity people who even take up a reproach about other people. It is just as bad to carry a rumor around after it starts as it is to start it."

You may be rebuked by this strong statement. You feel uncomfortable. Convicted. You've been unkind with your tongue.

What can you do?

Confess your unkind words to the Lord. Claim His forgiveness.

Stop grieving over past failures. But don't travel that same road again. Give Christ control of your life...including that dangerous tongue!

June

GIVE US THIS DAY OUR DAILY BREAD

While the earth remaineth, seedtime and harvest, and cold and heat, and summer and winter, and day and night shall not cease.

Genesis 8:22.

GIVING IN TROUBLE

MEMORY VERSE: *Of the gold, the silver, and the brass, and the iron, there is no number. Arise therefore, and be doing, and the LORD be with thee* (I Chronicles 22:16).

Some expect to be liberal givers to the Lord's work when they get through their present tight squeeze. They have the cart before the horse. People of faith have learned to give during difficult times and God has honored their faith.

Samuel Chadwick wrote: "Unless a man cultivates a habit of systematic giving when he has not much to give, he will give little when he is rich."

David instructed Solomon concerning his duty in building the temple and informed him that he had stockpiled the materials for the temple during troubled times: *"Now, behold, in my trouble I have prepared for the house of the LORD an hundred thousand talents of gold, and a thousand thousand talents of silver; and of brass and iron without weight; for it is an abundance: timber also and stone have I prepared; and thou mayest add thereto"* (I Chronicles 22:14).

Had David deferred his giving, he might never have prepared for the building of the temple. The reason? Trouble followed him all his life. And it is likely that we will never be completely free from difficulties. If we are ever to invest in the Lord's work, we must do so immediately.

Most of us do not have great fortunes to leave to Christian ministries after we finish this life and few have huge amounts to give now. The work of God is supported in large degree by widow's mites that He multiplies to reach the multitudes. But we do have something in our hands. And a share of that belongs to the Lord.

Even in troubled times!

WHY TROUBLE COMES

MEMORY VERSE: *I was not in safety, neither had I rest, neither was I quiet; yet trouble came* (Job 3:26).

Sometimes we know why trouble has come. A lady in a hospital bed once said to me, "I know why I'm here."

Trouble may come as a result of God's love and concern for us. Many will be in heaven because trouble enabled them to see the real issues of life more clearly. When their eyes had been washed with tears, they saw the folly of living without Christ and the emptiness of worldly gain or pleasure. A time of trouble became a signpost for heaven.

Trouble may come to a Christian because he is not living in the will of God: *"For whom the Lord loveth he chasteneth, and scourgeth every son whom he receiveth. If ye endure chastening, God dealeth with you as with sons; for what son is he whom the father chasteneth not?"* (Hebrews 12:6, 7). A professing Christian who seems to continue to get away with sin should examine himself to see if he is in the faith,

Trouble may come because God has a special purpose for it. Jesus met a man who had been born blind and His disciples thought the man's trouble was the result of some sin that he or his parents had committed. But Jesus told them that the blind man's trouble was not the result of his sins or the sins of his parents (John 9:3). His blindness was for the glory of God. Jesus restored his sight.

Trouble may come as an attack from Satan. That was the source of Job's trouble. He had not been presumptuous or backslidden. His trouble was an attack from the enemy.

We must be careful not to judge others in their times of trouble. If trouble comes to us because of sin, God will let us know so that we can confess it and be forgiven. Trouble that is not easily explained should be entrusted to the Lord.

His grace is sufficient for all!

ANSWERING JOB'S QUESTIONS

MEMORY VERSE: *Man that is born of a woman is of few days, and full of trouble* (Job 14:1).

Job was a good and prosperous man. He was both rich and righteous — a rare combination. His family consisted of seven sons and three daughters. Everything seemed to be going his way.

Then everything went wrong. Thieves stole his work animals. Lightning struck his sheep. A tornado hit his house where his children were gathered for a party and they were killed. His health failed. His wife became so depressed that she suggested that he end it all.

It is well known that Job came through this tough time triumphantly. Being human, however, he did ask some honest questions. Let's answer them.

QUESTION NUMBER ONE: *"Who can bring a clean thing out of an unclean..."* (Job 14:4).

ANSWER: God can. He specializes in it. We are all unclean. Yet Christ died for us and invites us to come for cleansing. *"Come now, and let us reason together, saith the Lord: though your sins be as scarlet, they shall be as white as snow... "* (Isaiah 1:18).

QUESTION NUMBER TWO: *"...yea, man giveth up the ghost, and where is he?"* (Job 14:10).

ANSWER: If he is a Christian, he is in heaven. *"We are confident, I say and willing rather to be absent from the body, and to be present with the Lord"* (II Corinthians 5:8).

QUESTION NUMBER THREE: *"If a man die, shall he live again?"* (Job 14:14).

ANSWER: Yes. He will be resurrected. For Christians, it will happen when Christ returns, and will bring blessing. *"...the dead in Christ shall rise first"* (I Thessalonians 4:16). The lost will be raised for judgment one thousand years later (Revelation 20:5).

THE REFUGE

MEMORY VERSE: *The LORD also will be a refuge for the oppressed, a refuge in times of trouble* (Psalm 9:9).

Troubled people often long for a place to hide. That is exactly what the Lord offers. Refuge here means "hill-fort." David must have been thinking of one of the hill-forts where he had sought refuge during one of his many times of trouble. See how many times he uses this precious likeness to our Lord:

"Ye have shamed the counsel of the poor, because the LORD is his refuge" (Psalm 14:6). *"...be merciful unto me: for my soul trusteth in thee: yea in the shadow of thy wings will I make my refuge, until these calamities be overpast"* (Psalm 57:1). *"But I will sing of thy power; yea, I will sing aloud of thy mercy in the morning: for thou hast been my defense and refuge in the day of my trouble"* (Psalm 59:16). *"In God is my salvation and my glory: the rock of my strength, and my refuge, is in God. Trust in him at all times; ye people, pour out your heart before him; God is a refuge for us"* (Psalm 62:7-8). *"I am as a wonder unto many; but thou art my strong refuge"* (Psalm 71:7). *"I will say of the LORD, He is my refuge and my fortress: my God; in him will I trust"* (Psalm 91:2). *"I cried unto thee, O LORD: I said, Thou art my refuge and my portion in the land of the living"* (Psalm 142:5).

Trouble can be going on all around one who is in a safe refuge and yet he will be secure. Perhaps your sea is storm-swept today. Unexpected problems have come upon you and you feel near the breaking point. You'd like to fly away somewhere and refuse to see anyone.

Here's good news. You do not need to flee to a different location to find peace and safety. Your refuge is available. Run to the hill-fort provided by Jesus.

He will keep you safe until the troubles are past!

IN HIDING

MEMORY VERSE: *For in the time of trouble he shall hide me in his pavilion: in the secret of his tabernacle shall he hide me; he shall set me up upon a rock* (Psalm 27:5).

Today you'd like to hang a "DO NOT DISTURB" sign on your door. You're embarrassed by a turn of events over which you had little or no control and you don't want to face people. You'd like to go into hiding. Interestingly, the Bible says that the Lord hides His own in His pavilion. What does that mean?

The pavilion of the king was a tent that was placed right in the middle of the army. An honor guard protected the pavilion and was charged with the king's protection as well. Guests of the king were privileged to stay in the pavilion and so they were assured of all the protection afforded by the king's army. The pavilion was a safe place to be.

The Psalmist also speaks of the safety of the tabernacle. Being inside the tabernacle speaks of the safety of the presence of the Lord. In the New Testament, Paul wrote: *"Set your affection on things above, not on things on the earth. For ye are dead, and your life is hid with Christ in God. When Christ, who is our life, shall appear, then shall ye also appear with him in glory"* (Colossians 3:2-4).

Finally, David declares that the Lord has set his feet up upon a rock. The Lord says that He is the Rock: *"He is the Rock, his work is perfect: for all his ways are judgment: a God of truth and without iniquity, just and right is he"* (Deuteronomy 32:4).

What protection in trouble! We are safe within the Lord's pavilion, safe within His tabernacle and standing on the Rock.

Don't you feel secure?

HE KNOWS

MEMORY VERSE: *I will glad and rejoice in thy mercy: for thou hast considered my trouble; thou hast known my soul in adversities* (Psalm 31:7).

You thought you were suffering alone.

The bills have been mounting. Your health has been shaky. Family problems eat away at your peace of mind. World conditions have made you worried. Your job isn't all that secure. And your savings are being depleted.

Take heart

God knows.

He also knows the state of your spiritual life. And intends that these burdens build you up in the faith. Matthew Henry has written: "God looks upon our souls, when we are in trouble, to see whether they are humbled for sin, and made better by the affliction. Every believer will meet with such dangers and deliverances, until he is delivered from death, his last enemy."

C. H. Spurgeon said, "Trials are the ballast of life. The burdened vessel may sail slowly, but she sails safely. Without the ballast of trial men are apt to blow over. Ballast yourself with sympathy, if you have no trials of your own.

Since God has considered your troubles... knows them, it is certain that they have not taken Him by surprise. Nothing slips up on God. And we belong to Him. He will not allow us to face more than we can bear. Henry Ward Beecher concluded: "No physician ever weighed out medicine to his patients with half so much care and exactness as God weighs out to us every trial, Not one grain too much does He ever permit to be put in the scale."

Rejoice. He knows and cares!

PRESERVED

MEMORY VERSE: *Thou art my hiding place; thou shalt preserve me from trouble; thou shalt compass me about with songs of deliverance* (Psalm 32:7).

When Mary Selleck of Chula Vista, California, neared her 100th birthday, she expressed poetically her trust in the provident care of God:

*"I do not know what the future holds
Of joy or pain,
Of loss or gain,
Along life's untrod way;
But I believe
I can receive
God's promised guidance day by day,
So I securely travel on.
And if, at times, the journey leads
Through waters deep,
Or mountains steep,
I know this unseen Friend,
His love revealing,
His presence healing,
Walks with me to the journey's end,
So I securely travel on."*

Heaven will hold many surprises. Looking back on earth's journey, we will be amazed and thankful at the knowledge that God has miraculously preserved us when trouble would have overtaken us. Our present burdens may seem heavy, but even these have been screened by the permissive will of our loving Lord.

THE UNFAILING ONE

MEMORY VERSE: *And the LORD, he it is that doth go before thee; he will be with thee, he will not fail thee, neither forsake thee: fear not, neither be dismayed* (Deuteronomy 31:8).

George Frederick Handel, the great musician, lost his health; his right side was paralyzed; his money was gone; and his creditors seized and threatened to imprison him. Handel was so disheartened by his tragic experiences that he almost despaired. But his faith prevailed. In his affliction, he composed his greatest work, *The Hallelujah Chorus*, which is part of his great, *Messiah*.

The list is long of those who have overcome handicaps and gone on to achievement and success through trust in the Lord. Annie Johnson Flint, afflicted with pain and suffering, wrote the much used "He Giveth More Grace," and many other wonderful poems. Fanny Crosby was blind but composed more than 8,000 published hymns. Helen Keller, shortly before her sixteenth birthday, expressed pity for the real unseeing, for those who have eyes still often do not see. She said, "If the blind put their hand in God's, they find their way more surely than those who see but have not faith or purpose."

What has been the secret of these conquerors?

They have understood that God is still in charge of the future. Refusing to be defeated by their fears, they have dared trust Him to accomplish great things in spite of their problems. And He has rewarded their faith.

Some choose to major on their problems, drawing back from contacts with other people and choosing the imprisonment of fear. Perhaps you are one of them. What a good day to place your future in the hands of the Unfailing One. He will not forsake you.

And you will not fail!

HOPE THOU IN GOD

MEMORY VERSE: *Why art thou cast down, O my soul? and why art thou disquieted within me? hope thou in God* (Psalm 42:11).

What was it that upset you last week? A harsh word? Fear of embarrassment of shame? Disappointment? Whatever it was that broke into your peaceful haven and made waves, you now know the result.

You lost hours of time that could have been filled with useful service. Your family was affected because you were upset. You said things that you cannot call back. You were less efficient in your daily work.

You should have learned a lesson from that experience, but, more than likely, you will be human enough to fall into that old trap again. When it happens, you may be disgusted with yourself. You may wonder why it has happened. You may find David's questions coming from your lips: *"Why art thou cast down, O my soul? and why art thou disquieted within me?"*

The answers to the psalmist's questions are not given. Only the antidote: *"...hope thou in God..."*

While we cannot prevent problems from coming our way, we can be prepared to meet them. Paul wrote: *"We are troubled on every side, yet not distressed; we are perplexed, but not in despair"* (II Corinthians 4:8). He had trouble, but was triumphant.

God is interested in the daily irritations that bug you. Tell Him about them. You'll find that sharing them with Him will ease the burden.

Hope thou in God!

HELP

MEMORY VERSE: *Give us help from trouble: for vain is the help of man* (Psalm 60:11).

Help from friends in times of trouble is always appreciated. Acts of love by others when we are in distress make us aware of the value of friends and fellow Christians, members of the family of God. There is a tie that binds our hearts in Christian love and in John Fawcett's great hymn, "Blest Be The Tie That Binds," he speaks of the blessing of helping one another.

"We share our mutual woes, Our mutual burdens bear;
And often for each other flows the sympathizing tear."

But there are times when the help of man is not enough. Times of trouble come that are beyond the reach of any earthly helping hand. The Psalmist saw those times and said of them, *"...vain is the help of man."*

Jesus specialized in helping those who had been given up by others. He healed ten lepers who were outcasts from their people. He raised the daughter of Jairus who had died. He restored health to a woman who had spent all her living on physicians seeking help. He called dead Lazarus from the grave after he had been dead four days.

You may be facing a problem that is beyond the help of man. Friends have been sympathetic, but your burden remains. Doctors have done their best to no avail. Financial experts have figured and refigured and have found no way out but bankruptcy. Counselors have exhausted their training and wisdom and your problems still is not solved.

It's time to call on the Lord in faith. Many have stood where you stand now and have been rescued by the Saviour. Long prayers are not required. Just call for help.

As the Lord answers, honor Him before others. Witness to His faithfulness. Your troubles will turn to triumph through the help of the Lord!

NOT AFRAID

MEMORY VERSE: *The LORD is my light and my salvation; whom shall I fear? the LORD is the strength of my life; of whom shall I be afraid?* (Psalm 27:1).

Chrysostom of Constantinople, threatened with exile or death, stated in a sermon at the time of his banishment: "What can I fear? Will it be death? But you know that Christ is my life. Will it be exile? But the earth and all its fullness is the Lord's. Will it be loss of wealth? But we brought nothing into the world and can carry nothing out. Thus all the terrors of the world are contemptible in my eyes, and I smile at all its good things."

He continued: "Poverty I do not fear. Riches I do not sigh for. Death I do not shrink from, and life I do not desire to save only for the process of souls. And so be if they banish me, I shall be like Elijah! If they throw me in the mire, more like Jeremiah. If they plunge me in the sea, like the prophet Jonah! If into the pit, like Daniel! If they stone me, it is Stephen I shall resemble! John the forerunner, if they cut off my head! Paul, if they beat me with stripes! Isaiah, if they saw me asunder."

The man of God had captured the meaning of David's question: *Whom shall I fear?*

Of whom are you afraid? Your boss? Your hot-tempered associate at work? Your husband? Your wife? Your creditors? Criminals? Communists?

They are but people. In Christ, you have the strength of the Lord. You do not need to be afraid!

UNSEEN ALLIES

MEMORY VERSE: *And he answered, Fear not: for they that be with us are more than they that be with them* (2 Kings 6:16).

Christians have immense resources in times of trouble. Sadly, we often forget this truth and react as if we had to face our problems alone. Angels must wonder at our frail faith. We have been promised protection and care, yet we fret and worry as if God did not exist. And worry is but another form of atheism.

Elisha and his servant found themselves surrounded by an army with horses and chariots bent on their destruction. The shaking servant seemed justified in his fears. But Elisha put away his fright by increasing his sight: *"And Elisha prayed, and said, LORD, I pray thee, open his eyes, that he may see. And the LORD opened the eyes of the young man; and he saw: and, behold, the mountain was full of horses and chariots of fire round about Elisha"* (2 Kings 6:17).

One of the surprises of heaven will be the revelation of God's goodness to us while we were on earth. When we get the answers to life's questions, it will amaze us to know how many times our Father has sent His angels to protect and help us in times of need.

Throwing in the towel when faced with difficulties disregards the effectiveness of our unseen allies. Christians ought not surrender, in view of their heavenly resources. We do not face obstacles alone.

The next time you're overwhelmed in a forest of fears, remember your unseen allies.

The woods are full of them. And their mission is for your good: *"Are they not all ministering spirits, sent forth to minister for them who shall be heirs of salvation?"* (Hebrews 1:14).

DISTRESS

MEMORY VERSE: *Then they cried unto the LORD in their trouble, and he delivered them out of their distresses* (Psalm 107:6).

Jesus meets the Christian who is in distress.

And He understands. He has been there.

Expose your distress to this message from Charles Spurgeon: "God is with us in sorrows. There is no pang that rends the heart, I might almost say, not one which disturbs the body, but what Jesus Christ has been with you in it all.

"Feel the sorrows of poverty? He 'had not where to lay His head.' Do you endure the griefs of bereavement? Jesus wept at the tomb of Lazarus. Have you been slandered for righteousness' sake and has it vexed your spirit? He said, 'Reproach hath broken Mine heart.' Have you been betrayed? Do not forget that He, too, had His familiar friend who sold Him for the price of a slave.

"On what stormy seas have you been tossed which have not roared about His boat? Never glen of adversity so dark, so deep, apparently so pathless, but what, in stooping down, you may discover the footprints of the crucified One! In the fires and in the rivers, in the cold of night and under the burning sun, He cries, 'I am with you; be not dismayed; for I am both thy Companion and thy God!'"

The dictionary defines distress as "Acute or extreme suffering or its cause; pain; trouble... an afflicted wretched or exhausted condition; a state of extreme need."

"Ah," you say, "that describes me and my troubles exactly."

Then take heart. You are not the first to endure such heartaches. God delivered others when in distress. That is the promise of our text.

And He will deliver you!

TRUST

MEMORY VERSE: What time I am afraid, I will trust in thee (Psalm 56:3).

David was no stranger to fear. He had been pursued by Saul who intended to kill him. Often, enemies had sought his life. Finally, rebellion racked his kingdom. He knew the twinge and tightening of fear. But he also knew what to do when fears came - *"What time I am afraid, I will trust thee."*

Trust. What a good word!

Hudson Taylor was so feeble in the closing months of his life, that he wrote a friend, "I am so weak that I cannot work; I cannot read my Bible; I cannot even pray. I can only lie still in God's arms like a little child and trust." This great man of God came to a place of physical suffering and weakness where he could only lie still and trust. And that is all God asks in that hour. James McConkey gave this advice to those in the fierce fires of affliction: "Do not try to be strong. Just be still."

How wonderfully the Bible meets us where we are! Scores of times the Scriptures advise us not to fear. Isaiah wrote: *"I will trust, and not be afraid"* (Isaiah 12:2). Yet, knowing that some would experience fear in spite of all assurances, direction is given to those already afraid. The call is for a move from trembling to trust.

But how does one trust when immobilized by fear?

There is but one answer. Fill your mind and heart with the promises of the Bible. Read the old familiar chapters that you love. Sing the old hymns that are full of Bible truth. Let God assure you with His Word.

Trust will grow — even in a trembling heart!

OUR REFUGE

MEMORY VERSE: *Therefore will not we fear, though the earth be removed, and though the mountains be carried into the midst of the sea* (Psalm 46:2).

In his book, *Two Thousand Hours in the Psalms*, Dr. Marion Hull says of Psalm 46, "No wonder the psalmist says 'therefore will not we fear.' What could man do to anyone who has such a source of strength and help as this?"

He explains that *refuge* means "a place to go quietly for protection." And that the Hebrew word translated trouble means "in tight places. "When we get in tight places we can go to the Lord and find a place of quiet protection.

This place of safety belongs to the children of God and is available even in convulsions of nature. One lady who slept through an earthquake was asked how she had such peace in the crisis. She replied that she rejoiced to have a God strong enough to shake the world.

Some are terrified at storms. The disciples expected to die in a watery grave during the storm that swept the Sea of Galilee. Jesus rebuked them for their lack of faith and also rebuked the wind and the waves. When they had entered the boat Jesus had said: "*Let us pass over unto the other side*" (Mark 4:35). His statement of sure crossing made the boat unsinkable in the face of any storm. Their fears were a waste of energy and a useless drain on their emotions. The Master of nature was on board. And in spite of their anxiety, all was well.

In all the storms of life, Christians have a refuge.

Flee to Him and leave your fears behind!

A TROUBLED FATHER

> **MEMORY VERSE:** *And he arose, and came to his father. But when he was yet a great way off, his father saw him, and had compassion, and ran, and fell on his neck, and kissed him* (Luke 15:20).

The prodigal's father must have spent many troubled nights, burdened about his son who had gone into the far country. He may have reviewed his life again and again wondering what he might have done differently, reliving a thousand situations and speculating at the possible results had he chosen a different course in regard to his son.

But this troubled father lived to see his son's return. His tears were changed to laughter; his regret to rejoicing. What was there about this father that brought the prodigal back from the pig pen?

HE WAS APPROACHABLE. The account given by Jesus seems to indicate that the mother had died, adding to the father's load. It is clear that the family was wealthy. There were servants and a sizeable inheritance. With all these responsibilities, the father evidently remained approachable. When the son decided to leave to seek his fortune, he was able to go to his father and tell him about his dreams. Some might have slipped away in the night, but he knew that his father would listen, that he could communicate with him.

HE WAS AFFECTIONATE. When the son returned home, he ran and fell on his neck and kissed him. Away with the nonsense that says manhood calls for hardness or that maturity calls for coldness. Spurgeon describes this scene as "prodigal love for the prodigal son." The son was welcomed by an affectionate father's open arms, not glaring stares of condemnation.

IN HIS SON'S MIND, HE WAS ASSOCIATED WITH HEAVEN. Even when wayward, the prodigal couldn't think about his father without being reminded of heaven: *"I have sinned against heaven, and before thee,"* he confessed.

No wonder the prodigal came home!

CHOOSE LESS

MEMORY VERSE: *Better is little with the fear of the LORD than great treasure and trouble therewith* (Proverbs 15:16).

A few years ago, a man stepped out into his back yard, and looking up saw a speck in the sky. It grew larger and larger. Then he discovered it was something alive, a struggling, living mass of something slowly descending to earth.

What he had first seen as a speck, had now revealed itself to be two large bald eagles in deadly combat. The huge birds were fighting in the sky over a fish. The fish finally dropped to the ground, but the birds continued their struggle until they were bloody and exhausted. With a last fatal scream and a plunge at each other, both birds came tumbling down to earth — dead, falling side by side, within a few feet of the man who had been witnessing the fierce battle of the sky. Greed had destroyed them.

Christians and churches are often destroyed like those birds. Testimonies are ruined. Congregations are divided. Reputations are destroyed. And all for the love of money, position or recognition. Someone demanded his rights... insisted on them, regardless of the destruction.

Here is a verse from the Bible that needs reviving: *"Now therefore there is utterly a fault among you, because ye go to law with one another. Why do ye not rather take wrong? why do ye not rather suffer yourselves to be defrauded?"* (I Corinthians 6:7).

That bit of advice would halt many a court battle between Christians and on a daily personal level would quiet many troubled seas. Strange that this practical verse seldom appears in Sunday School lessons or memorization programs. Perhaps too many would rather ignore its message.

In your present conflict, choose less, Take wrong!

JACOB'S TROUBLE

MEMORY VERSE: *Alas! for that day is great, so that none is like it: it is even the time of Jacob's trouble, but he shall be saved out of it* (Jeremiah 30:7).

Christ is coming soon. His return will usher in the world's most terrible time, known as the Tribulation or the Time of Jacob's Trouble. Of this time, Jesus said: *"For then shall be great tribulation, such as was not since the beginning of the world to this time, no, nor ever shall be"* (Matthew 24:21).

Some believe the church will remain on earth for the Time of Jacob's Trouble. Here are some reasons for rejecting that conclusion:

1. The return of Christ for His church is a sign less event. Even the New Testament writers expected the Lord's return at any moment. The moment the Tribulation begins, a timetable is evident. Date setting would be conclusive. Scripture would be violated.

2. The Tribulation is related especially to Israel. In Daniel 9:24-27, the prophet shares a vision of 70 weeks of years concerning Israel. Sixty-nine of those weeks have been fulfilled. When Christ returns for His church, the prophetic clock will tick again, fulfilling the final week.

3. The church is not the recipient of God's wrath: The Tribulation is a time when God's wrath is poured out on the earth. Paul assures us we will not go through that awful time: *"For God hath not appointed us to wrath, but to obtain salvation by our Lord Jesus Christ"* (I Thessalonians 5:9).

4. The world is ready for the Antichrist: The church is not all it ought to be but the world is better because it is here. When the influence of the Holy Spirit is removed at the Rapture of the church, the world will be ready for the final world dictator (II Thessalonians 2:7-8).

Your present trouble does not compare with the coming Tribulation.

Aren't you thankful?

REDEEMED

MEMORY VERSE: *But now thus saith the LORD that created thee, O Jacob, and he that formed thee, O Israel, Fear not: for I have redeemed thee, I have called thee by thy name; thou art mine* (Isaiah 43:1).

The old hymn says, "Redeemed, how I love to proclaim it!" And our redemption is worth proclaiming. The definition of *redeem* is "to regain possession of by paying a price." The price of our redemption was the blood of Christ: *"Forasmuch as ye know that ye were not redeemed with corruptible things, as silver and gold, from your vain conversation received by tradition from your fathers; But with the precious blood of Christ, as of a lamb without blemish and without spot"* (1 Peter 1:18,19).

To be redeemed is to belong to the Redeemer.

Since our Redeemer is Christ, we belong to Him.

This privileged position brings security. The Good Shepherd is our Redeemer and we are His sheep. Expose your fears to these promises: *"I am the good shepherd: the good shepherd giveth his life for the sheep. I am the good shepherd, and know my sheep, and am known of mine. As the Father knoweth me, even so know I the Father: and I lay down my life for the sheep. My sheep hear my voice, and I know them, and they follow me: And I give unto them eternal life; and they shall never perish, neither shall any man pluck them out of my hand. My Father, which gave them me, is greater than all; and no man is able to pluck them out of my Father's hand. I and my Father are one"* (John 10:11,14,15,27-30).

If you have been born again, you are one of the redeemed — one of His sheep. You belong to the Good Shepherd.

And here you are, afraid!

SECURITY

MEMORY VERSE: *Hearken unto me, ye that know righteousness, the people in whose heart is my law; fear ye not the reproach of men, neither be ye afraid of their revilings* (Isaiah 51:7).

The promises of God are given to a particular people, those who have received His Son as Saviour and Lord. Some mistakenly try to claim the promises without receiving the Saviour.

One may quote the beautiful Twenty-third Psalm and enjoy its description of green pastures and still waters, but it is vital to remember that the overflowing cup of the psalmist was based upon the first sentence of his expression of praise for provision: "The Lord is my shepherd."

Perhaps you have been reading the Bible to find peace and still your fears remain. Could it be that you have never been saved? My wife, Rexella, had a similar experience in her youth. Let her tell it:

"Following my solo in a church service — when I was sixteen — the moment of truth came. I left the service weeping and went to my parents' car to be alone. Concerned, my father followed me and asked what was wrong. 'Oh, Dad,' I sobbed, 'I've deceived my own heart. I've deceived our pastor and you and the whole church. I have known about the Lord all my life, but I don't really know Him.' Resisting the temptation to soothe my feelings, my father said: 'Be sure, Rexella.'

"A few days later, my older brother learned of my soul's distress when he heard me crying in my room. With genuine compassion and understanding, he led me through God's plan of salvation."

Tell the Lord of your doubts and uncertainty. Take Christ as your Saviour without delay. Trust Him to take away all your sins.

PEACE IN TROUBLED TIMES

MEMORY VERSE: *And ye shall hear of wars and rumours of wars: see that ye be not troubled: for all these things must come to pass, but the end is not yet* (Matthew 24:6).

Present world conditions incubate fears. And things are not likely to improve. Jesus said: *"And there shall be signs in the son, and in the moon, and in the stars; and upon the earth distress of nations, with perplexity; the sea and the waves roaring; Men's hearts failing them for fear, and for looking after those things which are coming on the earth: for the powers of heaven shall be shaken"* (Luke 21:25-26). But Christians do not need to be troubled.

The movements of men and nations in our day are but the outworking of our Father's plan. Perilous times, the explosion of knowledge, Israel as a nation, Russia a militaristic power with designs on the Middle East, China becoming a world power, the coming together of the nations of Western Europe, the slide of morals, the space programs and other developments are simply indications that God's Word is true and that our Saviour is coming soon.

What a great time to be alive!

Sometimes Christians become afraid when they read about a coming Antichrist, the mark of the beast and terrible persecutions that will come to believers during the Tribulation. But we must realize that we will not be here for that frightening time. Many will be converted after the Rapture of the church and will endure persecutions and martyrdom but Christians living at the time of Christ's return will escape the Tribulation (Revelation 3:10).

Look about you. See the fulfilling of prophecy. And rejoice!

The Lord is coming. He's coming for you!

THE OVERCOMER

MEMORY VERSE: *These things I have spoken unto you, that in me ye might have peace. In the world ye shall have tribulation: but be of good cheer; I have overcome the world* (John 16:33).

Christians will not go through the Tribulation but in this life they have tribulation. Being born again does not deliver one from all earthly trouble.

Christians have trouble because they have bodies that have been affected by the fall. Though the child of God is a citizen of heaven and will go there when he dies, his body still suffers the effects of the fall. We are all the children of Adam and Eve. Christians catch cold, get the flu, break bones when they fall, lose their teeth and hair with age and generally give evidence of being part of a fallen race. Sickness may not be the result of any particular sin or proof of the chastening of God, but simply an affliction that has come because our bodies are not what they were before the sin that brought about the fall.

Christians have trouble because they live in a troubled world. War that affects the general public also affects Christians. They should have greater peace in the midst of war, but inconveniences and injuries have come to Christians as to others during war. Christians have cars that don't start, washing machines that break down, pumps that give out, roofs that leak and other common irritations.

Christians have trouble in some cases because they are Christians. Jesus warned his disciples: *"If the world hate you, ye know that it hated me before it hated you. If ye were of the world, the world would love his own: but because ye are not of the world, but I have chosen you out of the world, therefore the world hateth you"* (John 15:18-19).

But Christians do not face their troubles alone. One overcoming Saviour gives us peace...even in troubled times!

DEVELOPING PATIENCE

MEMORY VERSE: *And not only so, but we glory in tribulations also: knowing that tribulation worketh patience* (Romans 5:3).

Some groan because of trials. Paul chose to glory in them. Writing on this text, Dr. Kenneth Wuest says: "Paul did not exult because of the tribulations themselves but because of their beneficial effect upon his Christian life. This the saint must learn to do. He must look at these trials and difficulties as assets that develop his Christian character. Paul says that they work patience."

George L. Rogers writes: "Most blessed is the ministry of affliction to those in the school of grace. Affliction produces endurance, the endurance of expectation (I Thessalonians 1:3), which, without fretfulness or complaint, heroically bears up under what God sends as being part of the all which He is working together for our good,"

Trials also build the patience of faith. Had we been asked to endure certain trials in advance, we might have thought we were unable or that God could not sustain us through them. However, when the trouble came, we held up because He gave grace for that occasion. After the trial, we knew that God was sufficient even for that unwanted affliction and therefore faith was stronger.

Annie Johnson Flint said from experience: "He giveth more grace when the burdens grow greater, He sendeth more strength when the labors increase." And had she not gone through times of increased burdens we would never have had her helpful and blessed song.

Trouble also increases patience in prayer. How quickly we want our answers! Yet God in His wisdom delays so that we will learn to pray with patient faith.

God is at work in your trials today!

VALUABLE

MEMORY VERSE: *Fear ye not therefore, ye are of more value than many sparrows* (Matthew 10:31).

We are bird-watchers. Beginning in the early fall, we stock our backyard bird feeder and watch the feathered drama there through the cold winter months. The beauty and temperament of God's flying creatures amaze and amuse us. The action there is a scene we wouldn't miss.

Jesus drew lessons from the birds and they play other prominent roles in the Bible. Noah dispatched birds to see if the flood had ended sufficiently to embark from the ark. Elijah was fed by the ravens during the long drought that had come upon his land.

God's care of the birds is revealed in the statement of Jesus that not one sparrow can fall to the ground without the Father's notice. Hence the song, "His Eye Is on the Sparrow." Nothing escapes the Father's view and all His creatures are objects of His concern and care.

But people are of more value than birds. Truth about the care of God for animals and birds should increase our confidence in the care of God for people. Every flying bird should remind us that God loves us and that He is concerned with our welfare and safety.

Martin Luther was once rebuked for being depressed by hearing a bird singing outside his window. A humorous sign says, "Cheer up! Birds have bills and they keep singing."

Put your fears to the sparrow test.

Know that He cares for you!

NOT IN DESPAIR

MEMORY VERSE: *We are troubled on every side, yet not distressed; we are perplexed, but not in despair.* It's not an easy road that we travel to heaven. And Paul's path was especially strewn with thorns. Stoning, scourging and shipwreck were a few of the hazards of his occupation — preaching the Gospel. Nevertheless, he did not despair (II Corinthians 4:8).

Why?

He remembered the resurrection: *"Knowing that he which raised up the Lord Jesus shall raise up us also by Jesus, and shall present us with you"* (II Corinthians 4:14). Paul served a living Saviour. And he never forgot it. He knew that he did not pass through his trials alone.

He remembered to refresh the inner man: *"For which cause we faint not; but though our outward man perish, yet the inward man is renewed day by day"* (II Corinthians 4:16). Times of trouble will overcome us if we do not give attention to spiritual needs. Never allow difficulties to keep you from the Bible, from prayer or the fellowship of your church. If you have slacked off in any of these areas, return to them immediately. No one is strong enough to neglect his Bible, his prayer life or the fellowship of other believers and stay strong.

He remembered that eternal values are greater: *"For our light affliction, which is but for a moment, worketh for us a far more exceeding and eternal weight of glory"* (II Corinthians 4:17). Time passes quickly. Eternity is more important. Looking beyond our present problems to blessings promised in the future, lightens the load and makes it bearable.

Your present situation may be difficult, but you are loved by your living Lord who has pledged His word and is preparing a place. Don't despair!

COMFORTING OTHERS

MEMORY VERSE: *Who comforteth us in all our tribulation, that we may be able to comfort them which are in any trouble, by the comfort wherewith we ourselves are comforted of God* (II Corinthians 1:4).

An old man once prayed, "Lord, bless the pastor for no man can be a blessing until he himself is first blessed of God." Here Paul gives somewhat the same requirement for those who long to comfort others in their times of trouble. Having experienced the comfort of God in tribulation, we are able to comfort those in need.

Jesus has set the example. Hear Peter's application of this good news: *"For what glory is it, if, when ye be buffeted for your faults, ye shall take it patiently? but if, when ye do well, and suffer for it, ye take it patiently, this is acceptable with God. For even hereunto were ye called: because Christ also suffered for us, leaving us an example, that ye should follow his steps: Who did no sin, neither was guile found in his mouth: Who, when he was reviled, reviled not again; when he suffered, he threatened not; but committed himself to him that judgeth righteously"* (I Peter 2:20-23). Because He suffered, He can help us in our suffering: *"For in that he himself hath suffered being tempted, he is able to succour them that are tempted"* (Hebrews 2:18).

Your suffering, then, may be given to open up a ministry to those who are passing through similar trials. Observe God's faithfulness to you during this experience so that you can share the message with those to whom you are sent.

Lean hard on His promises... and look for your opportunity to serve!

TEMPORARY TRIALS

MEMORY VERSE: *Wherein ye greatly rejoice, though now188 for a season, if need be, ye are in heaviness through manifold temptations* (I Peter 1:6).

All trials are temporary.

And fretting over them doesn't help.

Had John Bunyan spent his twelve long years in the Bedford jail stewing over his predicament, we would have been deprived of *"Pilgrim's Progress."* It was there in his greatest time of trouble that he produced his greatest work. Bunyan said, "I was at home in prison, and I sat me down and wrote and wrote, for the joy did make me write."

Sounds great for Bunyan. But rejoice in trials?

Let's face it. Trials themselves do not generally make us feel like rejoicing. But Peter's word here is that the Christian always has some things in which to rejoice, even during difficulties.

We can rejoice that we have living hope because of our living Saviour.

We can rejoice that we have an inheritance reserved in heaven that cannot be affected by trials here below.

We can rejoice that we are kept by the power of God and that eternal life is therefore certain.

We can rejoice that our trials are temporary...passing things.

We can rejoice that faith grows during times of trouble and that true faith comes forth as gold. Job understood that in the time of his severe trials: *"But he knoweth the way that I take: when he hath tried me, I shall come forth as gold"* (Job 23:10).

We can rejoice that our Lord is coming again ... perhaps today, and that it will be worth it all when we see Him.

A Christian can rejoice in times of trial because he has so many possessions that earthly trials cannot touch. Rejoice!

JOYFUL IN TRIBULATION

MEMORY VERSE: *Great is my boldness of speech toward you, great is my glorying of you: I am filled with comfort, I am exceeding joyful in all our tribulation* (II Corinthians 7:4).

The Christian lifestyle is different. The world rejoices when all is going well. Christians are taught to praise God — give thanks — and rejoice even in trouble. This message runs through both the Old and New Testaments. Note these examples:

"Although the fig tree shall not blossom, neither shall fruit be in the vines; the labour of the olive shall fail, and the fields shall yield no meat; the flock shall be cut off from the fold, and there shall be no herd in the stalls: Yet I will rejoice in the LORD, I will joy in the God of my salvation" (Habakkuk 3:17-18).

"Blessed are ye, when men shall revile you, and persecute you, and shall say all manner of evil against you falsely, for my sake. Rejoice, and be exceeding glad: for great is your reward in heaven: for so persecuted they the prophets which were before you" (Matthew 5:11-12).

"And not only so, but we glory in tribulations also: knowing that tribulation worketh patience" (Romans 5:3).

"Beloved, think it not strange concerning the fiery trial which is to try you, as though some strange thing happened unto you: But rejoice, inasmuch as ye are partakers of Christ's sufferings; that, when his glory shall be revealed, ye may be glad also with exceeding joy. If ye be reproached for the name of Christ, happy are ye; for the spirit of glory and of God resteth upon you: on their part he is evil spoken of, but on your part he is glorified" (I Peter 4:12-14).

Having a bad day?

The Lord understands.

Praise the Lord!

THE LIVING ONE

MEMORY VERSE: *And when I saw him, I fell at his feet as dead. And he laid his right hand upon me, saying unto me Fear not; I am the first and the last* (Revelation 1:17).

There is really only one question about life and death: *Did Jesus Christ rise from the grave?* And careful investigation allows only one answer: *He arose.* He lives!

Since Christ lives, those who trust in Him do not need to fear life's end. No one is more miserable than the person who lives in fear of some illness or accident that will bring death. An old epitaph says:

> *Here lies a man who lived to age,*
> *Yet still from death was flying;*
> *Who, though not sick, was never well.*
> *And died for fear of dying.*

Neither does a Christian need to fear life. Some are brave in death and cowards in life. Bible Christianity embraces all of life and faces the issues of death, preparing the believer for both. Paul said it well: *"For to me to live is Christ, and to die is gain"* (Philippians 1:21).

How can you prepare to live and die?

By receiving Jesus Christ as your Saviour by faith. Accept this invitation: *"If thou shalt confess with thy mouth the Lord Jesus, and shalt believe in thine heart that God hath raised him from the dead, thou shalt be saved"* (Romans 10:9).

When you take this step of faith, expect changes: *"Therefore if any man be in Christ, he is a new creature: old things are passed away; behold, all things are become new"* (2 Corinthians 5:17).

Wouldn't you like to be free from fear?

TROUBLES OVER TEARS GONE

MEMORY VERSE: *And God shall wipe away all tears from their eyes; and there shall be no more death, neither sorrow, nor crying, neither shall there be any more pain: for the former things are passed away* (Revelation 21:4).

We live in a world of grief and God has graciously provided tears as a safety valve for our emotional and physical survival. Were it not for the ability to weep, many would break down... come apart.

Nor is it a sign of weakness to shed tears, *Jesus wept* (John 11:35).

Still we look forward to that day when tears are unnecessary because all trouble is over. And that good day is coming!

Death will be gone.

Sorrow will be gone.

Pain will be gone.

Because sin will be gone.

What is it that has you upset today? Are you troubled about world conditions? Do family problems loom large before your mind? Are financial woes weighing you down? Has health taken wings? Are you in pain? Do you fear the outcome of some present conflict? Has a friend betrayed or deserted you? Have you lost a loved one in death? Do tears come unwanted?

Look upward and onward.

Christ is coming. Time is moving swiftly to its end. Signs of our Lord's return are all about. If you know Him as your Saviour, thank Him for that coming day when He will wipe all tears from your eyes.

If you have not received Him as your Saviour, do not delay one more day. Come to Him as you are, turning from your sins to Him and taking Him by faith as your personal Saviour and Lord. Prepare for that great day!

July

GIVE US THIS DAY
OUR DAILY BREAD

While the earth remaineth, seedtime and harvest, and cold and heat, and summer and winter, and day and night shall not cease.

Genesis 8:22.

TROUBLEMAKERS

MEMORY VERSE: *And Elijah came unto all the people, and said, How long halt ye between two opinions? if the LORD be God, follow him: but if Baal, then follow him. And the people answered him not a word* (I Kings 18:21).

Elijah's country was in trouble.

King Ahab thought the prophet was the cause of it all.

Actually, the wicked king was the guilty one. He had led the people in idolatry and had forsaken God's commandments. The drought announced by Elijah was but the natural consequence of the nation's sin. The famine in the land was directly traceable to the waywardness of the people. Israel was experiencing the law of sowing and reaping: *"Be not deceived; God is not mocked: for whatsoever a man soweth, that shall he also reap"* (Galatians 6:7).

Godly people are often thought of as troublemakers. They speak out against evils and seem not to fit in with many modern trends. They may seem out of step with the times ... unwilling to compromise proven standards. Dogmatic. Old fashioned.

Never mind. Convictions based on the Bible should be held even though they disturb others. God rewards righteousness and judges sin. His standards are unchanging because He is always the same.

Sin brings chastening... produces heartache... invites trouble. And no amount of rationalizing can change sin's wages. It is impossible to sin and win: *"For the wages of sin is death; but the gift of God is eternal life through Jesus Christ our Lord"* (Romans 6:23).

America needs some troublemakers... the righteous kind. We need people who will stand for truth and decency in spite of what others say.

May God raise up some troublemakers to keep the nation out of trouble!

DON'T FORGET

MEMORY VERSE: *The wicked shall be turned into hell, and all the nations that forget God* (Psalm 9:17).

The mighty Roman Empire was powerful and proud. People thought it would last forever. But it fell... and fell hard.

In 1787, Gibbon completed his masterful book, *"The Decline And Fall Of The Roman Empire."* He gave the following reasons for its fall: the rapid increase of divorce with resultant undermining of the home; higher and higher taxes and the spending of public money for free bread and circuses for the people; the mad craze for pleasure and sports which became more and more brutal; the building of gigantic armaments, when the real enemy was within, and the decay of religious faith which faded into formalism and became impotent.

Paul's letter to the Romans begins with the record of a fall for similar reasons, the most important of which was that of forgetting God... on purpose: *"And even as they did not like to retain God in their knowledge, God gave them over to a reprobate mind, to do those things which are not convenient"* (Romans 1:28).

Forgetting God is dangerous to the survival of nations.

Do you think America is guilty of forgetting God?

What evidences of forgetting God do you see about you?

Do you believe the religious life of our nation to be heartfelt or formalistic?

Have America's moral standards declined during your lifetime? In the last decade? During the past year?

How about your personal relationship to Christ? Is it vital or formalistic? Can you remember a better day?

What are you going to do about it? When?

SALVATION

MEMORY VERSE: *But I have trusted in thy mercy; my heart shall rejoice in thy salvation* (Psalm 13:5).

The joy of the Lord begins with salvation. The moment of new birth gives cause for rejoicing. Heaven rejoices: *"Likewise, I say unto you, there is joy in the presence of the angels of God over one sinner that repenteth"* (Luke 15:10). The newborn Christian can also be glad for many reasons.

We can rejoice in salvation because we have a home in heaven. Earthly homes are temporary. Fire or foreclosure may take away your home on this earth. Not so your heavenly home. The things that are seen are temporal but the things that are not seen are eternal. Each Christian has a title deed to a home in heaven that is indestructible.

We can rejoice in salvation because we have become heirs of God and joint-heirs with Christ (see Romans 8:17). During your earthly journey, you may never inherit anything valuable, but if you have been saved, you will share the inheritance of the saints. Praise the Lord!

We can rejoice in salvation because our names are written in heaven. Jesus said: *"Notwithstanding in this rejoice not, that the spirits are subject unto you; but rather rejoice, because your names are written in heaven"* (Luke 10:20). Many people do not know your name. You are probably not on a first-name basis with world leaders. But, if you have been born again, your name is known in heaven.

Rejoice in God's salvation!

TRUSTING

MEMORY VERSE: *But let all those that put their trust in thee rejoice: Let them ever shout for joy, because thou defendest them: let them also that love thy name be joyful in thee* (Psalm 5:11).

History records how George Washington found rest and relief in prayer during the trying times he and his soldiers passed through at Valley Forge. With all the cares and anxieties of that time upon him, he used to have recourse to prayer.

One day a farmer approaching the camp heard an earnest voice. On coming nearer, he saw George Washington on his knees, his cheeks wet with tears, praying. The farmer returned home and said to his wife: "George Washington will succeed!"

"What makes you think so, Isaac?" asked his wife.

The farmer replied: "I heard him pray, Hannah; you may rest assured he will."

One night during the Civil War, a guest in the White House reported that he had heard Lincoln praying in the next room. He said the President prayed: "Thou God, who heard Solomon in the night when he prayed and cried for wisdom, hear me! I cannot guide the affairs of this nation without Thy help. I am poor and weak and sinful. O God, save this nation."

We have a great heritage. Without question, God has defended America in the past. We ought to rejoice in our independence. But we must never forget that this freedom is a gift from God. The moment we stop trusting Him, liberty is in jeopardy.

Christians who serve God and rejoice in Him are America's most valuable asset. What will YOU do for your country?

GOD'S PROTECTION

MEMORY VERSE: *Blessed be the LORD, who hath not given us as a prey to their teeth* (Psalm 124:6).

God has protected America.

We ought to thank God daily for His care of our nation through more than two hundred years. We have escaped the march of foreign feet on American soil in time of war though two world conflicts have been fought in this century.

Even the destruction of the nation through civil war was averted through prayer. Walter Brown Knight has written: "The fate of the nation was hanging in the balances. General Lee and his army had surged forward to the environs of Gettysburg, where the fateful, decisive battle of the Civil War was in the making. The sorrows and burdens of the war-torn nation had exacted its terrible toll on the occupant of the White House, Abraham Lincoln. Yet on the eve of the crucial Battle of Gettysburg, he was calm and assured. His serenity was reassuring to his generals. When they inquired, 'How can you be so self-possessed in this hour of the nation's mortal peril and darkness?' Lincoln said, 'I spent last night in prayer before the Lord. He has given me the assurance that our cause will triumph and that the nation will be preserved.'"

And what blessing has followed America through these years. This good land has become the home base for missionary outreach all over the world. American printing presses as well as radio and television carry the Bible message to millions.

Still, many are becoming concerned about the future. Will America continue to experience such blessings? For how long?

God's blessings rest on those who obey His Word. Let's live in His will so that His protection will always preserve our land!

WHAT CAN I DO FOR MY COUNTRY?

MEMORY VERSE: *Righteousness exalteth a nation: but sin is a reproach to any people* (Proverbs 14:34).

De Tocqueville of France, over a century ago, visited America. Upon his return home he wrote: "I sought for the greatness of America in her harbors and rivers and fertile fields, and her mines and commerce. It was not there. Not until I went into the churches and heard her pulpits aflame with righteousness did I understand the greatness of her power. America is great because she is good: and if America ever ceases to be good, America will cease to be great."

But there is a sense in which America cannot be good.

Righteousness is not something that is accepted by a nation as a body. It is not legislated in congress or decided in the halls of justice. Good or bad decisions by a government may affect the conduct of its people in certain areas of life, but righteousness is an individual matter.

"In God We Trust" is a moving motto for our money, yet millions of Americans do not trust in God. Therefore, that official statement of faith is only meaningful for those to whom it has meaning. In whom do you trust?

Neither is it enough to decry conditions in the land. A serious situation does exist. Daily news reports are convincing proof of that. But the solution lies in personal repentance of sin and faith in Christ.

It is the righteousness of the people that exalts a nation. The sins of the people reproach the land.

As an individual American, what do you intend to do for your country?

HELPED

MEMORY VERSE: *The LORD is my strength and my shield; my heart trusted in him, and I am helped: therefore my heart greatly rejoiceth; and with my song will I praise him* (Psalm 28:7).

A Christian in Central Russia wrote the following: "After our commune was closed, I spent some time in the place where God's servants have to stay... (in prison). And yet, I assure you, that during that time in my heart it was as though I were living in the Garden of Eden... Scarcely a single night passed when I did not rise from my bed and thank God. And what was that which moved me to praise Him? Why, the consciousness of His wonderful presence. The only thing for me to do was to get upon my knees and praise God for His faithful and unfailing presence."

The world has a saying: "The Lord helps those who help themselves." Some mistakenly think that this statement is in the Bible. The truth is — the Lord helps those who cannot help themselves. He meets us where we are in our deepest needs.

Paul was helped when buffeted by a messenger from Satan, a thorn in the flesh. Though the physical problem was not removed, grace was promised for that particular test: *"My grace is sufficient for thee: for my strength is made perfect in weakness"* (2 Corinthians 12:9).

How have you been helped? Have prayers been answered? Has money been supplied for a special need? Have you recovered from a serious illness? Has a loved one been saved? Were you protected from an accident? Were you given strength for a difficult task?

Are you rejoicing over the help granted to you? Praise God for His goodness and rejoice in His help.

FREEDOM

MEMORY VERSE: *Is not this the fast that I have chosen? to loose the bands of wickedness, to undo the heavy burdens, and to let the oppressed go free, and that ye break every yoke?* (Isaiah 58:6).

No people have ever had so much and appreciated it so little as Christians in America. We belong to a privileged few who have been able to carry Bibles, attend church and live for Christ without fear of imprisonment or the loss of our lives. Other Christians in other centuries or in other lands have often paid with their lives or freedom for identifying with the Saviour.

Because of the persecutions brought by communistic governments, it is generally agreed that there have been more Christian martyrs in this century than in any other. Still Christians in America have been virtually untouched.

How strange it is then that we are so given to complaining! We gripe about so many things: the weather, our jobs, our wives or husbands, our homes, our churches, our pastors, our health, etc. What would we do if things were really difficult?

This question raises a frightening thought! If we are edgy in affluence, may God have to chasten us to allow us to see what blessings we have been experiencing? Must goods and loved ones be taken away before we appreciate them? Must freedom flee before we realize its importance?

One winter morning I was walking through a blizzard to my office and complaining silently about the storm. When I stepped inside my office my eyes fell on a tiny book in my library, entitled *Come Wind Come Weather*. Immediately my grumbling ceased, for the book I saw upon entering that warm room is the story of the persecution of the church in China. Our storms here are few. Thank God for freedom!

RENDER UNTO CAESAR

MEMORY VERSE: *Then saith he unto them, Render therefore unto Caesar the things which are Caesar's; and unto God the things that are God's* (Matthew 22:21).

Should Christians pay their taxes? Vote? Hold public office? Carry out civic responsibilities?

Yes!

Without a doubt!

Christians ought to be the finest citizens in the land. They have been commanded to give Caesar his due.

This command of Jesus is not meant to so separate the secular and the sacred that one can be loose in his conduct while caring for matters having to do with the government simply because that is in Caesar's department. Not at all. Every area of the Christian life is sacred. However, it is clear that carrying out earthly responsibilities does not interfere with dedication to the Saviour unless the government requires some act that is in conflict with the Bible. In those cases, we ought always to obey God rather than man (Acts 5:29).

On this text, Dr. John R. Rice has written: "Duty to government does not conflict with duty to God. Jews would sin if they went after Roman idolatry, but they would properly pay taxes to support the government then in power which furnishes them so many of the protections and facilities of the nation. Jesus Himself and Peter paid taxes (Matthew 17:24-27). Christians are urged to pray for rulers (I Timothy 2:1, 2). It is proper for Christians to vote and to use their influence for good government."

Citizens of heaven cannot ignore their duty as citizens of this earth!

AFTER BACKSLIDING

MEMORY VERSE: *Make me to hear joy and gladness; that the bones which thou hast broken may rejoice* (Psalm 51:8).

No load is heavier than the burden of backsliding. David had learned that lesson the hard way. After sin, the chastening of God had fallen upon him and he was tormented with conviction of his wrong doing.

At first he decided to ignore God's voice that called him to confession of sin. Listen to his description of that awful time: *"When I kept silence, my bones waxed old through my roaring all the day long. For day and night thy hand was heavy upon me: my moisture is turned into the drought of summer"* (Psalm 32:3,4).

Finally, tired of his backsliding, he made the right decision: *"I acknowledged my sin unto thee, and mine iniquity have I not hid. I said, I will confess my transgressions unto the LORD; and thou forgavest the iniquity of my sin"* (Psalm 32:5).

Psalm 51 is David's prayer of confession of sin. See his openness with God. Nothing is hidden. He calls for cleansing, forgiveness, a right attitude, and the joy of salvation. He fully intends to become an effective witness even though he has failed so badly: *"Then will I teach transgressors thy ways; and sinners shall be converted unto thee"* (Psalm 51:13).

How good it feels to be right with God! There is rejoicing in heaven over the return of the prodigal, but the prodigal also rejoices. Home is a wonderful word. And the Christian who returns to His Lord after backsliding has come home.

Come home. And rejoice!

IN THE LORD

MEMORY VERSE: *Rejoice in the LORD, 0 ye righteous: for praise is comely for the upright* (Psalm 33:1).

"Rejoice in the Lord" is a command given in both the Old and New Testaments. Paul admonished the Christians at Philippi: *"Rejoice in the Lord alway: and again I say, Rejoice"* (Philippians 4:4).

But how can one rejoice when all his castles are tumbling and everything seems to go wrong? Can we rejoice over unpaid bills? Poor health? A divided family? The loss of a job? Jangled nerves?

Perhaps not.

But we can rejoice in the Lord!

When everything seems to be coming apart, He is unchanged. Though others forsake us, He remains faithful. If financial reverses come, He provides for our needs. When earthly gain turns to loss, He offers permanent treasure in the bank of heaven. If death seems imminent, He has given eternal life. Though the love of those nearest us cool, His love is constant.

The rejoicing of the psalmist had to find expression. He played the harp, the psaltery, and an instrument of ten strings. He sang songs of praise. It was impossible to hold in his joy. Some may have thought him too emotional. Perhaps they preferred dead-pan religion. Nevertheless, the psalmist rejoiced in the Lord and announced his joy to others. His praise was public and he was not ashamed.

Regardless of the circumstances, we can rejoice in the Lord. Christians should never be "under the circumstances." Our Lord is above all. Today's problems have not taken Him by surprise. Praise the Lord!

MUST CHRISTIANS OBEY THE LAW?

MEMORY VERSE: *Let every soul be subject unto the higher powers. For there is no power but of God: the powers that be are ordained of God* (Romans 13:1).

Christians ought to obey the law. Though some laws may be irritating and seem senseless, if they do not conflict with the Bible, we are obligated to obey them.

Commenting on this text, Dr. H. A. Ironside wrote: "The position of the Christian in this world is necessarily, under the present order of things, a peculiarly difficult and almost anomalous one. He is a citizen of another world, passing as a stranger and a pilgrim through a strange land. Presumably loyal in heart to the rightful King, whom earth rejected and counted worthy only of a malefactor's cross, he finds himself called upon to walk in a godly and circumspect way in a scene of which Satan, the usurper, is the prince and god. Yet he is not to be an anarchist, nor is he to flaunt the present order of things. His rule ever should be: 'We must obey God rather than man.' Nevertheless he is not to be found in opposition to human government, even though the administrators of that government may be men of the most unrighteous type."

So clear is this text that one must understand that to disobey the law is to be out of the will of God.

And that logical conclusion presents another: you may not have found the will of God for your life because you are not obedient to the laws of the land.

Sound farfetched? Better reconsider.

We learn God's will through His word. Obey it. All of it. Even Romans 13!

PROSPERITY

MEMORY VERSE: *They drop upon the pastures of the wilderness: and the little hills rejoice on every side* (Psalm 65:12).

Sometimes those who prosper rejoice less than the poor. They hold earth's trinkets so tightly that the fear of losing them is ever with them. Often they have become slaves to the prosperity that has been their goal in life.

A few wealthy and prosperous people are free from the bondage of their possessions. A Christian doctor was asked what he had done during the past week. He replied, "On Monday, I preached the Gospel in Brazil. Tuesday, I ministered among the Mexican people in southwest Texas. Wednesday, I operated on patients in a hospital in Africa. Thursday, I taught in a mission school in Japan. Friday, I helped establish a new church in California. Saturday, I taught classes in our seminaries. Sunday, I distributed Bibles in Korea."

The astonished questioner asked, "How could you be in so many places, doing so many different things?"

"I wasn't," said the doctor with a twinkle in his eye, "for I have been busy with my patients every day. But, you see, I hold the dollars God has enabled me to earn in trust for God, and some of them have been channeled into the places of need I have mentioned."

Walter Brown Knight wrote: "There are two ways to be rich — one is to have all you want, and the other is to be satisfied with what you have."

The real secret of joy in prosperity is the ability of rejoicing in the One who gives the power to get wealth. Rejoice in Him! All we have is from His hand.

THE RIGHTEOUS

MEMORY VERSE: *But let the righteous be glad; let them rejoice before God: yea, let them exceedingly rejoice* (Psalm 68:3).

Righteousness is rewarded.

Sometimes it doesn't seem that way.

Knowing there would be times when it appeared the wicked were coming out winners, the psalmist wrote: *"Fret not thyself because of evildoers, neither be thou envious against the workers of iniquity. For they shall soon be cut down like the grass, and wither as the green herb"* (Psalm 37:1,2).

Things are seldom what they seem. Outward success is meaningless unless the heart is right. Sin detracts from delight. The so-called "beautiful people" are often among the worlds most unhappy.

Only the righteous can truly rejoice.

But it is sad when the righteous do not rejoice. Those who have every reason to be glad sometimes spend their days groaning about trivial matters. Equipped for daily victory they are continually defeated. Having become citizens of heaven they live like hopeless earthlings. Though heirs of God and joint-heirs with Christ, they have allowed themselves to take on the mental attitudes of spiritual paupers. They are more often found pouting than praising, fault-finding is their specialty and nothing escapes their criticism. They are part of the body of Christ and have great potential for service, but they spend their time murmuring and complaining instead of rejoicing and reaching out to the lost.

Let the righteous rejoice! This is the will of God for each one of His children.

OLD AGE

MEMORY VERSE: *My lips shall greatly rejoice when I sing unto thee; and my soul, which thou hast redeemed* (Psalm 71:23).

"Let it be our unceasing prayer that as we grow older we may not grow colder in the ways of God," said good George Muller.

Muller lived up into the late nineties — always bright, full of interest, hopeful, joyful. In his last years, he would often stop in the midst of his conversation to exclaim, "Oh, I am so happy!" And it was not a mannerism, nor was it feigned.

"As we advance in years," he had written long before, "let us not decline in spiritual power; but let us see to it that an increase of spiritual vigor and energy be found in us, that our last days may be our best days... Let the remaining days of our pilgrimage be spent in an ever-increasing, earnest consecration to God."

"The devil has no happy old people," it has been said. And that is understandable. How sad to have lived only for these few passing years and the thrills or compensations of them! In that case, old age is like a solemn countdown to the end. Treasures must be left behind. Moments must be drained of all good, for nothing good is expected beyond the grave.

In contrast, the Christian can rejoice in old age. He is still young in the light of eternity and every beat of his heart moves him closer to glory. He is not leaving his treasures but going to them. The end of life is but the end of his limitations. He savors every moment as another opportunity to serve his Lord and to be with loved ones, but he knows that better things are ahead and that a great reunion is coming in heaven.

Whether in church, his home, or in heaven, he can say, *"My lips shall greatly rejoice when I sing unto thee."*

A LOVING CHURCH

MEMORY VERSE: *And the multitude of them that believed were of one heart and of one soul: neither said any of them that ought of the things which he possessed was his own; but they had all things common* (Acts 4:32).

The great number of converts in Jerusalem after Pentecost created an economic emergency. Many of these believers had come from other places for the Jewish feast days and now that they had been born again, they remained but were unprepared financially for the longer stay. Others may have lost their means of livelihood because of being identified with Jesus.

No matter.

They would survive.

Why? And how?

Because the Christians in Jerusalem loved one another more than they loved their possessions. They sold their possessions and pooled their resources to meet this emergency.

Most American Christians know little of sharing with the needy in their fellowship. We have become so accustomed to having the government handle emergencies that we often neglect those near us in times of need.

How long has it been since you sent a gift to one in need?

What have you sacrificed in your church?

What do you intend to do about it?

"If a brother or sister be naked, and destitute of daily food, And one of you say unto them, Depart in peace, be ye warmed and filled; notwithstanding ye give them not those things which are needful to the body; what doth it profit" (James 2:15-16).

GOD REIGNS

MEMORY VERSE: *The LORD reigneth; let the earth rejoice; Let the multitude of isles be glad thereof* (Psalm 97:1).

God reigns.

Have you ever thought how sad the plight of planet earth would be if that were not true?

We would all be on a hopeless voyage through space with no destination.

Every grave would be a place of despair and total separation.

Life would be without purpose.

The universe would be like a giant clock winding down until the end.

No prayer would ever be heard or answered.

Man would always walk the dark valley of death alone.

All of life's horizons would be limited by time.

The trinkets and thrills of this life span would be the only things of value.

But God reigns.

Therefore the earth can rejoice.

We are the recipients of the love of God and the beneficiaries of His boundless grace.

We do not walk through life alone if we have been born again.

The dark valley has been changed to the valley of the shadow of death — and He — the Light of the World — walks there with us.

Heaven is a real place for a prepared people. Treasures can be sent on ahead for enjoying forever.

In every perplexing situation in life, we know that He is in charge.

God reigns! Rejoice!

BABIES IN THE CHURCH

MEMORY VERSE: *I have fed you with milk, and not with meat: for hitherto ye were not able to bear it, neither yet now are ye able* (I Corinthians 3:2).

God's plan for His children is birth, growth and maturity. The moment one receives Christ as personal Saviour, he is born again. There is rejoicing at the birth of a child and in heaven there is rejoicing in the presence of the angels when one is born again. Sadly, some who are born again never grow. They remain spiritual infants throughout life, missing the blessings of the abundant life.

Spiritual babies are concerned with self rather than service. They carry their feelings on their sleeves and have to be handled with care. They are like bombs, always ready to explode. Infancy shows in any crisis. The spiritual baby is upset over the smallest of things, expecting to be catered to by the pastor and other members of the church. The church baby examines everything as a receiver instead of a giver. He asks: "What is there in this for me?"

Spiritual babies are concerned with argument rather than action. Look for the trouble spot in the church and the ecclesiastical infant will be there. Gossip is his delight. Trifles touch off his temper. Often his self-righteous attitude masquerades as piety. He can sound so right that others follow him. But a real look at the church baby reveals that much of his fussing is a smoke screen to keep him from getting involved in the real mission of his church. It is always easier to be part of the faction than to get into the action.

Spiritual babies look to man rather than to God. An infant's world is small, revolving around a few people. Church babies also have small worlds, revolving around a few favorite preachers or leaders. They are more loyal to men than to the Master or the church.

God blesses people on the grow!

YE DID RUN WELL

MEMORY VERSE: *Ye did run well; who did hinder you that ye should not obey the truth?* (Galatians 5:7).

The church at Galatia had known better days. Once it had been vibrant and alive. Love for one another had been evident to all. Now they were locked into a system of legalism. And it had happened so easily. The logic of adding law to faith had appeared to be so right. But in adding to Christ, they had taken away from Him. They had traded the simple Gospel for a complex system of man-made rules.

Paul analyzed their problem... saw through their charade. He asked: *"O foolish Galatians, who hath bewitched you, that ye should not obey the truth, before whose eyes Jesus Christ hath been evidently set forth, crucified among you?"* (Galatians 3:1). He knew that their downward trek had begun when they had started to listen to a new voice, one given to a message that twisted the true Gospel. Now he was calling them back to the truth.

Has your church known better days?

Can you pinpoint the time the decline began?

Has warm fellowship given way to cold legalism?

The way back is the way of surrender. Stop following religious pied pipers who offer methods and doctrines built on human effort and exalting man's ability: *"Are ye so foolish? having begun in the Spirit, are ye now made perfect by the flesh?"* (Galatians 3:3).

Come back to the simple, wonderful, Gospel message. And share it with others. Take the lead in calling your church back to the Saviour by rededicating your own life to Jesus and by reaching out to the lost.

You did run well.

And that means you can serve your Lord again!

THE BIBLE

MEMORY VERSE: *I rejoice at thy word, as one that findeth great spoil* (Psalm 119:162).

In our youth, most of us have fancied finding buried treasure. As adults, millions buy lottery tickets or gamble in other ways in the hope of receiving great treasure. The psalmist valued God's Word far more than any earthly bonanza.

If you have difficulty rejoicing today, praise God for the Bible. Think about its worth. Dwell on its riches. Apart from this divine revelation, we would know little of the personality of God. We might conclude that He is powerful and the Creator, for *"the heavens declare the glory of God; and the firmament sheweth his handywork"* (Psalm 19:1), but we could never understand His love and would therefore miss life's greatest blessing.

The Bible reveals God's plan of the ages. We do not have to stumble through life ever questioning the direction of history and fearing the future. God has explained His plan. History is His story. We do not fear what the future holds because we know the One who holds the future. And it has been revealed to us in the Bible.

The earth has some traumatic days ahead. Christ is coming. The dead will be raised. Christians will be raptured. Tribulation will overtake the earth. Political and religious chaos is sure to come. But none of these things will take God by surprise, and students of the Bible have been given a preview of these events.

Christians who read God's Word are "in the know." They are better informed than the world's most able news analysts.

What a book! Rejoice in it. Praise God for it. Let its message rule your life today!

RELIGIOUS CANNIBALS

MEMORY VERSE: *But if ye bite and devour one another, take heed that ye be not consumed one of another* (Galatians 5:15).

Many a missionary has come back from the foreign field with thrilling stories of the power of the Gospel to change cannibals to Christians. Missionary books abound with like accounts. That kind of transformation in people gives proof of the reality of salvation. How wonderful to think of a man feeding his soul on the Word of God, who once fed his body on the flesh of his fellowman?

Interestingly, Paul speaks of another kind of cannibalism.

The Galatian church had once been a center of dynamic Christianity. Paul, himself, had ministered there. The Gospel had been presented clearly and the work of the Holy Spirit in the lives of the people had been evident. The love of Christ was an active force in personal relationships. Paul said they had loved him so much that they would have been willing to pluck out their eyes and give them to him to improve his poor vision, if that had been possible.

Sadly, things changed. The church became legalistic and love left. Paul lamented their spiritual poverty.

Observing their bickering and infighting, he warns that if they keep eating away at one another they will eventually consume one another. They had become Christian cannibals.

There is no room for cannibals among Christians. Instead, we are to *"...love one another with a pure heart fervently"* (I Peter 1:22).

When Christians conquer their spiritual cannibalism, another great missionary story will be told. Those observing real love among the people of God will turn to the Saviour. The church will fulfill its mission at home. And this will enlarge its missionary ministry the world around!

HUSBANDS AND WIVES

MEMORY VERSE: *Let thy fountain be blessed: and rejoice with the wife of thy youth* (Proverbs 5:18).

Here is a good test for married couples. Estimate the number of years you have left together. Figure the number of hours that totals. Divide the number by three and subtract the answer from the total to find the number of waking hours together. Now divide the remaining amount by two to arrive at the approximate time apart because of work. How do you intend to spend the hours that remain?

How many hours do you intend to spend arguing? In hand-to-hand combat? Pouting? Administering the "silent treatment"? Grumbling? Finding fault? Putting one another down? Criticizing one another before friends? Being apart unnecessarily? Now that you've removed the clutter, what will you do with the time that is left to invest?

How many hours have you reserved for expressing your love for each other? Holding one another? Complimenting? Walking together? Laughing? Sharing projects of mutual enjoyment? Relaxing together? Planning new adventures? Enjoying your children or grandchildren? Praying together? Studying the Bible? Attending church services? Telling others of God's blessings?

Generally, we do not think about how quickly life escapes. The Bible speaks about the importance of "redeeming the time." Unless priority is given to rejoicing together, as God intends, couples may waste most of their lives in unpleasant tasks or sour attitudes, thereby missing God's will for their lives.

"Rejoice with the wife of thy youth." And enjoy your husband while he's with you. It's the Bible way to live!

CHURCH WITH A FLAW

MEMORY VERSE: *Nevertheless I have somewhat against thee, because thou hast left thy first love* (Revelation 2:4).

The last book of the Bible records seven letters from Jesus to seven local churches. They contain truths for churches of all ages.

The church at Ephesus was commended for a number of excellent qualities. This was a fundamental church; sound in doctrine, faithful, separatist in position, not afraid to expose false teachers and labouring in God's name.

Interestingly, the Lord commended the church before raising any word of criticism. One commentator explains that the Lord loves to number our accomplishments by His grace. There is a lesson here: we ought to look for the best in our fellow Christians. That is the way of love.

The Lord's criticism of the church at Ephesus was a serious one: *"thou hast left thy first love."* Diminishing love is always critical. When love reigns there is communication, consideration and compassion. When love declines all service becomes mechanical, a burden... vain.

The cure prescribed for the church was plain. They were to remember, repent and return: *"do the first works."*

One day Henry W. Grady, the great newspaperman, left his editorial room and went to see his aged mother. He told her he was confused religiously and asked her for help. She told him to sit beside her as he had done as a child while she told him the story of Jesus again. That night she had him sleep in his old bed and pray his childhood prayer. In the morning, when he came down to breakfast, Mr. Grady said, "It's all right, Mother. I'm back with God again."

Remember, repent and return!

PERSECUTION

MEMORY VERSE: *Blessed are ye, when men shall hate you, and when they shall separate you from their company, and shall reproach you, and cast out your name as evil, for the Son of man's sake* (Luke 6;22).

Pastor J. H. Crowell, when about sixteen, shipped on a sailing vessel where he was the only Christian in a crew of twelve. Before leaving his mother he promised to meet her three times a day at the throne of grace, and so he regularly went below and prayed knowing that his mother was praying at the same time at home beside her bed.

The other crew members were furious over his praying and persecuted him severely. They threw wood at him and poured buckets of water over him, but they could not put out the fire in his soul.

Finally, they tied him to the mast and laid thirty-nine stripes on his back. Still he prayed on. At last, they tied a rope around him and threw him overboard. He swam as best he could, and when he took hold of the side of the ship, they pushed him off with a pole. When his strength gave way and he thought he would die, he called out: "Send my body to my mother and tell her I died for Jesus."

The wrath of the angry sailors seemed finally to be exhausted and they pulled the young Christian up on the deck and left him there unconscious. Shortly after he revived, conviction began to seize his companions on the ship. Before night, two of them were saved. Within a week, everyone on board, including the captain, had been born again.

The persecution was difficult, but J. H. Crowell met it as a Christian, counting it joy to suffer for Christ. The Lord rewarded him with the conversion of his persecutors.

Can you rejoice in opportunities to suffer for the Lord? (See 2 Timothy 3:12.)

THE DEAD CHURCH

MEMORY VERSE: *Be watchful, and strengthen the things which remain, that are ready to die: for I have not found thy works perfect before God* (Revelation 3:2).

The church at Sardis was dead.

Active, but dead.

C. H. Spurgeon once said: "Have you ever read 'The Ancient Mariner?' I dare say you thought it one of the strangest imaginations ever put together, especially that part where the old mariner represents the corpses of all the dead men rising up to man the ship — dead men pulling the rope, dead men steering, dead men spreading the sails. I thought what a strange idea that was. But do you know I have lived to see that time. I have gone into churches, and I have seen a dead man in the pulpit, a dead man as a deacon, a dead man handling the plate, and dead men sitting to hear."

Paul wrote that the last days would be characterized by dead religion instead of living faith: *"Having a form of godliness, but denying the power thereof"* (II Timothy 3:5).

The Gospel gives life but just going through the motions brings death. Jesus did not come to found social clubs, organizations to fill the time of members to keep them from boredom or religious corporations given to successful money raising. He came to save the lost... to impart spiritual life to those who were dead in sin. And He gives life to those who trust Him: *"...I am come that they might have life, and that they might have it more abundantly"* (John 10:10),

If your church is dead, start sharing the Gospel with others. When people are saved through your faithful Gospel witness, the church will come alive!

CHURCH WITH A FEW FAITHFUL

MEMORY VERSE: *But that which ye have already holdfast till I come* (Revelation 2:25).

The church at Thyatira contained some bad people. The Lord's letter warns them of coming judgment. Nevertheless there was a faithful remnant there. And the Lord lets them know that they have not been overlooked. He knows His own sheep.

Nearly every church has a faithful few who serve the Lord because they love Him and are not upset by the failures and compromises of other members. If there are two groups in your church, join the faithful few.

Chester Shuler's, "The Faithful Few," concludes:

"God bless, I pray, the faithful few,
And may their tribe increase —
They must be very precious to
The blessed Prince of Peace."

George Eliot shared his secret of remaining faithful as follows:

"I will try this day to live a simple, sincere and serene life, repelling promptly every thought of discontent, anxiety, discouragement, impurity, self-seeking; cultivating cheerfulness, magnanimity, charity and the habit of holy silence; exercising in expenditure, generosity in giving, carefulness in conversation, diligence in appointed service, fidelity in every trust, and a childlike faith in God.

"In particular I will try to be faithful in those habits of prayer, work, physical exercise, eating and sleep, which I believe the Holy Spirit has shown me to be right.

That all my powers with all their might To God's sole glory may unite."

THE HARVEST

MEMORY VERSE: *And he that reapeth receiveth wages, and gathereth fruit unto life eternal: that both he that soweth and he that reapeth may rejoice together* (John 4:36).

Early one morning, William Gladstone was at his desk at No. 10 Downing Street, London. A timid knock on the door called him from preparing an important speech he was to deliver that day in Parliament.

Standing at the door was a little boy whose friendship Gladstone had won by little deeds of kindness. The boy said, "My brother is dying. Won't you please come and show him the way to heaven?"

Leaving his important work for the most important work any Christian can do, Gladstone went to the bedside of the dying boy. In a matter of moments, the boy was rejoicing in his newly found Saviour!

Returning to his office, Gladstone wrote at the bottom of the speech he had been preparing: "I am the happiest man in London today!" He had been the human instrument in the hands of God, to lead a boy to the Saviour.

Gladstone was there in the hour of reaping and rejoiced. Some, however, miss the moment of reaping, yet share in the winning of lost people. They are the sowers.

Sowers may have difficulty finding courage or words for the moment of decision in soul wining, but they faithfully witness and give out the gospel. Some sowers mail scores of letters with enclosed tracts. Other sowers live consistent Christian lives and show compassion to those in need.

In the harvest, the sowers and reapers rejoice together! (See John 4:37,38.)

REJOICING IN HEAVEN

MEMORY VERSE: *Likewise, I say unto you, there is joy in the presence of the angels of God over one sinner that repenteth* (Luke 15:10).

The man who knelt beside me was the son of a preacher of the gospel. His father had gone to heaven long ago. Now the son, a grandfather, was asking the Lord Jesus to save him. When he had finished his prayer of faith, I rejoiced with him in his salvation and then said, "Your father knows that you have been born again."

"I hope so," he sighed.

"I guarantee it," I said reassuringly. Then I shared our memory verse with him.

There is no doubt about it. Those in heaven know when any person on earth is saved and it brings great rejoicing there. The angels are glad and joy breaks out among the saints. Another soul will share heaven with them.

I would like to have been there when that former circuit-riding preacher was notified of the salvation of his son, Bill. I'm sure he had led many to Christ in days gone by and had rejoiced to see them saved, but always there had been that longing over his son. Through life he had prayed for him, expecting his conversion year after year but never seeing it happen. Perhaps he had experienced times of doubting that his prayer would ever be answered. Preachers are human enough to go through valleys of doubt and depression. Sometimes he may have felt like giving up — but always he went back to his knees. It was all he could do. Then, finally, his earthly sojourn ended and he went to heaven without his prayer answered. It may have been the only touch of sadness that he felt in arriving there. But now the victory had come.

Heaven rejoiced!

THE LUKEWARM CHURCH

MEMORY VERSE: *I know thy works, that thou art neither cold nor hot: I would thou wert cold or hot* (Revelation 3:15).

Some churches are prosperous outwardly but are poverty stricken as to real spiritual values. They see themselves as successful but God sees them as failures. They are religious, perhaps even sound in Bible doctrine, but they have no fire. They are lukewarm.

Long ago, Joseph Seiss lamented: "Many consider themselves Christians, and Christians of the better sort, who are quite indifferent to the doctrines they hold. They make nothing of creed, despise it, and want nothing to do with those who are in any wise strict and earnest about it. Their religion is a mere goodish ness, which has something of moral warmth in it, but which when tested is only a tepid sentimentalism, having nothing of the solid backbone of Christianity in it.

"Others are very rigid and punctilious about sound doctrine. They make orthodoxy everything, and are ready to fight and suffer for it, but are not so particular about their lives. They stickle earnestly for the creed and the unadulterated truth; and so far they are warm. But when it comes to orthodoxy of practical godliness, they are anything but warm, and hence must be classed with the lukewarm."

Some churches are sound, but as Spurgeon said, "sound asleep."

Paul was on fire for Christ. There was nothing lukewarm about his life. He suffered the loss of all things for His Saviour and did so gladly. The world still feels the impact of his life and ministry.

Is your church lukewarm?

Be a thermostat... not a thermometer.

Raise the spiritual temperature of your Church!

CHURCH WITH AN OPEN DOOR

MEMORY VERSE: *I know thy works: behold, I have set before thee an open door, and no man can shut it: for thou hast a little strength, and hast kept my word, and hast not denied my name* (Revelation 3:8).

A minister was once asked by a friend, whom he met in a distant city: "How many members do you have in your church?"

"One thousand," the preacher replied.

"Really." the friend exclaimed, "And how many of them are active?"

"All of them are active," was the response. "About two hundred of them are active for the Lord; the balance are active for the devil."

Few churches take full advantage of the opportunities given for service. Some are even guilty of looking for ways to trim their outreach in order to save money.

Someday we will all stand at the Judgment Seat of Christ and give an account of our service. There the Lord will remind us of all the doors that were open but that we shunned.

Since our Lord knows the potential of each of His children, it is reasonable to conclude that He will open doors for any church that will employ all the talents and gifts of the people in that congregation. A church is not really active unless the members are being used to the ultimate of their ability and dedication. Activity for Christ cannot be determined by how busy the church schedule appears or how full the calendar, rather the true test is the use of the members in the areas of service for which they are equipped by the Holy Spirit.

Is there a door of service open through which you have not passed?

How will you handle this at the Judgment Seat?

IN TROUBLE

MEMORY VERSE: *Wherein ye greatly rejoice, though now for a season, if need be, ye are in heaviness through manifold temptations* (1 Peter 1:6).

Though Christians will not pass through the Tribulation, in this world we have tribulation. This is not strange. Salvation transforms sinners into citizens of heaven but it does not deliver them from earthly trials.

Some seem to have more than their share. Perhaps you feel you are one of them.

Still, God is faithful and has promised that He will not allow us to be tempted above what we are able. Henry Ward Beecher wrote: "No physician ever weighed out medicine to his patients with half so much care and exactness as God weighs out to us every trial. Not one grain too much does He ever permit to be put in the scale.

So, the Bible says we can rejoice in our trials.

Does this seem contradictory?

Not at all! These trials are designed to try our faith. And through them all we are kept by the power of God (see 1 Peter 1:5).

Like Peter, who began to sink when he looked at the wind and the waves while walking on the sea to Jesus, we may waver at times. But He never wavers. Our faith may sometimes be weak. But the object of our faith — Jesus — is strong.

No wonder we can rejoice in our temporary troubles. We have everlasting life! And we are in the care of our Eternal God.

August

**GIVE US THIS DAY
OUR DAILY BREAD**

*The Lord is
my helper,
and I will not
fear what
man shall do
unto me.*

Hebrews 13:6.

LOVE GOD

MEMORY VERSE: *And thou shalt love the Lord thy God with all thine heart, and with all thy soul, and with all thy might* (Deuteronomy 6:5).

An old Indian chief constantly spoke of the Lord Jesus and what He meant to him. "Why do you talk so much about Jesus?" asked a friend. The old chief did not reply, but slowly, deliberately gathered some sticks and bits of grass, making a circle of them. In the circle he placed a caterpillar. Still silent, he struck a match and lit the sticks and grass. As the fire caught around the circle, the trapped caterpillar began to crawl around rapidly, seeking a way of escape.

As the fire advanced, the helpless caterpillar raised its head as high as it could. If the creature could have spoken, it might have said, "My help can only come from above."

Then the old chief stooped down. He extended his finger to the caterpillar which crawled up his finger to safety.

"That," said the chief glowingly, "was what the Lord Jesus did for me! I was lost in sin. My condition was hopeless. I was trapped. Then the Lord Jesus stooped down, and in love and mercy drew me out to safety. How can I help but love Him and talk of His wondrous love and care?"

Moses' call to love God is but a call to respond to God's love. He loved first. John said it well: *"Herein is love, not that we loved God, but that he loved us, and sent his Son to be the propitiation for our sins"* (I John 4:10).

Though we love God with heart, soul and might, our love will still fall short of His great love for us. He deserves complete devotion with deepest emotion.

How much do you really love your Lord?

NOT ASHAMED

MEMORY VERSE: *For I am not ashamed of the gospel of Christ: for it is the power of God unto salvation to every one that believeth; to the Jew first, and also to the Greek* (Romans 1:16).

What is the Gospel?

"Good news," someone answers.

True, but what is this good news?

Let Paul answer: *"Moreover, brethren, I declare unto you the gospel which I preached unto you, which also ye have received, and wherein ye stand...how that Christ died for our sins according to the scriptures; And that he was buried, and that he rose again the third day according to the scriptures"* (1 Corinthians 15:1,3,4).

Isn't it strange that there are so many divisions over this simple and wonderful message? Why do cults rise with far-out formulas for salvation?

Blindness.

Christ died for you and me. He was buried and rose again according to the Scriptures. That message produces the new birth. All who go to heaven arrive there because of this message. God has made His way of eternal life understandable. How sad that man makes it complicated.

To believe the Gospel is to receive Christ by faith.

So, we do not follow the theological concoctions of some self-styled religious charlatan. Our faith rests in the everlasting gospel. And that is good news worth sharing.

Let the whole world know.

Don't be ashamed of the Gospel of Christ. It's the power of God unto salvation...needed by all. Cut through meaningless conversation. Speak up for Christ today.

THE GOODNESS OF GOD

MEMORY VERSE: *Or despisest thou the riches of his goodness and forbearance and longsuffering; not knowing that the goodness of God leadeth thee to repentance?* (Romans 2:4).

Repentance is misunderstood. Some think of it as a time of deep sorrow for sin and long crying. Sorrow and tears may be a part of repentance but one may shed buckets of tears and never repent. To repent is to make an about-face. Repentance is a change of direction...a change of mind about sin and about the Saviour.

Many repent during difficult times or after experiencing some great loss, but others turn to Christ because He has been so good to them. "The goodness of God" leads them to repentance.

And God has been good to us all.

The eloquent DeWitt Talmage wrote: "It is high time you began to thank God for present blessing. Thank Him for your children, happy, buoyant, and bounding. Praise Him for fresh, cool water, bubbling from the rock, leaping in the cascade, soaring in the mist, falling in the shower, dashing against the rock, and clapping its hands in the tempest. Love Him for the grass that cushions the earth, and the clouds that curtain the sky, and the foliage that waves in the forest. Thank Him for the Bible to read, and a cross to gaze upon, and a Saviour to deliver."

Talmage had a way with words. But your silent song of thanksgiving rising to God from a grateful heart may outdo the great orator and preacher if you give thought to all of God's wondrous blessings.

Has God been good to you?

Isn't it time you became serious about repentance?

LOVE THY NEIGHBOR

MEMORY VERSE: *Thou shalt not avenge, nor bear any grudge against the children of thy people, but thou shalt love thy neighbor as thyself: I am the LORD* (Leviticus 19:18).

The natural result of love for God is genuine love for others. Anything less is hypocrisy. Assurance of salvation is rooted in love for other Christians, made possible through the new birth: *"We know that we have passed from death unto life, because we love the brethren. He that loveth not his brother abideth in death"* (I John 3:14).

Strong words! But inescapably true.

Love for others cannot be vengeful. To talk of Christian love while seeking to get back at a brother is but empty conversation. Words of brotherly affection accompanied by gossip and backbiting are exposed for what they really are. And the speaker is revealed for what he is!

Only eternity will let us know how much of the blessing of God has been forfeited through holding grudges. But right now the grudge-holder is unmasked and is held up in contrast to the one who loves brethren.

The Bible is a mirror in which we can see ourselves as God sees us. A man reading the Bible is face to face with himself. James wrote: *"But be ye doers of the word, and not hearers only, deceiving your own selves. For if any be a hearer of the word, and not a doer, he is like unto a man beholding his natural face in a glass: For he beholdeth himself, and goeth his way, and straightway forgetteth what manner of man he was. But whoso looketh into the perfect law of liberty, and continueth therein, he being not a forgetful hearer, but a doer of the work, this man shall be blessed in his deed"* (James 1:22-25).

What kind of reflection do you see in God's mirror? If the face is one lined with grudges and revenge, put away these hindrances to love.

EVERLASTING LOVE

MEMORY VERSE: *The Lord hath appeared of old unto me, saying, Yea, I have loved thee with an everlasting love: therefore with loving kindness have I drawn thee* (Jeremiah 31:3).

An old Scottish woman who was alone for the greater part of each day was asked, "What do you do during the day?"

"Well," she replied, "I get my hymn book, and I have a little hymn of praise to the Lord." "Then," she added, "I get my Bible and let the Lord speak to me. When I am tired of reading, and I cannot sing anymore, I just sit still and let the Lord love me."

The length of love is often celebrated. We congratulate those who have been married for twenty-five or fifty years. In this day of trial marriages and easy divorces, couples who experience lasting love are somewhat rare.

But God's love lasts!

The love of God doesn't diminish with the passing of time. His love for you and me is as strong as it was yesterday, last month or last year. And this in spite of our many failures along the way.

That's only part of the story.

God's love is everlasting. He'll love us as much in ten thousand years as today. Our walk with Him can be bathed in love through all our days on earth and then when we arrive in heaven immediately after death, His loving arms will greet us home.

Many long for love. Life has been hard and sometimes despair has become an unwelcome companion. That may describe your life.

Here's good news: GOD LOVES YOU! And His love never changes. Respond to His love and His lovingkindness will be your experience forever!

GOD FORBID

MEMORY VERSE: *For what if some did not believe?*
shall their unbelief make the faith of God without effect?
(Romans 3:3).

A minister proclaimed the Gospel in an open-air meeting in Glasgow, Scotland. At the conclusion of his message, an unbeliever stepped from the crowd and said: "I don't believe what the minister said. I don't believe in heaven or hell. I don't believe in God or Christ. I haven't seen them."

Then a man, wearing dark glasses, came forward and said: "You say there is a river near this place — the River Clyde. There is no such thing. You say there are people standing here, but it cannot be true. I haven't seen them — I was born blind! Only a blind man could say what I have said. Likewise you are spiritually blind and cannot see. The Bible says of you, *"But the natural man receiveth not the things of the Spirit of God: for they are foolishness unto him: neither can he know them, because they are spiritually discerned"* (1 Corinthians 2:14).

Christians often are shaken over the arguments of atheists. That is a mistake. Their unbelief does not change the truth of God. What if atheists finally outnumbered believers? Would unbelief by the majority make the Bible less dependable?

God forbid.

What if all the scientists in the world determined that God does not exist? Would their unbelief eliminate the Almighty?

God forbid.

And what if some should doubt that God will take you safely through your present crisis? Will their unbelief cancel the promises of God?

Nor for a moment. God forbid.

You're safe in His care.

NOT OFFENDED

MEMORY VERSE: *Great peace have they which love thy law: and nothing shall offend them* (Psalm 119-165).

The Bible contains the greatest love story ever written. Nothing in literature can compare with the Bible because it was given by inspiration of God. All that we know about the love of God is contained in the Bible.

People who love God love the Bible. It is impossible to hate the Word of God and love the Author. Your love for the Lord can be measured by your attitude toward the Bible.

Exposure to the Bible in a devotional sense changes lives. The Bible has power to give daily victory over temptation. Many have despaired of ever conquering some besetting sin. Following David's formula in Psalm 119:9-11 would have solved the problem and ended constant defeat: *"Wherewithal shall a young man cleanse his way? by taking heed thereto according to thy word. With my whole heart have I sought thee: O let me not wander from thy commandments. Thy word have I hid in mine heart, that I might not sin against thee. "*

One of the great benefits of loving God's Word is in experiencing its power to deliver us from super sensitivity. Those who love the Bible will stop carrying their feelings on their sleeves. It is impossible to love the Bible, read it regularly and take it into life, without overcoming the sensitivity syndrome.

Christians do not have the right to be offended. We are not allowed to get our feelings hurt over trifles. Supersensitive saints are missing something in their walk with God. They need to fall in love with the Bible and its message so that feelings are subject to God's Word and will.

If this truth offends you, better hurry back to the Bible for help!

LOVE YOUR ENEMIES?

MEMORY VERSE: *But I say unto you, Love your enemies, bless them that curse you, do good to them that hate you, and pray for them which despitefully use you, and persecute you* (Matthew 5:44).

Two Christian men had a disagreement and one of them began to slander the other throughout the neighborhood. Upon hearing of it, the object of the gossip went to his indignant brother and said: "Will you be kind enough to tell me my faults to my face, that I may profit by your Christian candor and try to get rid of my errors?"

When the slanderer agreed, the man under attack went a step further. "Before you begin telling me what you think is wrong in me, will you please bow down with me and let us pray over it, that my eyes may be opened to see my faults as you will tell them?" he asked.

Upon finishing the time of prayer, the one seeking reconciliation said: "Now proceed with what you have to complain about."

But the other replied, "After praying over it, I now feel that in going around talking against you, I have been serving the devil and have need that you pray for me and forgive me the wrong I have done you." Love had won.

Perhaps the most difficult instruction in the Bible to follow is that of loving those who wrong us. Yet, this is God's way. He loved us while we were enemies through sin: *"For if, when we were enemies, we were reconciled to God by the death of his Son, much more, being reconciled, we shall be saved by his life"* (Romans 5:10).

An atheist once said about Christians: "They are not as good as their Book." It's time to start following God's Word instead of yielding to the fallen nature within.

When you start loving your enemies, who will be first on the love-list?

DISCIPLES

MEMORY VERSE: *By this shall all men know that ye are my disciples, if ye have love one to another* (John 13:35).

Love is a requirement of discipleship. It is the identifying Christian characteristic. The world is able to recognize one who is disciplined to Christ by his daily and practical acts of Christian love.

Real Christianity suffers when religion gets in the way. It has always been so. We are so given to accepting outward claims to piety that we often conclude the best Christians are those who put on the most religious airs. Platform prowess may convince the general public as to who is the spiritual one in town or in the local church. But polish and performance will not count at the Judgment Seat of Christ.

Heaven will contain many surprises. The old song says: "Everybody talkin bout heaven ain't goin there." Many talk about heaven who have climbed the religious ladder to high positions in Christian work but are bankrupt of love. They are quick to judge and they major on criticism. The eloquent DeWitt Talmadge observed: "There are in every community, and every church, watch dogs, who feel called upon to keep their eyes on others and growl. They are always the first to hear of anything wrong. Vultures are always the first to smell carrion. They are self-appointed detectives. I lay this down as a rule without exception, that those people who have the most faults themselves are the most merciless in their watching of others. From scalp of head to soles of foot, they are full of jealousies, or hypercriticism." In such cases, heaven may not be the destination. People who are truly born again have the Holy Spirit within. And the fruit of the Spirit is love (Galatians 5:22-23).

THE WORLD'S LOVE

MEMORY VERSE: *If ye were of the world, the world would love his own: but because ye are not of the world, but I have chosen you out of the world, therefore the world hateth you* (John 15:19).

The world loves its heroes, but even this love is temporary. One may be king of the mountain one day and cast down the next. Big names of the past are often the moral and financial wrecks of today. Faces that once graced top magazine covers now sell cheap sensational papers with stories of the former star's present predicament. The world's love is fickle and dependent on fortune.

God's love is enduring. The ups and downs of life do not affect it: *"Who shall separate us from the love of Christ? shall tribulation, or distress, or persecution, or famine, or nakedness, or peril, or sword? Nay, in all these things we are more than conquerors through him that loved us. For I am persuaded, that neither death, nor life, nor angels, nor principalities, nor powers, nor things present, nor things to come, nor height, nor depth, nor any other creature shall be able to separate us from the love of God, which is in Christ Jesus our Lord"* (Romans 8:35, 37-39).

Which love shall we choose?

Responding to the love of God by receiving Christ can put one at odds with others. Some will not understand. The love of the world will be forfeited. In some cases this may cost popularity or money. In many parts of the world it means imprisonment or even death. Nevertheless, it will be worth it all when we meet the Lord.

Forfeiting the world's love to serve Christ is a small loss compared to eternal gain. Wise ones choose the love that lasts!

BROTHERLY LOVE

MEMORY VERSE: *Be kindly affectioned one to another with brotherly love; in honour preferring one another* (Romans 12:10).

In the first century after Christ, Tertullian, the Christian theologian wrote: "It is our care for the helpless, our practicing of lovingkindness, that brands us in the eyes of our opponents. 'Look,' they say, 'how they love one another. Look how they are prepared to die one for another!'"

But is that reputation alive and well today?

In some areas and individual situations it is! Sadly, in others the missing dimension is love that really cares.

Note the tenderness of Paul's wording: *"Be kindly affectioned one to another with brotherly love."* Commenting on the words, "kindly affectioned," Dr. Kenneth Wuest points out that the Greek word used is "philostorgos." He then explains: "The word here represents Christians as bound by a family tie. It is intended to define more specifically the character of 'philadelphia' (brotherly love) which follows, so that the exhortation is, 'love the brethren in the faith as though they were brethren in blood.'"

The world is looking for a brotherhood. Witness the existence of dozens of lodges, clubs and other organizations that claim to be fraternal. Here is another example of human effort to produce a remedy for the need of man. All brotherhoods or sisterhoods call out for the real thing. The bond between Christians, made possible through the love of Christ and the indwelling of the Holy Spirit, produces genuine brotherhood. How sad when this powerful truth and experience is neglected!

Nothing is gained through bemoaning the absence of Christian love. Action is required. The place to begin is here. The time is now.

LOVE FOR OTHERS

MEMORY VERSE: *So when they had dined, Jesus saith to Simon Peter, Simon, son of Jonah, lovest thou me more than these? He saith unto him. Yea, Lord, thou knowest that I love thee. He saith unto him. Feed my lambs* (John 21:15).

In preparing Peter for his work in the early church, the Lord asked Peter if he loved Him. Peter had to learn that genuine love for Christ required acts of love and concern for others. He would he called on to feed and care for thousands of new converts. These members of the New Testament church would be known for their warm fellowship and love for one another. Peter must set the example.

It is easy to speak or sing of our love for the Lord, but real love must act. James reminded his readers that faith without works is dead. The same might be said of love. At the end of a sermon by Dr. Harry Ironside, the congregation was singing, "OH HOW I LOVE JESUS." As they sang softly, a skid row derelict made his way to the front of the church, coming all the way from the last pew. His clothes were ragged and dirty and he reeked with the smell of booze. A call was made for a personal worker to come and talk to him about Christ — but not one person moved. It was one thing to sing about love for Jesus and another to kneel beside this down and outer who had come to learn of Him. But *real* love for Christ *reaches out to others* — especially those in great need.

What can you do today that will demonstrate your love for Jesus? Will you be asked to feed His lambs, His sheep? Awaiting you in your day's activities are people with hungry hearts. Some need the Gospel. Others are Christians who need help and encouragement. While you're deciding whether or not to get involved, face the question: *"Lovest thou me?"*

FULFILLING THE LAW

MEMORY VERSE: *Love worketh no ill to his neighbour: therefore love is the fulfilling of the law* (Romans 13:10).

Jesus once shocked the Pharisees, saying: *"...thou shalt love the Lord thy God with all thy heart, and with all thy soul, and with all thy mind. This is the first and great commandment. And the second is like unto it, Thou shalt love thy neighbor as thyself. On these two commandments hang all the law and the prophets"* (Matthew 22:37-40). They had hoped to trap Him in some contradiction concerning the law given to Moses. His answer silenced them.

Explaining Paul's effort to drive home this same great truth to the Christians at Rome, Dr. H. A. Ironside wrote: " 'Thou shalt love thy neighbor as thyself.' He who thus loves could, by no possibility, ever be guilty of adultery, murder, theft, lying, or covetousness. It is impossible that love should be manifested in such ways as these. 'Love worketh no ill to his neighbor: therefore love is the fulfilling of the law.' It is in this way that the righteous requirement of the law is fulfilled in us who walk not after the flesh but after the Spirit."

Year after year, legislatures and parliaments grind out laws designed to keep the populace in line and to preserve the common peace. These laws, containing rules and sentences, are prepared and passed to keep citizens from wronging or hurting one another. How unnecessary most laws would be if love reigned! Billions in tax monies would be saved if love determined actions. Prisons and jails would he empty if love was a way of life.

We cannot control the way others live, but we can fulfill the purpose of God in our lives by loving one another.

And our neighbors will notice!

LIBERTY

MEMORY VERSE: *But if any man love God, the same is known of him* (I Corinthians 8:3).

Many Christians wrestle constantly with the question of what they can or cannot do in the Christian life. Their understanding of "the world" is fuzzy and they struggle to know the difference between dedicated Christian living and compromise with sin. Often it appears they have drawn an imaginary line as close to danger as possible and are crowding it continually, yet giving the impression they want to do it right. They run from one counselor to another seeking guidance, sometimes with the purpose of finding a Christian leader who will soothe their consciences by lowering the standard just a bit. They appear to want to get away with as much as they can and still make it to heaven.

There is another group of saints who are sincere and dedicated but confused. They honestly want to live for Christ and honor Him in their words and actions, but they have trouble knowing what to do in a number of situations. The clear-cut issues are no problem to them, but the "gray" areas keep them off balance. In the text above, Paul dealt with just such an issue. Christians were troubled about whether or not to eat meat that had been offered to idols. There was nothing wrong with the meat because the idols were but images made with hands. Still, there was an area of doubt.

Paul settled the "what to do" issue by appealing to their love for the Lord. Liberty would have allowed them to eat the meat. But how would this have affected those who didn't really understand Christian liberty? Therefore liberty had to be tempered with love.

Let love temper Christian liberty and the "gray" will go away.

UNFEIGNED LOVE

MEMORY VERSE: *By pureness, by knowledge, by longsuffering, by kindness, by the Holy Ghost, by love unfeigned* (II Corinthians 6:6).

"I love him, but..." often precedes a tirade of sanctified slander. Sometimes the gossip is guised as a prayer request or finished with a postscript: "I just thought you ought to know — I've said this in Christian love."

But is this love? Not at all! It is Pseudo love — fake love — malice masquerading as love. And God hates it (Proverbs 6:19).

Genuine Christian love is not fake. It is unfeigned. Real love doesn't have to be explained. Excuses are not needed when acts of heartfelt love are performed. All who hear or see Christian love in action know it is the real thing.

Love does not defend itself. It takes wrong rather than cast doubt on another. Love flows outward, seeking opportunities to serve rather than expecting to be served. Like Jesus, those who love live to minister, not to be ministered unto.

Paul's love for Christ and the souls of men kept him going in all kinds of difficulties. Beatings, imprisonments, hunger, labours and distresses were his way of life. No matter. Christ and others were more important than his comfort or even his life.

No wonder churches were planted and multitudes saved through the ministry of this man of God. His was a service of love. Love unfeigned.

What is the quality of your love? Have you been pretending?

Allow the love of Christ to flow through you today. Others will notice and know it is love unfeigned.

PROVING LOVE

MEMORY VERSE: *I speak not by commandment, but by occasion of the forwardness of others, and to prove the sincerity of your love* (II Corinthians 8:8).

A popular bumper sticker says: Honk! If You Love Jesus."

Perhaps a better one would be: "Tithe! If You Love Jesus."

A wealthy businessman and an attorney were traveling around the world. One morning as they walked along a country road in Korea, they saw a boy pulling a plow which was steered by an old man. The attorney was so moved by the scene that he took a picture of the plowing pair and later showed it to a missionary in the next village.

"It seems a very strange way to plow a field," said the missionary, "but I happen to know the boy and the old man very well. They are very poor. However, when the little church was built here in the village, they wanted to contribute something. Having no money, they sold their ox and gave the money to the church building fund, and now, minus the valuable animal, they have to pull the plow themselves."

The travelers looked at each other for a moment, and then the attorney said, "But what a stupendous sacrifice! Why did you allow it?"

"They did not feel that way about it," replied the missionary. "They regarded it as a great joy that they had an ox to give to the Lord's work."

Giving is one way of proving our love for Christ. It is one thing to talk of love and loyalty to Christ and quite another to prove our love by digging deeply into our treasures and sharing them as He directs. Still, it is the only way to convert earthly treasures into wealth that lasts forever!

NO DIFFERENCE

MEMORY VERSE: *For there is no difference between the Jew and the Greek: for the same Lord over all is rich unto all that call upon him* (Romans 10:12).

The *Pacific Garden Mission News* carried the following article: "Remember, the man on Skid Row is not different IN KIND from the rest of us. He is merely worse in degree. On Skid Row we see fallen man at his dismal worst. In the better neighborhoods we see him at his polished best, but he is the same man for all his disguise. In the gutter we find him chained by dope and drink and dirt. On the Avenue we find him bound by pride and greed and lust. To God there is no difference. He sees beyond appearances and He knows what is in every man. His remedy for every man is the same, a new birth and the impartation of a new kind of life. (See John 3:5,7.)

"The Gospel is the power of God operating toward the moral and spiritual transformation of man. And it works! Thousands will testify that it does. No man who wants to climb up out of his past and find a new and better life should overlook the Gospel. It is God's way out, and there is no other."

The Gospel meets men where they are; all men. And they are all found in the same need. The ground is level at the cross. All need to be saved and all can be saved.

But do we see all people the same?

Are we as likely to witness to the poor as to the rich? Are we as eager to reach those who have little and therefore can give little? Does our concern go out equally to people of all races? Do we long to share heaven with all people? Even those who are not kind to us?

In the sight of God there is no difference (see Romans 2:11).

Let us see all those we meet today as people in need of the Saviour.

THE FRUIT OF THE SPIRIT

MEMORY VERSE: *But the fruit of the Spirit is love, joy, peace, longsuffering, gentleness, goodness, faith* (Galatians 5:22).

The Christian's body is the temple of the Holy Spirit. This Divine Person within is not only a resident, but a resource. It is His purpose to reproduce the life of Jesus Christ in each of us. The Bible tells us what to expect when we allow that to happen: *"But the fruit of the Spirit is love, joy, peace, longsuffering, gentleness, goodness, faith, meekness, temperance..."* (Galatians 5:22-23). What cannot be attained through trying to keep the law, becomes ours through yielding to the Holy Spirit.

Notice that love heads the list. In his commentary on the New Testament, Alford says of this text: "Love — at the head, as chief." He then refers the reader to I Corinthians 13 for a study of what love is and what it does.

It is the work of the Holy Spirit to speak of Christ. *"Howbeit when he, the Spirit of truth, is come, he will guide you into all truth: for he shall not speak of himself; but whatsoever he shall hear, that shall he speak: and he will shew you things to come. He shall glorify me: for he shall receive of mine, and shall shew it unto you"* (John 16: 13-14).

No wonder the life that is surrendered to the Holy Spirit is filled with love! The Spirit of God within is at work conforming the Christian's life to that which honors the loving Saviour.

Have you had difficulty loving others? Is the fruit of the Spirit missing from your life? Do you find yourself bitter and defeated instead of joyful and loving? Stop trying to pump-up love. Yield to the Holy Spirit and allow His fruit to be evident in you!

FAITH WORKING BY LOVE

MEMORY VERSE: *For in Jesus Christ neither circumcision availeth any thing, nor uncircumcision; but faith which worketh by love* (Galatians 5:6).

The church at Galatia was a troubled church. At one time it had been flourishing. Love had lived there. The bond between Paul and these Christians had been so strong that he said they would have been willing to pluck out their eyes to give them to him had that been called for or helpful. Now they were torn by strife.

False teachers had come to Galatia and had confused the church. They hovered between law and grace, not knowing or experiencing real Christian liberty. While claiming to adhere to the law in an effort to attain righteousness, they had forsaken the truth. Fellowship had disappeared in this legalistic atmosphere and they had become Christian cannibals — eating away at one another's reputations.

Sadly, these Christians, in trying to become more righteous, had missed the point of God's great plan. The law had been but a schoolmaster to bring them to Christ. To retreat back to the law would not bring righteousness — Christ had died to deliver them from the law. Their need now was to allow the Holy Spirit to produce works of love through them. Faith had come in response to God's love. Now they must stop trying to do through the law what God intended to bring about as a result of their faith.

Perhaps the reason for your failure in the Christian life has been your legalistic approach: *"Are ye so foolish? having begun in the Spirit, are ye now made perfect by the flesh?"* (Galatians 3:3). It is time to get back to the basics of salvation. Success lies in faith which works by love!

LOVE IS POWERFUL

MEMORY VERSE: *Though I speak with the tongues of men and of angels, and have not charity, I am become as sounding brass, or a tinkling cymbal* (1 Corinthians 13:1).

All Christian service is powerless without love.

No matter how you speak — you are weak without love. No matter your words — they are worthless without love. Eloquence may move men and nations for political causes, but in Christian work even the ability to speak as an angel cannot bring true success without love.

Spiritual gifts are useless apart from love. The exercise of God-given gifts will be empty of edification unless love is present. Even faith is unable to move hearts when moving mountains without love.

Sacrifice without love is senseless. It has been said: "You can give without loving, but you cannot love without giving." What may be missed is the lack of purpose in a gift that is given without love. Even martyrdom — for the sake of martyrdom or making a name — accomplishes nothing of lasting value!

This is the century of tools and gimmicks. More means of getting the Gospel to the world exist today than ever before. Bible schools and colleges for training Christian soldiers abound. Printing presses produce attractive literature, written to capture interest and convince all skeptics. Radio and television make it possible to preach the message to every corner of the globe. Still, millions remain unreached.

Why?

Could it be a lack of love? Logistics, without love, fail! Is love the missing ingredient in your teaching? In your preaching? In your witnessing? In your home?

LOVE IS PRACTICAL

MEMORY VERSE: *Charity suffereth long, and is kind, charity envieth not; charity vaunteth not itself, is not puffed up* (1 Corinthians 13:4).

But how do we know when love is present? What are the practical effects of love?

Love suffers long. That is love reacting. Love puts up with many things. Peter had to learn a lesson in love when he asked how many times he should forgive, Love doesn't ask.

Love is kind. Here is the positive side of love's patience. A great preacher of the past said: "If you are not very kind, you are not very spiritual."

Love does not envy, does not vaunt itself and is not puffed up. All envy and pride spring from selfishness — catering to self. Love is not selfish. Therefore the loving person behaves properly and does not seek the place of prominence.

Love is not easily provoked. What small things shake and break us. Why? The absence of love.

Love does not look for weakness in another. It is not glad when faults are found. It is not lurking like a detective, hoping to find some shortcoming in a brother or sister in Christ. Love would rather be wronged than to wrong another.

Love bears all things. And believes all things. That is, love endures the slights and attacks of others and then expects the best of them. Love is optimistic about the future of those who wound it.

The practical effects of love help us to understand its power. There is only One who perfectly demonstrated love at all times. In looking to Him (Hebrews 12:2), we can be living examples of His love!

LOVE IS PERMANENT

MEMORY VERSE: *Charity never faileth: but whether there be prophecies, they shall fail; whether there be tongues, they shall cease; whether there be knowledge, it shall vanish away* (1 Corinthians 13:8).

Love will never become obsolete.

Some gifts are described here as temporary. But not love.

Our love for Christ and for the saints will increase through the ages of eternity. John Newton wrote:

> "When we've been there ten thousand years
> Bright shining as the sun;
> We've no less days to sing God's praise
> Than when we first begun."

Not only is love permanent while other gifts are temporary, it is superior to faith and hope: *"And now abideth faith, hope, charity, these three; but the greatest of these is charity"* (I Corinthians 13:13).

A day will come when faith will be lost in sight. We will see our Saviour face to face: *"Behold, he cometh with clouds; and every eye shall see him, and they also which pierced him: and all kindreds of the earth shall wail because of him. Even so, Amen"* (Revelation 1:7).

Hope that lifts our eyes daily above the struggles of life as we await His return, will be unnecessary when Jesus comes again. In that day all will be perfect. There will be no reason to look for a better day. Hope will be a relic of bygone days. We will be with Him: *"Then we which are alive and remain shall be caught up together with them in the clouds, to meet the Lord in the air: and .so shall we ever be with the Lord"* (I Thessalonians 4:17).

But love will endure.

Love lasts. Better enjoy it now. It's going to be in style forever!

LOVE YOUR WIVES

MEMORY VERSE: *Husbands, love your wives, even as Christ also loved the church, and gave himself for it* (Ephesians 5:25).

Christian couples should remember that their love for each other is to be a demonstration of Christ's love for the church. There are some parallels between the love of Christ for the church and the love of a man for his wife that contain valuable lessons for married people.

The love of Christ is a sacrificial love. A lady once said that her marriage was completely changed by a preacher's statement. He had said, "You may be asking whether or not you are getting enough out of your marriage, when that is not even the question. You should be asking whether or not your husband or wife is getting all that he or she should be getting out of your marriage." The preacher's thought provoker had turned their marriage around and made them givers instead of receivers. And that's what love is all about.

The love of Christ is an enduring love. It is sad to meet couples whose love suffered a blow from which it has never recovered. One or the other became offended at some careless word or act and the wound has never healed. Communication died. They are still husband and wife but only in the legal sense of the word. They smile and seem happy in public. Most of their friends do not know about their problem. But when they are alone the wall between them is real. How unlike the love of Christ their love has become! He forgives, and forgives again.

The love of Christ is a love that is expressed often. How long has it been since you expressed your love to your marriage partner? If it has been a long time since you communicated your love, you are not living as God intended. Look for opportunities to show your love today!

THE LOVE OF MONEY

MEMORY VERSE: *For the love of money is the root of all evil: which while some coveted after, they have erred from the faith, and pierced themselves through with many sorrows* (1 Timothy 6:10).

"Money is the root of all evil" is the common misquoting of 1 Timothy 6:10: Here, as in other areas of life, leaving out love perverts truth. The truth is: *"...the love of money is the root of all evil."*

The word translated love in this verse means lust. A lust for money is the root of all evil. In Alford's commentary on the New Testament, he quotes Chrysostom on this verse as follows: "Lusts are thorns: and as among thorns, whenever one touches them, one's hands are bloodied and wounds are made; so he who falls among lusts shall suffer the same and shall surround his soul with griefs."

Only eternity will reveal how many have suffered as a result of lusting for money. Families have been neglected, friends lost, futures sacrificed and lives taken all because of the love of money.

If you make money your goal, you are certain to be disappointed. If you do not get a large amount of money in life you will be disappointed because you will think you would have found happiness had you done so. If you do acquire a large amount of money, you will be disappointed because you will have discovered that money doesn't satisfy. Either way you lose!

Money and all it can buy is tied to time. A dying queen once cried, "Millions in money for an inch of time." She should have gladly given her wealth for another day. But money cannot buy time when that day arrives.

A few follow the advice of Jesus and will meet their treasures later. Money or the Master, which will it be?

PROVOKING LOVE

MEMORY VERSE: *And let us consider one another to provoke unto love and to good works* (Hebrews 10:24).

"Provoke" and "love" are not usually associated. Paul explained that love is not easily provoked (I Corinthians 13:5). What then does the writer of Hebrews mean when he says: *"And let us consider one another to provoke unto love..."* Is this a contradiction?

Not at all! In his book, "Hebrews Verse By Verse," William R. Newell wrote: "You say, consider one another to provoke, is strange language for Christian guidance. Yes, brother, if we turn to human reasoning and practice, there is plenty of considering others — their faults, their failures, in merciless criticism, which provokes. But this passage reads, '...to provoke unto love and to good works.' How can we provoke one another unto love? By loving others constantly and tenderly. They will find it out, and will be provoked to return love. The same is true concerning good works. We provoke others to good works by constant good works toward them. As I look back through the years, my heart lights upon one and another, and another, whose tender love and constant goodness 'provoked' everyone to imitate them."

How interesting that the Holy Spirit directed the inspired writer to use the word "provoke." We all understand that word in its less pleasant usage. Some irritating person has "provoked" us into foolish action or a regretted response by continuing to do something displeasing.

Applying Newell's explanation, we are faced with great opportunity. Just as our nerves have become frayed, causing us to want to repay in kind when we are irritated — provoked — so our hearts become full when others continually show love and good works.

Many Christians need provoking — pleasantly.

ALMOST DAWN

MEMORY VERSE: *The night is far spent, the day is at hand: let us therefore cast off the works of darkness, and let us put on the armour of light* (Romans 13:12).

Each passing day in this dark world brings us nearer to the time when Christ, the Light of the World, shall appear. The works of darkness may be prevalent now but a better day is coming...the day of our Lord's return.

The night is far spent. If that was true in Paul's day, how much more in ours. The works of darkness surround us and are the topic of nearly every daily paper: crime, war, greed, and lust. Since the night of sin's reign is nearly over, we must cast off the works of darkness. Children of light do not always live up to their name. Compromise with the world and its degrading practices is on the increase.

But this is no time for compromise.

It is almost dawn.

How quickly the darkness flees at the first light of the morning. Christians must separate from the works of darkness because their Lord may soon appear, the "Dayspring from on high." Upon His return we must all stand before the Judgment Seat of Christ. It is time to get right with God (see 2 Corinthians 5:10).

Honesty of heart is needed.

Drunkenness, envy, and strife must be put away and all else that grieves our Lord. Instead of these dark pastimes, we ought to occupy ourselves with the Lord Jesus.

Christ may return today.

Are you walking in the light?

OUR MOST IMPORTANT ENGAGEMENT

MEMORY VERSE: *So then every one of us shall give account of himself to God* (Romans 14:12).

It is a sobering thought that every Christian must one day stand before the One who has saved him to have his service reviewed. We are all accountable to Jesus for our stewardship of time and talents. The Judgment Seat of Christ will be examination day for the saints.

God has not left us on this planet to waste our lives in useless chatter and earthbound projects. We are to be carrying the Gospel to our world. We have been commissioned to occupy until He comes. We are to be as lights in a dark place. Our earthly vocations should be but the means of support that make it possible for us to be witnesses in our communities.

If all that seems too great a load to bear, remember that one day it will be worth it all. Paul's life was filled with hardship and suffering, yet at the end of the road he eagerly anticipated his departure, and looked forward to the Judgment Seat of Christ. He spoke of it as "that day." He expected to receive eternal rewards that would outweigh any trial he had experienced along the way.

The judgment of the children of God will take place at the Lord's return for His Church. Jesus said, *"And, behold, I come quickly; and my reward is with me, to give every man according as his work shall be"* (Revelation 22:12).

The Judgment Seat of Christ is your most important coming engagement. It will be a revealing day: *"For we must all appear before the judgment seat of Christ; that every one may receive the things done in his body, according to that he hath done, whether it be good or bad"* (2 Corinthians 5:10).

What on earth are you doing for heaven's sake?

CONTINUE IN LOVE

MEMORY VERSE: Let brotherly love continue
(Hebrews 13:1).

For an experiment, babies in an orphanage were divided into two groups. Both groups received all the routine care provided by the nurses and matrons. They were fed on schedule and given proper medical attention.

But one group was given personal, loving care above the routine duties. The babies in Group One were held and cuddled as they were fed, changed and put to sleep. The babies in Group Two had their basic physical needs met but were shown no love at all. They had nothing more than routine care.

It did not take long for marked differences to develop. All the babies in Group One thrived. They developed bright, sunny personalities. But some of the babies in Group Two developed signs of serious emotional maladjustment. Their physical condition suffered, too.

The experiment demonstrated that love is vitally important for healthy growth and development.

Those who are born again need to grow and develop properly. This will be impossible without a continual experience of Christian love. Sometimes we are guilty of giving ourselves completely to the winning of persons to Christ and then neglecting these spiritual babes. New converts need guidance and love.

But brotherly love ought also to continue among those who have been Christians for many years. We never outgrow our need for love. Many have become backslidden after years of service because they have been snubbed by Christians who should have known better.

Reach out to some neglected one. Let brotherly love continue!

LOVE NOT THE WORLD

MEMORY VERSE: *Love not the world, neither the things that are in the world. If any man love the world, the love of the Father is not in him* (1 John 2:15).

Some find it difficult to reconcile John's warning: *"Love not the world,"* with *"For God so loved the world"* (John 3:16). Just what is the "world" that we are not to love?

It certainly is not the world of nature. Jesus loved the beauties of creation and spoke of the lilies of the field, the birds of the air and other wonders of nature. Creation manifests the wisdom and goodness of God: *"The heavens declare the glory of God; and the firmament sheweth his handywork"* (Psalm 19:1).

In answer to the question, "What then is the world?" Dr. H. A. Ironside wrote: "It is that system that man has built up in this scene, in which he is trying to make himself happy without God."

So, many things may qualify as "the world." John Wesley said: "Whatever cools my affection toward Christ is the world." Dr. J. Wilbur Chapman declared: "Anything that dims my vision of Christ, or takes away my taste for Bible study, or cramps my prayer life, or makes Christian work more difficult, is wrong for me and I must, as a Christian, turn away from it."

Choosing the world over Christ is bad judgment. This world is shallow and temporary: *"For all that is in the world, the lust of the flesh, and the lust of the eyes, and the pride of life, is not of the Father, but is of the world. And the world passeth away, and the lust thereof; but he that doeth the will of God abideth forever"* (I John 2:16-17).

What, then, is the world for you? Answer carefully. The truth may touch some of your favorite pastimes!

FEAR AND LOVE

MEMORY VERSE: There is no fear in love; but perfect love casteth out fear; because fear hath torment. He that feareth is not made perfect in love (1 John 4:18).

The following poem was found among the possessions of an atheist after his death:

> *"I've tried in vain a thousand ways*
> *My fears to quell, my hopes to raise;*
> *But what I need the Bible says*
> *Is Jesus, only Jesus. "*

Why did an atheist have this poem? Who gave it to him? Did he heed its message before death? We do not know the answers to these questions. Perhaps he wrote these lines in a time of great fear and desperation, having found his atheism bankrupt.

Fear is an enemy of man. All men. And who has not experienced fear? It stalks us all and steals the joy and peace that God intends for us to have and enjoy.

The Bible is filled with "fear nots." It is said that there is one for every day of the year. Real release from fear comes through resting in the perfect love of God. As we relax in His love, we become settled in the truth that nothing can reach us without passing through the protective wall of His love: *"And we know that all things work together for good to them that love God, to them who are the called according to his purpose"* (Romans 8:28). Acceptance of this great promise depends on confidence in the love of God.

Perfect love casts out fear.

And His love is perfect!

FIRST LOVE

MEMORY VERSE: *Nevertheless I have somewhat against thee, because thou hast left thy first love* (Revelation 2:4).

First love. How warm and wonderful it is!

Do you remember the day you were born again? And what about that special time afterward?

You wanted to tell the world of your discovery. The secrets of the Bible beckoned and you wanted to devour its entire message. Your friends all became prospects for salvation and you sought them out to share the Gospel. You thought about fulltime Christian service. You loved the church, the pastor and all Christians. Missionary projects were accepted and carried out with zeal. Clerks, gas station attendants, business associates and your neighbors all received tracts from your hand and a personal witness. You became a soul winner and soon some of those you love were rejoicing with you.

Then something began to happen. It's hard to pinpoint the exact time the decline set in. But its reality is inescapable. All those good things became fewer in number and less important.

Why? Who can say? Perhaps you just began to look about and see that you were one of the few on fire and found it a lonely feeling.

Maturity set in. Or was it lethargy? At any rate, it seemed to be a general condition among those who had been around for awhile.

Sometimes you think about those good days and long to return to them. Here's good news: YOU CAN!

There is no need to go on in this awful condition. Turn from the direction you are going. Return to your first love. Christ has not changed.

Return today!

September

He shall cover thee
with his feathers,
and under his
wings shalt thou
trust: his truth
shall be thy shield
and buckler.

Psalm 91:4

GOD HEARS

MEMORY VERSE: *O thou that hearest prayer, unto thee shall all flesh come* (Psalm 65:2).

The tin-roofed tabernacle in Waterloo, Iowa, roared under a driving rain when Dr. Charles E. Fuller stepped up to the microphone to pray, "Lord, if you don't stop the rain the Old Fashioned Revival Hour will not be able to go out over the air. For Jesus' sake, please stop the rain!"

Within three minutes the rain stopped abruptly and the program was broadcast without interference. But five minutes after the service was over a downpour drenched the home going crowds.

In Pontiac, Michigan the final night of the Jack Van Impe Crusade was scheduled for Wisner Stadium, an outdoor arena. Rain was forecast and had it come it would have been necessary to move the meeting to a church building holding less than half the capacity of the stadium. Christians were asked to pray. On that closing night, the clouds were threatening and dark. Rain fell in torrents throughout the area — except in a four block radius surrounding Wisner Stadium. God had heard the prayers of His people and was pleased to answer. The news media covered the story of the miracle.

Examples might be multiplied where earnest prayer has been heard and answered. Why then are we so timid in our asking? A. B. Simpson wrote: "Our God has boundless resources, the only limit is in us. Our asking, our thinking, our praying are too small. Our expectations are too limited."

God hears. And here you are carrying that load!

Give your burden to Jesus. Ask and receive. *Prove His promises.* The God Who holds back the rain can also give showers of blessings!

ADAM AND EVE

MEMORY VERSE: *And Adam said, This is now bone of my bones, and flesh of my flesh; she shall be called Woman, because she was taken out of Man* (Genesis 2:23).

Eve was made, "not from Adam's head to be over him; nor from his feet to be trampled by him; but from his side to be next to him; from under his arm to be protected by him; and near to his heart to be loved by him."

God has established the home, not the herd.

No earthly bond is so close and wonderful as that special relationship existing between a man and a woman who have been joined in marriage.

Adam must have been the most handsome of men and Eve the most beautiful of all women. They lived in a world untouched by sin. Grief and tears were unknown until after the fall. We struggle to understand such ideal conditions. Nevertheless, Christian marriage can be a taste of heaven. When two people are in love and express their affection continually while living in an atmosphere of faith in Christ and dedication to His will, they experience something of the blessing shared by Adam and Eve in the Garden of Eden.

Adam said that Eve was bone of his bone and flesh of his flesh. Paul said the same is true of Christ and the Church. *"For we are members of his body, of his flesh, and of his bones. This is a great mystery: but I speak concerning Christ and the church"* (Ephesians 5:30,32).

Grasping this truth makes living the Christian life an adventure in faith. F. J. Huegel has written: "What is impossible to me as an imitator of Christ becomes perfectly natural as a participant of Christ."

Now don't you feel close to Jesus?

PRAYING GROUND

MEMORY VERSE: *If my people, which are called by my name, shall humble themselves, and pray, and seek my face, and turn from their wicked ways; then will I hear from heaven, and will forgive their sin, and will heal their land. Most have heard preachers speak of the importance of staying on "praying ground." But what does that mean? What is praying ground?* (II Chronicles 7:14).

To be on praying ground is to be right with God. It calls for confession of all sin and a total dedication of life to Christ. The whole concept of "praying ground" is built on the teaching that one is more likely to have prayers answered if he is living in the will of God. And there is Bible basis for this conclusion: *"If I regard iniquity in my heart, the Lord will not hear me: But verily God hath heard me; he hath attended to the voice of my prayer. Blessed be God, which hath not turned away my prayer, nor his mercy from me"* (Psalm 66:18-20).

At the dedication of Solomon's temple, the Lord assured the king that his prayer of dedication was heard. He foresaw, however, that in the future Solomon's people would backslide and so gave instruction for their return to praying ground. They were to humble themselves, turn from their wicked ways and seek His face. Prayer accompanied by that kind of repentance was guaranteed to bring healing to the land.

America is far from God. How shall we return to praying ground? By humility. And where should it start? By turning from our wicked ways. And who will make the first move toward righteousness by seeking God's face? And who will seek God above all else?

I conclude it's my move. How about you?

ENOCH

    MEMORY VERSE: *And Enoch walked with God: and he was not; for God took him* (Genesis 5:24).

Enoch must have been a remarkable man. He was one of only two chosen to escape death. The New Testament names him as a man of faith and says that his life pleased God: *"By faith Enoch was translated that he should not see death; and was not found, because God had translated him: for before his translation he had this testimony, that he pleased God"* (Hebrews 11:5).

This man of faith was taken to heaven before the flood came and is a type (picture) of the Church and its coming rapture before the Tribulation. Many expect Enoch to return to the earth as one of the two "witnesses" spoken of in Revelation 11:3-12. These two will announce the coming of Christ in power and great glory to set up His kingdom. Their ministry will come during earth's most difficult time. The Antichrist will be furious and attempt to destroy these Tribulation prophets but God will protect them until their mission is fulfilled.

Should Enoch be one of these "olive trees," he will be able to declare the same message that he heralded before the flood: *"And Enoch also, the seventh from Adam, prophesied of these, saying, Behold, the Lord cometh with ten thousands of his saints, to execute judgment upon all, and to convince all that are ungodly among them of all their ungodly deeds which they have ungodly committed, and of all their hard speeches which ungodly sinners have spoken against him"* (Jude 14,15).

How interesting that God let Enoch in on scenes of the end time!

It pays to walk with God.

And only those who walk with Him below will walk with Him above.

PROTECTION

MEMORY VERSE: *Now when Daniel knew that the writing was signed, he went into his house; and his windows being open in his chamber toward Jerusalem, he kneeled upon his knees three times a day, and prayed, and gave thanks before his God, as he did aforetime* (Daniel 6:10).

Daniel's prayers brought him to the lion's den. And God preserved him there.

Peter began walking on the water to go to Jesus and his brief prayer: *"LORD SAVE ME!"* brought help in his time of need.

King Hezekiah, facing death, prayed and the Lord added fifteen years to his life.

Missionary experiences involving God's protection through prayer are well known. Often the deliverance from accident or attack came as a result of someone in the homeland being especially burdened for that particular missionary so that time was taken for special prayer at the very moment of danger.

Parents have the privilege of praying for God's protection for their children. Husbands or wives can pray for each other while apart. Members of congregations can pray for their pastor or other staff members while busy in the Lord's service. There are many opportunities to pray for protection for those whom we love.

If God someday allows us to look back on scenes of our earthly sojourn, we will be amazed to discover how many times lives have been spared and injuries prevented in answer to prayer.

Prayer changes things. It does not just change the person who is praying. Prayer can change circumstances and can deliver those in danger.

Who needs the protection afforded by your prayers today?

KEEP ON PRAYING

MEMORY VERSE: *Evening, and morning, and at noon, will I pray, and cry aloud; and he shall hear my voice* (Psalm 55:17).

Some pray earnestly about a matter for a time and then grow discouraged and stop praying. The Bible calls for persevering prayer.

In his book, *"Getting Things from God,"* the late Charles Blanchard shared the following experience: "In one of our church prayer meetings not long ago, a lady rose and said: 'My father is a drunkard. I have prayed seven years that God would save him and he is not saved. It seems as if God did not hear or did not care and I am discouraged. I do not know what to do.'

'She had only taken her seat when a lady rose and said: 'My father was a drunkard for fifteen years and I prayed for him all through those fifteen years. Then he was saved, not alone from drink but from all other sins. Now for fifteen years he has been a happy Christian. I think my sister ought not to be discouraged, but to pray on.'"

It is said that George Mueller prayed for two men to be saved and the years passed without his prayers being answered. Still, Mueller prayed on. When George Mueller died, he had been praying daily for these two men for sixty- two years. Shortly after his death they were both born again.

You have been praying long and faithfully for someone or for the meeting of some special need. The answer has not come and you are about to give up. You do not understand the delay.

But faith does not need to understand. Persevere in prayer.

Keep on praying.

God will answer. And right on time!

I WILL ANSWER

MEMORY VERSE: *Call unto me; and I will answer thee, and shew thee great and mighty things, which thou knowest not* (Jeremiah 33:3).

Dr. Thomas N. Carter, an ex-convict, told a thrilling story of his mother's faith. He had been wayward for many years and finally was sent to prison. On one occasion, while he was there, his mother received a telegram from the prison stating that her son was dead and asking what she wanted done with his body.

Carter's mother had prayed for years that he would one day be saved and become a preacher of the Gospel. Stunned at the receipt of the telegram, she immediately went to her prayer closet, instructing other members of the family not to disturb her.

Opening the Bible, she placed the telegram beside it and began to pray. "0 God," she began, "I have believed the promise you gave me in your Word, that I would live to see Tom saved and preaching the Gospel, and now a telegram has come saying he is dead. Lord, which is true, this telegram or your Word?"

When the faithful mother rose from her knees, having definite assurance of God's answer, she wired the prison as follows: "There must be some mistake. My boy is not dead."

And there was a mistake. Tom Carter was alive and when he had finished his time in prison, he became a preacher of the Gospel. God honored the trusting prayer of his mother.

Some make prayer too difficult. The Bible formula is simple. Our responsibility is to pray. God has promised to answer.

What "great and mighty" things do you need?

Ask God for them today!

LOT

MEMORY VERSE: *And while he lingered, the men laid hold upon his hand, and upon the hand of his wife, and upon the hand of his two daughters; the LORD being merciful unto him: and they brought him forth, and set him without the city* (Genesis 19:16).

Lot lingered in Sodom when judgment was imminent.

His investments were there.

Had Peter not revealed that Lot was a righteous man (see 2 Peter 2:8), we might have concluded he was a bad man, a lost man. But the Scriptures declare him righteous. Peter says Lot was uncomfortable in Sodom, vexing his righteous soul from day to day with the sinful acts of the citizens there. Nevertheless, he stayed. And his staying cost him dearly.

Writing of Lot's misery, J. C. Ryle says: "Make a wrong choice in life — an unscriptural choice — and settle yourself down unnecessarily in the midst of worldly people, and I know no surer way to damage your own spirituality, and to go backward in your eternal concerns. This is the way to make the pulse of your soul beat feebly and languidly. This is the way to make the edge of your feeling about sin become blunt and dull. This is the way to dim the eyes of your spiritual discernment, till you can scarcely distinguish good from evil, and stumble as you walk. This is the way to bring a moral palsy on your feet and limbs, and make you go tottering and trembling along the road to Zion, as if the grasshopper was a burden. This is the way to...give the devil vantage-ground in the battle...to tie your arms in fighting...to fetter your legs in running...to dry up the sources of your strength."

Facing an important decision today?

Make it prayerfully and carefully. And don't compromise!

LOT'S WIFE

MEMORY VERSE: *Remember Lot's wife* (Luke 17:32).

In the setting of His second coming, Jesus said, Remember Lot's wife. Mrs. Lot is then a beacon for our day.

What a strange choice!

One would think the Lord would have chosen a woman who was known for her faith. Instead, the woman we are to remember is Lot's wife.

Remember her privileges. She had a righteous husband. She had lived in the company of godly Abraham and his family. She had known faithful Sarah and had probably gathered with the family of the friend of God for times of worship and praise. She had been the object of Abraham's prayers. Yet, surrounded by spiritual opportunities, she remained aloof and spiritually cold. Today, more tools for getting out the gospel are being used than ever before. Especially in America, the average person is offered the gospel time and again. Ours is a day of religious privilege. Still, many ignore God's message of love.

Remember her possessions. Lot was a successful man. His wife evidently had no lack of this world's goods. Sadly, she failed to see that all earth's toys are temporal. Like many today, she was caught up in the merry-go-round of getting. Affluence is often the enemy of spirituality. And in the abundance of things, many are missing the abundant life made so available in these last days.

Remember her perishing. When warned of the coming destruction of Sodom and given instructions for safety, she looked back and became a pillar of salt. Ignoring the clear direction for deliverance, she died.

Week after week, the message of Christ's return goes out from the pulpits and over radio and television. Don't reject God's offer of salvation. Turn to Christ while there is time.

Remember Lot's wife.

THE CLOSET

MEMORY VERSE: *But thou, when thou prayest, enter into* • *thy closet, and when thou hast shut the door, pray to thy Father which is in secret; and thy Father which seeth in secret shall reward thee openly* (Matthew 6:6).

Sir Isaac Newton said: "I can take my telescope and look millions and millions of miles into space; but I can lay my telescope aside, go into my room and shut the door, get down on my knees in earnest prayer, and I see more of heaven and get closer to God than I can when assisted by all the telescopes and material agencies on earth."

Here is a good rule for public and private praying: "Make public prayers short and private prayers long." The person who prays in public to impress others will not abide by that rule. He sees an invitation to pray much like a call to preach. Often he lectures his listeners while supposedly communing with God. Like the Pharisee who went to the temple to pray, he prays with himself.

But the earnest child of God will spurn such carnal exhibitions and choose humility in public and genuine communication when alone with God. He will have a time each day when he "shuts the door" to pray to his Father who sees in secret. His companion there is likely to be an open Bible so that His Father can speak to him as he speaks to his Father.

The quiet place is the Christian's source of power and victory. To neglect the closet is to invite daily defeat. We all need Newton's long look through the telescope of prayer. Without it, spiritual anemia is sure to set in.

The closet is where the Father opens the door to His blessings!

BE DEFINITE

MEMORY VERSE: *Therefore I say unto you, What things soever ye desire, when ye pray, believe that ye receive them, and ye shall have them* (Mark 11:24).

What can one properly pray about?

Are there limits on what we may ask of God in prayer?

In his book, *"Prayer — Asking and Receiving,"* Dr. John R. Rice says: "Anything you have a right to want, you have a right to pray for. If you do not have a right to pray for it, then it is wrong to want it. About any particular matter, the Christian ought to ask for what he wants, or quit wanting it."

Proper wanting, then, is very important to proper praying. James expressed this in his epistle: *"Ye ask, and receive not, because ye ask amiss, that ye may consume it upon your lusts"* (James 4:3).

But how can we keep our wanting right?

Wanting is kept correct by continued exposure to the Bible. Outside influences are directed toward spiraling materialism. Generally, the more we get, the more we want. And American affluence keeps the cycle going.

The Bible reminds us of the temporary nature of all things and offers a lifestyle of giving instead of getting. Try these want-adjusters:

"Seeing then that all these things shall be dissolved, what manner of persons ought ye to be..." (II Peter 3:11).

"Lay not up for yourselves treasures upon earth..." (Matthew 6:19).

"...It is more blessed to give than to receive" (Acts 20:35).

Now, what do you want?

Ask for it. Be definite. Believe. Receive!

HEALING

MEMORY VERSE: *And he put forth his hand, and touched him, saying, I will: be thou clean. And immediately the leprosy departed from him* (Luke 5:13).

Some are afraid to pray for healing. But all healing comes from God. He may heal through doctors, through medicine (as in the case of Hezekiah in II Kings 20:7), or through instantaneous answer to prayer. God is sovereign. And He has invited us to pray for all our needs, including healing of our bodies.

A study of the life of Christ reveals many answers to prayer for healing. He opened blind eyes, made the lame walk, restored paralytics and cleansed lepers. To conclude that He would or could not answer prayer for healing today is inconsistent with the Biblical teaching that God is un- changing.

In his excellent book: "Prayer — Asking and Receiving," Dr. John R. Rice wrote: "I think I ought to say that in literally hundreds of cases I have had my prayers for the sick answered, some slowly, some suddenly, some at once, and others only after long waiting on God."

As in all praying, prayer for healing should be subject to the will of God. And it is not always God's will to heal. That is evident from Paul's thorn in the flesh (II Corinthians 12:7), Timothy's frail health (I Timothy 5:23), and the fact that Paul left his friend Trophimus at Miletum sick (II Timothy 4:20). To quote Dr. Rice again: "One who comes to pray for healing, either for himself or for another, must come saying, '...nevertheless not as I will, but as thou wilt' " (Matthew 26:39).

In praying for healing, then, let us ask God for the most and then leave the results with Him.

THE SINNER'S PRAYER

MEMORY VERSE: *And the publican, standing afar off, would not lift up so much as his eyes unto heaven, but smote upon his breast, saying, God be merciful to me a sinner* (Luke 18:13).

The Pharisee and the publican picture all people who pray. The Pharisee approached God on the basis of his own righteousness and thought that was safe ground. The publican came just as he was, admitting his sin and claiming God's mercy.

There are but two kinds of religion: that which says "Do" and the other that says "It is done." Multitudes hope to get to heaven because of their good works and therefore go out of their way to perform religious and righteous acts. Sadly, their good works will avail nothing. Heaven's gates are not hinged on the accomplishments of men. How clearly Isaiah has explained the futility of seeking God's favor through good works: *"But we are all as an unclean thing, and all our righteousnesses are as filthy rags; and we all do fade as a leaf; and our iniquities, like the wind, have taken us away"* (Isaiah 64:6).

The publican understood that he was a sinner. This is absolutely necessary. *"For all have sinned, and come short of the glory of God"* (Romans 3:23). Only sinners can be saved. And ALL are sinners: *"As it is written, There is none righteous, no, not one"* (Romans 3:10).

But God has been merciful to sinners. Christ died for sinners. There on the cross the debt of sin was paid. You can come to the Saviour just as you are. There is no need to reform or change in any way to be received of Him. Come with repentant heart and trust in Christ as your personal Lord and Saviour. You do not even have to pray a prescribed prayer: *"...Believe on the Lord Jesus Christ, and thou shalt be saved... "* (Acts 16:31).

THY WILL BE DONE

MEMORY VERSE: *And being in an agony he prayed more earnestly; and his sweat was as it were great drops of blood falling down to the ground* (Luke 22:44).

The four most difficult words to pray are these: THY WILL BE DONE. Our stubborn wills resist submission. Yet if we are to follow in His steps, those four difficult words must describe our purpose in living.

Consider the circumstances under which Jesus prayed "not my will, but thine, be done."

Judas had agreed to betray Him for thirty pieces of silver. The illegal and unjust trial lay just ahead of Him and beyond that the cross with its pain and shame. Nevertheless, His will was submitted to His Father's.

We do not know what tomorrow holds. Dark clouds may be gathering on the horizon and a storm of trouble may threaten. We have but one thought — deliverance from difficulties. Still, none face such misery as He faced when He prayed in submission to the Father's will.

While submission comes hard for most, it helps to remember that our Heavenly Father loves us. We are not surrendering to a tyrant bent on our destruction when we pray "Thy will be done." This is a case of giving one's self over to the One who always does right and who loves us with an everlasting love.

Submission to God's will does not guarantee an easy road in the immediate future. But it does promise a blessed eternity. Rewards await those who stop trying to save their lives and dare to risk everything with Jesus. Then we will rejoice in the blessings that will be ours from having earnestly prayed, "THY WILL BE DONE!"

IN JESUS' NAME

MEMORY VERSE: *And whatsoever ye shall ask in my name, that will I do, that the Father may be glorified in the Son* (John 14:13).

What does it mean to pray in the name of Jesus? It means to come to God relying on the merits of Jesus, having no confidence in our own righteousness. It also involves praying so that Jesus may be glorified in the answer. On the latter, the late Dr. Charles Blanchard shared the following in his book, *"Getting Things from God:"*

"Again, praying in the name of Jesus is praying in order that the name of Jesus may be glorified, His kingdom built up, His church established. This test again causes many of our supposed prayers to disappear."

Keeping this in mind, what was the motive in your praying yesterday? Did you come to the throne of grace in the merits of Jesus, or did you pray feeling that God really ought to answer because you deserve it for your faithful service? Did your praying have the glory of God as its motive? If not, you did not really pray in the name of Jesus.

The promise of answered prayer that is made in the name of Jesus is both thrilling and frightening. The promise is so broad and unlimited that its possibilities are exciting. The danger lies in loosely using the name of Jesus as a habit of prayer or a magic phrase without thought or reverence and in so doing taking the name of Christ in vain.

To pray in the name of Jesus, then, involves the attitude of the heart. If you have come in His merits and for His glory, ask boldly in His name. He is responsible to keep His promise of answered prayer.

ASK WHAT YE WILL

MEMORY VERSE: *If ye abide in me, and my words abide in you, ye shall ask what ye will, and it shall be done unto you* (John 15:7).

At first glance, this appears to be another wide open promise of answered prayer — "ask what ye will." Further investigation shows it to be a conditional promise.

The first condition is abiding in Christ. This has to do with consecration and continual confession of all known sin. In other words, it does not deal with salvation only, but with a daily dedicated walk with Christ. There is no room for hypocrisy here. One who abides in Christ in the sense given in this stern chapter makes Christ Lord of all. His life is separated from the world and unto God. He cares not the persecution. Consistency in Christian living is his aim. And his abiding in Christ produces fruit to the glory of God the Father.

The second condition is God's Word abiding in us. That does not happen by a two-minute perusal of a prepared devotional, however helpful. For the Word of God to abide in us, there must be a time set aside for extensive Bible reading and preferably for Bible memorization and meditation. Since the Bible is God's revelation of His will and purpose for man, it deserves our attention. Sadly, it often rates below the newspaper and the television set in priority. No wonder prayers go unanswered.

This prayer promise calls for a new commitment. Are YOU willing to surrender all to Christ, making Him Lord of all in your life? Are you ready to give His Word its proper priority? If so, expect answered prayer!

ELIJAH

MEMORY VERSE: *For thus saith the LORD God of Israel,*
The barrel of meal shall not waste, neither shall the cruse of oil
fail, until the day that the LORD sendeth rain upon the earth
(1 Kings 17:14).

Elijah was a powerful prophet. He announced a drought because of
the sins of his people and there was neither dew nor rain for three
and one half years. James reveals that Elijah prayed for the drought to
come: *"Elias [Elijah] was a man subject to like passions as we are, and*
he prayed earnestly that it might not rain: and it rained not on the
earth by the space of three years and six months. And he prayed again,
and the heaven gave rain, and the earth brought forth her fruit"
(James 5:17,18).

During the drought, God took care of Elijah and others who were
faithful. God is as able to provide our needs in times of famine or
depression as in times of prosperity. Christians ought not waste time
worrying about the state of the economy or the outcome of
international politics. God's plan is unfolding and our responsibility is
to be faithful in witnessing for Christ while there is time.

On one occasion, God used a widow to feed His servant. The widow
had but a handful of meal and a little oil but God would stretch those
meager provisions and make them last until rain came. The widow's
act of faith in providing for Elijah has caused her to be remembered
to this day.

Finally, Elijah called for a contest to prove how foolish it was to
worship the false god, Baal. In his call, he challenged the people to
get off the fence and worship the Lord. *"How long halt ye between two*
opinions? if the LORD be God, follow him" (1 Kings 18:21).

Take Elijah's advice and give your all to Jesus.

PRAYING FOR ME

MEMORY VERSE: *I pray for them: I pray not for the world, but for them which thou hast given me; for they are thine* (John 17:9).

Here is the longest recorded prayer of Jesus. It is known as His great intercessory prayer. He prays for His disciples and for all who will believe as a result of their ministry.

He prays that I will be kept from evil (verse 15). Temptation whirls around all, inviting shame and destruction. The enemy is strong and the flesh is weak. But Jesus has prayed for us. We do not enter the day alone or in our own strength. His Spirit and His prayers follow us every step of the way.

He prays that I will be sanctified through the truth. To be sanctified is to be set apart from the world and for God. Sanctification is in three dimensions — positional, progressive and perfect. As to position, we are sanctified at the moment of new birth. When we are saved through faith in Christ, we are set apart for God. Progressive sanctification continues throughout life. This has to do with growing in the grace and knowledge of Christ. Perfect sanctification takes place when the Lord returns. Then we shall be perfect for we shall be like Him.

Progressive sanctification is the aim of the prayer of Jesus for you and me. He is praying for growth and development in His own. And notice the instrument of sanctification — THE WORD OF GOD (verse 17). His Word gives growth. It contains the vitamins and minerals of soul health.

Our daily growth and Christian victory are concerns of Christ. Prayer concerns. Certainly there is then no excuse for defeat.

I expect to conquer and grow. Jesus prayed for me.

And His prayers continue to this day!

OF ONE ACCORD

MEMORY VERSE: *These all continued with one accord in prayer and supplication, with the women, and Mary the mother of Jesus, and with his brethren* (Acts 1:14).

Christians praying together — of one accord — in a local church can expect the mighty power of God in their witnessing. But too many churches are torn by strife and divisions. As a result, the Spirit of God is grieved and the church plods week after week on its weak way.

As the day of Pentecost approached, the disciples laid aside all differences and united their hearts in believing prayer. We remember that day when the Holy Spirit came as promised and we cherish the account given in the Bible of the thousands saved and the fellowship that was theirs.

- What would it take to get your church praying in one accord?

- Who would have to make the first move?

- What petty grievances would have to be forsaken?

- What do you intend to do about it?

Many Christians flit from church to church trying to find one that conforms to their idea of a perfect church. Some are genuinely concerned and are seeking a fellowship like that set forth in the Book of Acts. They feel they could serve the Lord and live victoriously if only they could find a church where the spiritual temperature was conducive to Christian victory and growth.

The disciples were the most unlikely group on earth with which to start a revival. Yet history speaks for the great work of God among them because they were of one accord.

Stop tramping. Start where you are and do what you can to get the saints together in earnest prayer — united in love. That of praying will change your church. And end your search!

A PRAYING CHURCH

> **MEMORY VERSE:** *And they continued stedfastly in the apostles' doctrine and fellowship, and in breaking of bread, and in prayers* (Acts 2:42).

The church at Jerusalem was made up primarily of new converts. One hundred twenty disciples had begun witnessing on the day of Pentecost and their efforts produced 3000 converts, Nevertheless, these new converts were involved in the prayer life of the church immediately.

It is a mistake to suppose that those newly converted cannot be expected to pray earnestly and powerfully. True, as they grow in grace their maturity will show in prayer, but babes in Christ should be taught to pray without delay. Attendance at the prayer meetings of the church should be expected of all members — new and old.

The New Testament church was powerful because it was a praying church. If the power of your church depended on your prayer life, how powerful would the church be? Would your church be strong in prayer if every member prayed as you pray? What percentage of your fellowship would be present at the prayer meeting service if all members attended as faithfully as you attend?

Five ministerial students were visiting in London on a hot Sunday in July. While they were waiting for the doors of the Metropolitan Tabernacle auditorium to open, a man approached them and asked if they would like to see the heating plant of the church. Thinking it strange to be speaking of a heating system in July, they followed him out of curiosity. He opened a door and whispered: "There it is, sirs!" Seven hundred people were kneeling in prayer.

Some heating system!

Why not install one in your church?

ESTHER

MEMORY VERSE: *And who knoweth whether thou art come to the kingdom for such a time as this?* (Esther 4:14).

God is always on time.

In the darkest day, God makes a way. The Jews were faced with extinction because of the evil plan of a Jew hater named Haman. He was not the first nor the last to attempt to destroy the Jews. History's graveyards are filled with those who hoped to do away with the children of Israel.

Esther was the queen but had never revealed her racial identity to the king. Now Mordecai, her relative who had raised her, came to ask her to intercede on behalf of her people. It was a risky request, placing Esther's life in danger.

God uses a woman or a man to fulfill His plan. Throughout history, God has raised up people to carry out His will. Moses' mother defied Pharaoh's law and spared the life of her son, who was destined to deliver his people. David arrived at the camp of Israel when Goliath had intimidated the armies of Saul. John Wesley was converted and his heart was set afire for Christ in time to save England from revolution. John Knox was there when Scotland needed him. Esther must face the challenge of rescuing her people.

Esther's cry was to do or die. She laid her life on the line. Read again her response to the call of duty: *"Go, gather together all the Jews that are present in Shushan, and fast ye for me, and neither eat nor drink for three days, night or day: I also and my maidens will fast likewise; and so will I go in unto the king, which is not according to the law: and if I perish, I perish"* (Esther 4:16).

Esther rose to the occasion and saved her people.

"Who knoweth whether thou art come to the kingdom for such a time as this?" (See Acts 1:8).

PRAYING BIG

MEMORY VERSE: *Peter therefore was kept in prison: but prayer was made without ceasing of the church unto God for him* (Acts 12:5).

Persecution was daily fare for the early church. Stephen was stoned to death. James, the brother of John, was executed by King Herod. Imprisonment was common, the only crime being telling the good news of the Gospel.

When Peter was arrested and jailed it was probably no surprise. Still, the church was not willing to ho-hum the matter just because the practice was common. They began to pray unceasingly for Peter's release from prison.

Meanwhile, back at the slammer, Peter was sound asleep — a good indication that he wasn't overcome by his difficulties. The one who had been such a coward before the crucifixion now relaxed awaiting the will of God to unfold. Clearly, he had traded fear for faith.

God answered the prayer of the church. An angel freed the sleeping apostle from his chains and set him free. It all happened so quickly and miraculously that Peter wasn't sure he was awake. He thought he might be seeing a vision (verse 9).

Finally, certain that this was for real, Peter hurried to where the church was at prayer — praying big — asking for Peter's release. However, when their prayer was answered they could hardly believe it. Rhoda, who answered the door when Peter knocked, was thought mad when she reported that Peter had arrived.

These early Christians learned two important lessons. First, it pays to pray big. Second, God is greater than our faith. They asked, but didn't really expect an answer. In spite of their frail faith, God answered.

Ask big. The answers may surprise you!

POWER

MEMORY VERSE: *And when they had prayed the place was shaken where they were assembled together; and they were all filled with the Holy Ghost, and they spake the word of God with boldness* (Acts 4:31).

Dr. F.B. Meyer was on his last visit to America. A large audience had assembled in a New York City church to hear him speak. Dr. Meyer's health was failing and he had to be helped to the platform by two men. He was so weak and wobbly that he was seated in an elevated chair from which he was to preach.

As the faithful servant of God began to preach, however, the audience witnessed a miracle of God's power. Dr. Meyer stood to his feet and preached with the vigor of youth for more than an hour. God had enabled him for that occasion. Here was living proof of Isaiah 40:29-31: *"He giveth power to the faint; and to them that have no might he increaseth strength. Even the youths shall faint and be weary, and the young men shall utterly fall: But they that wait upon the LORD shall renew their strength; they shall mount up with wings as eagles; they shall run, and not be weary; and they shall walk, and not faint."*

All ministers could be empowered in their pulpits through the prayers of their congregations. Though weak and wobbly in their own strength, they would become channels of blessing if their people would be faithful in prayer. Nothing is more tragic than church and pastor attempting to do God's work in human strength.

In the early church, they prayed and the place was shaken. Many places need shaking today. We are in need of an earth-shaking revival that can only come through prayer. It's time to pray!

JOB'S WIFE

MEMORY VERSE: *But he said unto her, Thou speakest as one of the foolish women speaketh. What? shall we receive good at the hand of God, and shall we not receive evil? In all this did not Job sin with his lips* (Job 2:10).

Job's wife may be the most maligned woman in the Bible.

It's not fair.

What she said was bad, but one must remember when she said it. Her children had just lost their lives. She and her husband had lost all their property. And now the man she loved had lost his health. Under such conditions many would have said foolish things. Depression often causes words to drop from our lips that would never be uttered under normal circumstances.

We must be careful not to judge the man by the moment. Or the woman.

Job understood his wife's state of mind and spoke to her tenderly. He didn't call her a fool. He knew her too well for that...and loved her. He simply told her that she was talking like one of the foolish women. He reminded her that she was out of character. This was not like her. There is not a touch of bitterness in his word of correction. This patient and good man knew the load of grief being carried by his deprived wife and he had compassion on her.

And now a good word for Mrs. Job. It is said that whenever a man reaches the top a good woman is holding the ladder. And Job had become a prosperous and respected man. Mrs. Job had evidently been a loyal and helpful companion through the years, a good homemaker and mother. She doesn't deserve the criticism heaped on her for her single lapse of judgment during a time of deep depression.

To attack others when they are down is to act like the foolish ones. *"Husbands, love your wives"* (Ephesians 5:25).

THE BATTLE

MEMORY VERSE: *Praying always with all prayer and supplication in the Spirit, and watching thereunto with all perseverance and supplication for all saints* (Ephesians 6:18).

We're at war!

Though at peace with God and experiencing the peace that passes all human understanding, all Christians are in conflict with spiritual foes bent on their destruction: *"For we wrestle not against flesh and blood, but against principalities, against powers, against the rulers of the darkness of this world, against spiritual wickedness in high places"* (Ephesians 6:12).

There is no discharge in this war until death.

If the sounds of battle discourage you, remember that you are equipped for victory. Casualties are unnecessary. We have a conquering Captain and all needed armour to insure safety is provided. The enemy cannot overcome the Christian soldier whose defense is salvation, faith, truth, the Gospel of peace and the Word of God. Only neglect of God's furnished protection can result in defeat.

This protection is provided through prayer. To neglect prayer in the fight of faith is to ignore the importance of constant contact with the Commander-in-Chief.

Some are pressed with the struggle. Circumstances have seemed against them. Temptation has been especially strong. Depression hovers like a dark cloud. Efforts to exercise faith or to advance with the truth have been futile. What can be done?

Pray.

And in your prayer, remember others who are struggling, too!

PRISON BREAK

MEMORY VERSE: *And at midnight Paul and Silas prayed, and sang praises unto God: and the prisoners heard them* (Acts 16:25).

In adversity it is normal to pray. But to praise?

Paul and Silas, jailed for Jesus, greeted midnight with a doxology. That's victorious Christian living!

Reacting differently than expected, attracts attention. When God's imprisoned servants began praying and praising, the other prisoners heard them and were affected by their testimonies. Following the earthquake and the opening of the prison doors, their fellow prisoners were more interested in hearing Paul and Silas than in escaping.

Praising God in difficulties gives evidence of submission to God's will. Too many live "under the circumstances." Praise is foreign to those who succumb to their trials. They pray and pout. No wonder others are not influenced to trust Christ through their witness.

Prayer that breaks bonds comes from praising hearts. If that sounds too positive to be realistic, meditate on Paul's instruction to the persecuted church at Philippi: *"Finally, brethren, whatsoever things are true, whatsoever things are honest, whatsoever things are just, whatsoever things are pure, whatsoever things are lovely, whatsoever things are of good report; if there be any virtue, and if there be any praise, think on these things"* (Philippians 4:8).

But in what can one rejoice in prison? Perhaps in the truth that he has been set free from sin through the death of Christ on the cross. At any rate, with backs bleeding and their feet in stocks, Paul and Silas made that dungeon a place of praise and prayer.

And here you are pouting about your problems!

YOU DIDN'T ASK

MEMORY VERSE: *Ye lust, and have not: ye kill, and desire to have, and cannot obtain: ye fight and war, yet ye have not, because ye ask not* (James 4:2).

What surprises heaven will bring! When the shadows flee away and all is made plain, we'll discover how much we missed by not asking for it. No wonder God will have to wipe away tears.

Interestingly, many of the things we strive for are among the things we might have had if we had asked for them. Fussing over supposed deserved offices in the church, material possessions, and other gains might well have been ours had we sought them in prayer. All the mileage rolled up on life's odometer was unnecessary — the arguing, complaining and bitterness. Ernest prayer could have provided what conflict denied... *"...ye have not because ye ask not."*

Some do not ask because their first recourse is not to prayer. When desire surfaces, human effort is the first avenue taken for achievement. The phrase "All we can do now is pray," is the child of such carnal reaction. The opposite ought to be true. Prayer should be the first means of securing the desires of our hearts.

Others do not ask because they have limited prayer to spiritual needs. They think it right to pray about things for the church or for things that have to do with witnessing, but God is ruled out as a supplier of daily needs or wants. Such reasoning has no basis in Scripture and should have no place in the Christian life. To the child of God there must be no separation of the sacred and secular. Everything must be done for the glory of God. All desires are either subjects for prayer or they are wrong.

What are you missing that you ought to have? It's possible that you have not, because you ask not!

FERVENT PRAYER

MEMORY VERSE: *Confess your faults one to another, and pray one for another, that ye may be healed. The effectual fervent prayer of a righteous man availeth much* (James 5:16).

Too much praying is only form.

Many who scorn written prayers are as guilty of formalism as those who read their supplications to God. Having fallen into the habit of repeating the same prayers over and over again, they do not really pray from their hearts. They mean well — but they do not pray well. This is not to imply that prayers are better because of eloquence. On the contrary, it is a call for communication with God in prayer rather than rote recitations that rise no higher than the ceiling.

Elijah was a prophet who prayed fervently. His recorded prayers were brief but powerful. His prayer on Mount Carmel is contained in two Bible verses: *"...LORD God of Abraham, Isaac, and of Israel, let it be known this day that thou art God in Israel, and that I am thy servant, and that I have done all these things at thy word. Hear me, O LORD, hear me, that this people may know that thou art the LORD God, and that thou hast turned their heart back again"* (I Kings 18:36:37), That fervent prayer brought fire down upon the sacrifice that had been prepared and in a short time the awful drought that had lasted for so long had ended.

How does your prayer fare in the "fervent" examination?

Is it time to trade form for fervency?

Remember: *"The effectual fervent prayer of a righteous man availeth much."*

LOVE AND HATE

MEMORY VERSE: *Ye that love the LORD, hate evil: he preserveth the souls of his saints; he delivereth them out of the hand of the wicked* (Psalm 97:10).

Those who love the Lord must learn to hate evil. Some envision one who loves God as a person who has a wishy-washy attitude toward everything — even sin. Nothing could be further from the Biblical truth. The Bible says: *"The fear of the LORD is to hate evil: pride, and arrogancy, and the evil tray, and the froward mouth, do I hate"* (Proverbs 8:13).

It is not strange that those who truly love the Lord hate certain things. There are a number of things that God hates. Here are some examples: *"These six things doth the LORD hate: yea, seven are an abomination unto him: A proud look, a lying tongue, and hands that shed innocent blood, an heart that deviseth wicked imaginations, feet that be swift in running to mischief, a false witness that speaketh lies, and he that soweth discord among brethren"* (Proverbs 6:16-19).

To say that we love God while loving or participating in the things He hates is hypocrisy.

You say you love God? Are you ruled by pride? Is your walk consistent with your talk? Do you have a loose tongue? Are you guilty of causing divisions and trouble among brethren? Does your love for God stand the test of consistency?

Wise Solomon explained that there is a time to love and a time to hate (Ecclesiastes 3:8).

It is time to love God.

It is time to hate evil!

END-TIME PRAYING

MEMORY VERSE: *But the end of all things is at hand: be ye therefore sober, and watch unto prayer* (1 Peter 4:7).

In these last days, prayer ought to have priority.

We live in turbulent times. Iniquity is increasing. War threatens. The Middle East is explosive. Signs of the countdown are all about.

During the crucial hours preceding His betrayal, Jesus instructed His disciples to remember the importance of prayer in times of crisis: *"Watch and pray, that ye enter not into temptation: the spirit indeed is willing, but the flesh is weak"* (Matthew 26:41).

The end time is a crisis time. Though the Rapture of the church is itself sign less, evidences of the Lord's return to set up His Kingdom are already here. And the Rapture of the church precedes the establishment of the Kingdom by seven years. His coming for His own may take place momentarily.

As the clock of prophecy ticks off the final moments, there are many things to be done. Souls must be won. His Word must be given to as many as possible while time remains. Laborers are needed in the whitened harvest.

How shall we ever meet the demands of these trying hours?

Prayer is the only answer.

So, pray!

Pray earnestly, fervently, and continually. Pray in faith. Pray for others. Pray for pastors and evangelists. Pray for missionaries. Pray for revival.

The Lord is coming! Watch and pray!

GIVE US THIS DAY
OUR DAILY BREAD

The Lord himself shall descend from heaven with a shout, with the voice of the archangel, and with the trump of God: and the dead in Christ shall rise first: Then we which are alive and remain shall be caught up together with them in the clouds to meet the Lord in the air: and so shall we ever be with the Lord. Wherefore comfort one another with these words.

I Thessalonians 4:16-18.

CONSENT NOT

MEMORY VERSE: *My son, if sinners entice thee, consent thou not* (Proverbs 1:10).

No one expected that Fire Base Mary Ann in Vietnam would be hit by the enemy. This was especially true of the men of the 1st Battalion, 46th Infantry, who manned it. Yet the base was hit and more than forty GI's perished!

In speaking of the tragic incident, an officer commented, "There were so many holes in the perimeter wire around the base that the GI's seldom bothered to use the gates. They walked right through the wire to go to the water hole. Many of the claymore mines did not work because their electric wires were corroded, Their guards against the enemy were down."

Many go down in defeat because of failure to keep their guards up. They live in ease and indifference, while the enemy, Satan, never takes a vacation. He is ever alert and aggressive. The Bible says: *"Be sober, be vigilant; because your adversary the devil, as a roaring lion, walketh about seeking whom he may devour"* (I Peter 5:8).

There is no haven on planet earth where temptation is unknown. Even the blessed Garden of Eden was invaded by the enemy. No one is immune from temptation. It is important then to keep up a good defense. And to learn to say "No!"

Probably some contact today will offer opportunities to do wrong. Few like to sin alone. Misery loves company and those who are overcome by temptation often seek to lure others into the same trap, thus bolstering their sagging self esteem. "Everybody's doing it" seems to make sin less sinful.

But Solomon's advice is as good today as when it was given: *"...if sinners entice thee, consent not."*

WISDOM

MEMORY VERSE: *For the LORD giveth wisdom: out of his mouth cometh knowledge and understanding* (Proverbs 2:6).

Wisdom is defined as: "The power of true and right discernment."

And we need it.

Somewhere along the line, man decided that education could be his saviour. But experience has taught us that full heads and empty hearts bring tragic results. We need more than an accumulation of facts to solve our problems.

We can build luxurious homes that are beyond the wildest dreams of our forefathers. But more homes are coming apart than ever before.

We have produced an army of experts on the causes of crime. The crime rate soars in spite of our know-how.

Knowledge of the atom, hoped to solve the energy needs of the world and be the miracle fuel of the latter part of the century, has been disappointing. The chief use of this mind-boggling breakthrough continues to be the continual buildup of armaments and a steady march toward Armageddon.

Man's wheel-spinning predicament in the last days, in spite of his great knowledge, is foretold in this one descriptive statement in Paul's revelation concerning the end time: *"Ever learning, and never able to come to the knowledge of the truth"* (II Timothy 3:7).

But what is the reason for this contradiction? A lack of wisdom.

And where is that available? From the Lord: *"If any of you lack wisdom, let him ask of God, that giveth to all men liberally, and upbraideth not; and it shall be given him"* (James 1:5).

THE CORDS OF SIN

MEMORY VERSE: *His own iniquities shall take the wicked himself, and he shall be holden with the cords of his sins* (Proverbs 5:22)

S. D. Gordon says that there are seven simple facts that everyone ought to know about sin: The first is that "sin earns wages." The second, "sin pays wages." The third, "sin insists on paying." You may be quite willing to let the account go, but sin always insists on paying. Fourth, "sin pays wages in kind. Sin against the body brings results in the body. Sin in the mental life brings results there. Sin in contact with other people brings a chain of results affecting others. It is terribly true that 'no man sinneth to himself.' Sin is the most selfish of acts. It influences to some extent everyone whom we touch." Fifth, "sin pays in installments." Sixth, "sin pays in full, unless the blood of Jesus washes away the stain." Seventh, "sin is self-executive, it pays its own bills. Sin has bound up in itself all the terrific consequences that ever come. The logical result of sin is death; death to the body, death to the mind, death to the soul."

Sin deceives. Promising freedom, it gives slavery — bondage. Promising thrills and pleasure, sin brings grief. Promising an escape from the routine of living, sin develops its own cycle of despair.

What then is the way of liberty and release? It is the path of righteousness and obedience. In doing right we gain all the freedom promised by the tempter — without the grief.

Complete dedication to Christ and day by day living for Him keeps one free from the restricting cords of sin. Jesus said: *"If the Son therefore shall make you free, ye shall be free indeed"* (John 8:36). Christ frees from the cords of sin!

KEEP THY HEART

MEMORY VERSE: *Keep thy heart with all diligence; for out of it are the issues of life* (Proverbs 4:23).

A lady who had been mistreated by her husband, said: "He's mean but he has a good heart." Her pastor corrected her. "No," he said, "he has a bad heart."

The pastor was right. Our actions reveal what is in our heart. Jesus said: "*...out of the abundance of the heart the mouth speaketh. A good man out of the good treasure of the heart bringeth forth good things: and an evil man out of the evil treasure bringeth forth evil things*" (Matthew 12:34-35).

The human heart has immense potential for evil: "*The heart is deceitful above all things, and desperately wicked: who can know it?*" (Jeremiah 17:9).

Salvation is the result of believing in one's heart: "*That if thou shalt confess with thy mouth the Lord Jesus, and shalt believe in thine heart that God hath raised him from the dead, thou shalt be saved. For with the heart man believeth unto righteousness; and with the mouth confession is made unto salvation*" (Romans 10.9-10).

One who has been born again must be careful to keep his heart right. Sin must be confessed. Forgiveness of others must be his continual experience. The Psalmist prayed well: "*Let the words of my mouth, and the meditation of my heart, be acceptable in thy sight, O LORD, my strength, and my redeemer*" (Psalm 19:14).

How can we keep our hearts right? Here's the answer: "*With my whole heart have I sought thee: O Let me not wander from thy commandments. Thy word have I hid in mine heart, that I might not sin against thee.*" (Psalm 119:10-11).

GOD IS HOLY

MEMORY VERSE: *And one cried unto another, and said, Holy, holy, holy, is the LORD of hosts; the whole earth is full of his glory* (Isaiah 6:3).

A lady once prayed: "0 Lord, forgive us. We do so many things now that we used to think were wrong." Her prayer is a commentary on many lives.

When Isaiah was given a vision of the Lord, he was most impressed with God's holiness. That is not surprising since, in his vision, the creatures about the throne were occupied day and night with that attribute of God.

The holiness of God is taught throughout the Bible. Sodom and Gomorrah could not be allowed to continue in their wickedness. The angels that left their first estate were not spared. The world in Noah's day had but one hundred twenty years to turn from wickedness before destruction. Nineveh had to repent in forty days in response to the preaching of Jonah or be overthrown.

The most powerful illustration of God's holiness is found in the death of Christ on the cross. Sin could not be excused. It had to be judged. There was but one way for God to be just and the justifier: The Innocent One had to atone for the guilty. Christ died for us, taking our place: *"For he hath made him to be sin for us, who knew no sin; that we might be made the righteousness of God in him"* (2 Corinthians 5:21).

Live carefully. The price of sin is high. And one day soon we must stand before our Holy God (see Romans 14:12).

GOD IS TRUE

MEMORY VERSE: *And they sing the song of Moses the servant of God, and the song of the Lamb, saying, Great and marvelous are thy works, Lord God Almighty; just and true are thy ways, thou King of saints* (Revelation 15:3).

Dr. Philpot once had the sad duty of going to tell a Christian woman that her husband had died in battle. After greeting her he said, "I am the bearer of sad tidings. Your dear husband has been slain in battle!" The woman fell to the floor and wept uncontrollably. The faithful pastor did all he could to bring comfort to her but the grief-stricken woman, seemingly deaf to his words, would only cry out, "Is it true after all?" Thinking that she doubted the sad news, he said: "Yes, my good woman, it is true. Your husband has given his life in the service of his country." "Oh, Pastor," she sobbed, "I know that my husband is gone, but is it really true that there is a God who cares?"

There are many difficult experiences in life and in some of them we may be tempted to doubt the goodness and wisdom of God. Castles tumble. Plans do not work out. Health flees. Everything seems to go wrong. What is the answer?

The answer lies in our inability to know all the details of any given situation as God knows them. Our information is incomplete. God, knowing the future and all the results of every possible set of events, brings about what is best for His own (see Romans 8:28).

When we meet Him, we'll join the heavenly chorus singing: *"Great and marvelous are thy works, Lord God Almighty; just and true are thy ways, thou King of saints."*

GOD IS LOVE

MEMORY VERSE: *He that loveth not knoweth not God; for God is love* (1 John 4:8).

Many claim the name "Christian" who are not genuine. Some who profess Christ as Saviour are filled with bitterness, malice, selfishness, hatred, and envy. They are quick to gossip and they delight when others stumble along the way. Often these people are themselves deceived, and are of the opinion that their religious charade commends them to God.

Christians are people who have been born again through faith in the Lord Jesus Christ. This new birth is possible because of God's love for us. His love is seen in His many blessings and provisions but especially in the death of His Son on the cross: *"But God commendeth his love toward us, in that, while we were yet sinners, Christ died for us"* (Romans 5:8).

The love of God is placed in our hearts by the Holy Spirit: *"And hope maketh not ashamed; because the love of God is shed abroad in our hearts by the Holy Ghost who is given unto us"* (Romans 5:5).

It is totally inconsistent for one who has been saved to be filled with ire, bitterness, and malice. John wrote: *"If a man say, I love God, and hateth his brother, he is a liar: for he that loveth not his brother whom he hath seen, how can he love God whom he hath not seen?"* (1 John 4:20).

Since God loves us, let us communicate His love to others. John put it all together well: *"Beloved, if God so loved us, we ought also to love one another"* (1 John 4:11).

THE TRINITY

MEMORY VERSE: *Go ye therefore, and teach all nations, baptizing them in the name of the Father, and of the Son, and of the Holy Spirit* (Matthew 28:19).

Cults often attack the Trinity. Yet, teaching about the Father, Son, and Holy Spirit is found throughout the Bible.

The first verse in the Bible contains the plural form of the word that is translated God, *elohim.* Plurality is also indicated in such statements as: *"And God said, Let US make man in OUR image, after OUR likeness..."* (Genesis 1:26). *"And the Lord God said, Behold, the man is become as one of US"* (3:22).

Still, the Bible insists that God is ONE: *"Hear, O Israel: The LORD our God is one LORD"* (Deuteronomy 6:4). In short, then, the Hebrew words used for God and to describe God call for a plurality in unity.

But who are the persons of this plurality?

One Person is the Father. *"Doubtless thou art our father"* (Isaiah 63:16).

One Person is the Son. *"I will declare the decree: the LORD hath said unto me, Thou art my Son; this day have I begotten thee"* (Psalm 2:7).

One Person is the Holy Spirit. *"And the earth was without form and void; and darkness was upon the face of the deep. And the Spirit of God moved upon the face of the waters"* (Genesis 1:2).

Paul's benediction at the end of his second letter to the Corinthians makes it clear: *"The grace of the Lord Jesus Christ, and the love of God, and the communion of the Holy Ghost, be with you all. Amen"* (2 Corinthians 13:14).

Who could ask for more?

THE GREAT CREATOR

MEMORY VERSE: *All things were made by him; and without him was not any thing made that was made* (John 1:3).

Napoleon said: "I marvel that whereas the ambitious dreams of myself, Caesar, and Alexander should have vanished into thin air, a Judean peasant — Jesus — should be able to stretch His hands across the centuries and control the destinies of men and nations." But the dismayed fallen leader had forgotten to take into consideration the fact that Jesus was far more than a Judean peasant.

Had Jesus been but a man, He could not have atoned for the sins of the world. It was the great Creator who came down in human form to redeem His creation. No wonder He spoke with authority. No wonder the wind and waves were subject to Him. No wonder death could not hold Him.

John explains that Christ is the source of light and life. Doubters used to attack the reliability of the Bible account of creation because light is said to have been created before the sun. Now we know that there are other sources of light in the universe. How foolish to suppose that the Creator would be dependent upon the sun for illumination. That fiery ball is but one of His deputies assigned to provide light and physical life to planet earth.

At the moment of new birth, the same creative power that called the universe into existence becomes active within the believer: *"Therefore, if any man be in Christ, he is a new creature: old things are passed away; behold, all things are become new"* (2 Corinthians 5:17).

GOD IS OMNISCIENT

MEMORY VERSE: *Thou knowest my downsitting and mine uprising; thou understandest my thought afar off* (Psalm 139:2).

God knows all.

He knows all the past. While historians and archaeologists study and dig to solve the stubborn secrets of antiquity, God knows all about them. Questioning Job, the Lord said: *"Where wast thou when I laid the foundations of the earth? declare, if thou hast understanding. Who hath laid the measures thereof, if thou knowest? or who hath stretched the line upon it?"* (Job 38:4,5).

He knows all about the present. Philosophers puzzle over present problems. Politicians probe for answers. Stargazers try to discern the signs of the times in order to advise the public on their horoscopes. But God knows. Nothing takes Him by surprise. Everything is open before His gaze.

He knows all about the future. No crystal ball is needed for God to chart our tomorrows. He sees them more clearly than we remember yesterday. And He holds the future in His hands. All events still to come are written in His history book. The movements of the nations, the rise and fall of political leaders, and the personal triumphs and tragedies of us all are already in His mind.

Knowing Him, then, we can feel safe. We do not need to fear what the future holds for we know the One who holds the future. Even in times of trial, we can experience the confidence and assurance that carried Job through such great loss. In the darkest of hours, he declared: *"But he knoweth the way that I take: when he hath tried me, I shall come forth as gold"* (Job 23:10).

GOD IS OMNIPOTENT

MEMORY VERSE: *Behold, I am the LORD, the God of all flesh: is there any thing too hard for me?* (Jeremiah 32:27).

God is all-powerful. Theologians call this attribute "omnipotence." To most of us that just means that God can do anything.

The first verse in the Bible guarantees God's limitless power: *"In the beginning God created the heaven and the earth"* (Genesis 1:1). Still, the mind of man has continually staggered at God's ability to perform many of the miracles recorded in His Word.

How inconsistent!

The God who formed the seas could easily open one of them for His people to cross dry-shod. The God who feeds the angels could easily drop enough from heaven's table to feed the Israelites in the wilderness. The God who called forth water from the first spring could easily open a new fountain in a rock so that thirsty people could drink. The God who filled the seas with life could easily prepare a great fish perfectly designed to swallow backslidden and disobedient Jonah. The God who laid the foundations of the earth could easily cause it to tremble beneath the walls of Jericho until the mighty fortress fell. The God who holds the wind in His hands could easily call for a calm on the Sea of Galilee when it was raging in a storm. The God who engineered the human body could easily give ability to the lame to walk and the blind to see. The God who gave life could easily return it to one from whom it had taken flight.

And the God who knows your tomorrows can easily carry you through the darkest day.

HATE

MEMORY VERSE: *The fear of the LORD is to hate evil: pride, and arrogancy, and the evil way, and the froward mouth, do I hate* (Proverbs 8:13).

Is it ever wise to hate?

Cradled in a chapter exalting wisdom, is an injunction to hate.

Surprising?

Not when the righteous character of God is considered.

The fear (reverential trust) of the LORD causes one to hate what He hates. We are not shocked when instructed to love what God loves. Logic leads from love to hate. God hates evil, therefore it is wise for His children to hate evil too.

But hating sin is not popular in our day. Evil is simply renamed to make it more acceptable. Nevertheless, God's standards have not changed. Judgment will not be an exercise in semantics. Evil is evil. Sin is sin! And the child of God is called upon to declare his loyalty to the God of righteous- ness.

Now let's get personal.

It is not so difficult to hate evil, pride and arrogancy in another. Despising the froward mouth of a neighbor or fellow church member may come easily. But what if these awful acts and attitudes are our own?

- Have you learned to hate pride when you see it in the mirror?

- Have you caught yourself being disgustingly arrogant?

- Do you face the issue when you have spoken wrongly?

Thankfully, these serious transgressions of God's will can be confessed, forgiven and forsaken. No one has to live in defeat. Like all sins, these can be put away and overcome — if you hate them enough!

COVERING SINS

MEMORY VERSE: *Hatred stirreth up strifes: but love covereth all sins* (Proverbs 10:12).

A pastor was approached by one of his members who wanted to repeat to him some of the wrongdoings of another in the church. The pastor said, "Does anybody else know about this?" "No," answered the talebearer. "Then," advised the wise preacher, "go home and hide it away at the feet of Jesus, and never speak of it again unless God leads you to speak to the person himself."

What good advice! The talebearer acts out of hate and is in heart a murderer: *"Whosoever hateth his brother is a murderer: and ye know that no murderer hath eternal life abiding in him"* (I John 3:15). The Christian who covers sin is motivated by love. He cannot bring himself to repeat the wrongs of others in the family of God.

Peter reminded his readers of the importance of Solomon's instruction: *"And above all things have fervent charity among yourselves: for charity shall cover the multitude of sins"* (I Peter 4:8). How grateful this servant of God must have been for God's forgiveness and the love demonstrated by his brethren. After his three denials of Christ, he was forgiven and made the spokesman for the early church.

Shall we act today in hate or love? Will our conversations stir up strife or cover sins? Will the church be divided or helped because we have lived another day?

Does love then simply ignore wrongs in a brother or sister? Not at all. We have two obligations. The first is that of prayer for the one who has sinned. The second is to go to the one in need and make an effort to restore: *"Brethren, if a man be overtaken in a fault, ye which are spiritual, restore such an one in the spirit of meekness; considering thyself, lest thou also be tempted"* (Galatians 6:1).

WINNING SOULS

MEMORY VERSE: *The fruit of the righteous is a tree of life; and he that winneth souls is wise* (Proverbs 11:30).

Not many win souls.

It is estimated that only about 5% of Christians ever lead another to the Saviour. This means 95% do not win souls.

Had the early church advanced at such a snail's pace, Christianity would have died out in the first century! Those fiery souls were out to win the world and because they were faithful, we have received the Gospel. They had been commissioned to minister in Jerusalem, Judea, Samaria and the uttermost parts of the earth. And they took the charge seriously.

When persecution came to early Christians, they seized their scattering as an opportunity to preach the Gospel in new fields. Under pressure, they produced. Imprisoned, they sang praises to God and won other prisoners.

Why do so few win souls today? Why is fruit so scarce compared to the harvest of the first century?

There are undoubtedly a number of factors that contribute to fruitlessness. But one of the most important is that we do not make soul winning our most desired goal. We are quite content if all is going well at the church and we have few troubles at home. Financial targets get priority. We must get our incomes up to that of our friends. After overtime, there is little time to reach lost people. Church visitation and soul winning programs languish while we cater to our carnal desires of gain and ease.

But when all is said and done — who is wise?

All our earthly trinkets will someday be dissolved. But he that winneth souls is wise — having lasting treasure.

GOD IS OMNIPRESENT

MEMORY VERSE: *Whither shall I go from thy spirit? or whither shall I flee from thy presence?* (Psalm 139:7).

God is everywhere.

A celebrity attended the services of an old minister in a small church. The aged preacher spoke with his accustomed earnestness and seemed unshaken by the presence of the visitor. At the close of the service, some members of the congregation said, "Pastor, we had a distinguished visitor today, but you did not seem embarrassed." Their wise pastor replied: "I have been preaching in the presence of Almighty God for forty years, and do you think, with Him as one of my constant Hearers, any man can embarrass me by his presence?"

The ability of God to be everywhere is hard for us to grasp. Our minds struggle with such infinite information. Yet it is true. A number of Bible verses confirm it. Solomon wrote: *"But will God indeed dwell on the earth? behold, the heaven and heaven of heavens cannot contain thee; how much less this house that I have builded"* (1 Kings 8:27). The psalmist declared: *"Nevertheless I am continually with thee; thou hast holden me by my right hand. Thou shalt guide me with thy counsel, and afterward receive me to glory. Whom have I in heaven but thee? and there is none upon earth that I desire beside thee. My flesh and my heart faileth: but God is the strength of my heart, and my portion for ever"* (Psalm 73:23-26).

Though it is beyond our understanding, we can claim the promise of His presence. He will never leave us nor forsake us (see Hebrews 13:6). And so the child of God is never alone.

GOD IS UNCHANGING

MEMORY VERSE: *Every good gift and every perfect gift is from above, and cometh down from the Father of lights, with whom is no variableness, neither shadow of turning* (James 1:17).

God is the same today as He was yesterday. In all our tomorrows, He will be the same. Dr. Lewis Sperry Chafer wrote: "In no sphere or relationship is God subject to change. He could not be less than He is, and, since He filleth all things, He could not be more than He is. He could be removed from no place, nor is His knowledge or holiness subject to change."

The Bible says of God: *"For I am the LORD, I change not; therefore ye sons of Jacob are not consumed"* (Malachi 3:6); *"Of old hast thou laid the foundation of the earth: and the heavens are the work of thy hands. They shall perish, but thou shalt endure: yea, all of them shall wax old like a garment; as a vesture shalt thou change them, and they shall be changed: But thou art the same, and thy years shall have no end"* (Psalm 102:25-27).

In my youth, I would often kneel to pray in our humble home in Detroit. There I unloaded many burdens and asked for many blessings. Since that time, most things have changed. The community has changed. The neighbors have changed. I have changed. But God remains the same. He is as ready to bear the burdens of this preacher as He was to hear the prayer of that boy so long ago. Events of the day may change the course of our lives, but God is unchanging: *"Jesus Christ the same yesterday, and today, and forever"* (Hebrews 13:8).

POVERTY AND RICHES

MEMORY VERSE: *There is that maketh himself rich, yet hath nothing: there is that maketh himself poor, yet hath great riches* (Proverbs 13:7).

The love of money can be as great a pitfall to the poor as to the rich. Some who have little put on airs and pretend to be rich. Impressions are important to them. They want others to think they are successful.

Some who are very rich travel incognito. They keep their wealth secret. Finally, after death, the truth is known. Newspapers frequently carry stories of people leaving large estates to the surprise of friends and relatives. Their lifestyles had not given a true story of their resources. Living like paupers, they had stored immense fortunes.

What is the lesson here?

It is the folly of making money life's goal.

The poor person pretending to be rich reveals his belief that wealth determines personal worth. If only he could be rich, he thinks, life would have yielded him its best. Therefore, he spends beyond his means trying to get his message across. Finally, debt ridden, he comes to the end of his days never having been satisfied.

The wealthy person living as a pauper never feels secure enough to give of his abundance. He is ever looking for a rainy day and therefore lives under a cloud of fear. His security lies in that bank account or in his hidden treasure. He never learns the joy of leaning only upon God in a time of need. He misses the miracle of God's provision when there is no place else to turn. Pity him.

Resting in Jesus we can be ourselves. Secure in Him, we need not feign riches or poverty. Rich or poor we belong to Him. Hallelujah!

GOD IS INFINITE

MEMORY VERSE: *For as the heavens are higher than the earth, so are my ways higher than your ways, and my thoughts than your thoughts* (Isaiah 55:9).

God has no boundaries. No limits. He has always existed and He will always exist. He cannot be bound by time or space for they are His creations. His knowledge is beyond us.

We have many limits. There are things we do not comprehend. So many things we cannot do. We are limited in knowledge, in strength, and in ability. Even the strongest have areas of weakness. It is the way of mankind. We are a fallen race, still suffering from the effects of that traumatic tumble. We are finite beings.

How wonderful that the infinite God loves us as we are! How interesting that He should desire to have fellowship with us! The thought seems too great to take in.

Yet it is true.

At first glance, the gap seems too wide to bridge — from God to man — from the Holy One to sinners. And that first evaluation would stand were it not for the cross. There on that rugged hill, reconciliation was made, the barrier to blessing broken down: *"For through him we both have access by one Spirit unto the Father"* (Ephesians 2:18).

Amazing grace? And then some! Reaching from the heights to the depths. Linking us to the Lord of heaven and earth, when we respond by faith. Making us partakers of the divine nature (see 2 Peter 1:4), children of the King (see John 1:12), joint-heirs with Christ (see Romans 8:17).

And that is infinitely more than we deserve.

THE GOD OF NATURE

MEMORY VERSE: *The heavens declare the glory of God; and the firmament sheweth his handywork* (Psalm 19:1).

A man sat in the heat of the day under a walnut tree looking at a pumpkin vine. He began to muse, "How foolish God is! Here He puts a great heavy pumpkin on a tiny vine without strength to do anything but lie on the ground. He puts tiny walnuts on a tree whose branches could hold the weight of a man. If I were God, I could do better than that!" Suddenly a breeze knocked a walnut from the tree. It fell on the man's head. He rubbed the bump, a sadder and wiser man. He remarked: "Suppose there had been a pumpkin up there instead of a walnut! Never again will I try to plan the world for God. I shall thank Him that He has done it so well!"

Everything in nature carries in it the mark of the Creator. The psalmist says that the entire earth is given witness to the glory of God through the beauty and action in the sky. Still men turn their eyes from the heights and scan the earth trying to find support for a theory that disregards the Creator and traces the history of man to a beginning other than that stated in the Bible.

With the testimony of nature so strong, one wonders why men reject the reality of God's existence. Desire must be father to their action. Some would rather not accept the truth of God for fear of being accountable to Him for their sins.

Their escape route is a deception. They are still accountable. As are we all.

A MERRY HEART

MEMORY VERSE: *A merry heart doeth good like a medicine: but a broken spirit drieth the bones* (Proverbs 17:22).

In his book *"None of These Diseases,"* Dr. S. I. McMillen says that mental stress has taken the center of attention away from bacteria as the believed cause of disease. He ex- plains that emotions cause visible changes in the body, such as strokes, blindness, toxic goiters, fatal clots in the heart, bleeding ulcers, kidney disease and other serious conditions.

Isn't it interesting that the Bible is always far ahead of the discoveries of the scientific world? Job wrote of the world being suspended in space (26:7). Isaiah spoke of the roundness of the earth (40:22). Moses revealed that the life principle is in the blood (Leviticus 17: 11). We should not be surprised then to find that God's Word has again upstaged medical science in announcing that the state of the heart affects the general health — *"a merry heart doeth good like a medicine."*

Christians have good reason to be merry — happy — rejoicing. The most important issues of life have been settled for the child of God. He knows why he is here — the purpose of existence — and where he is going. His sins are forgiven, he is never alone and his destination is certain — heaven. Nevertheless, some who have become citizens of heaven become defeated and depressed. That is when they are not living as God intended.

How sad to have our bodies suffer from bad mental and heart attitudes when we are children of the King. Let's remember who we are and what we have. It's just good sense — and good medicine!

PRAYING FOR OTHERS

MEMORY VERSE: *Moreover as for me, God forbid that I should sin against the LORD in ceasing to pray for you; but I will teach you the good and the right way.* (I Samuel 12:23)

God has given us the privilege of praying for others. The protection and prosperity of others may rest in the hands of real prayer warriors. Paul requested prayer from others so that his ministry would be effective: *"Finally, brethren, pray for us, that the word of the Lord may have free course, and be glorified, even as it is with you: And that we may be delivered from unreasonable and wicked men: for all men have not faith"* (II Thessalonians 3:1-2).

Churches would come alive if Christians prayed more earnestly for one another and for pastors, church leaders and evangelists. In his book *"Prayer -- Asking and Receiving,"* Dr. John R. Rice wrote: "In many, many cases when I have been used of God in a blessed revival campaign in some locality, one or two saintly Christians have told me, 'I have been praying for two years that God would bring you here for these meetings,' or 'This campaign is the answer to my daily prayer for years.' Oh, if people would but pray, pray earnestly, pray effectively, pray with a holy abandon, God's work would not lanquish. The decay in the churches, the cooling of revival fires, the lukewarmness in the churches are the fruit of our prayerlessness."

But there is another serious side of praying for others that must be considered -- the lack of prayer for others is sinful. Prayer is an opportunity, but also a responsibility. It is sinful to neglect prayer for others. *And we are accountable to God for this inconsistency in Christian living.*

It's time to dust off the prayer list that has been neglected. Let's be faithful in prayer -- for others!

FORGIVE

MEMORY VERSE: *And when ye stand praying, forgive, if ye have ought against any: that your Father also which is in heaven may forgive you your trespasses* (Mark 11:25).

Those who have been forgiven have a right to pray with confidence — providing they forgive others.

Bitterness, malice and hatred are all hindrances to prayer. Answers long denied may be forthcoming when prayer finally comes from a forgiving heart. We deprive ourselves of God's bounty when we refuse to forgive.

Jesus stressed the importance of forgiving others by linking it to prayer. For a Christian, prayer is as normal as breathing. It is his opportunity to communicate with his Heavenly Father. In the experience of prayer, he unburdens his heart and taps the power of God for daily living. But — every time he prays he must forgive all who have wronged him: *"And when ye stand praying, forgive."*

One is uncomfortable in prayer when he harbors ill feeling toward another. Though he may be eloquent in expressing his needs to God, there is something empty about his praying. When the unforgiving person finishes his prayer he is uneasy. It is as if the one who is still unforgiven has been listening in on his conversation with God. He has prayed, but not well. In his praying, he has been disobedient. When he began to pray he should have forgiven his adversary. He has gone through a religious exercise to no avail. The un- forgiven one stands as a roadblock — obstructing the answer to his prayer.

Do you want to get things from God through prayer? Do you long to pray effectively. If so, you must first learn to forgive!

STRIFE

MEMORY VERSE: *It is an honour for a man to cease from strife: but every fool will be meddling* (Proverbs 20:3).

Many churches are filled with strife. How strange a report about groups of people who claim to be saved as a result of the love of God. No wonder the world remains unreached and millions mock the church.

Strife is serious. See what the Bible has to say about it: *"Let us walk honestly, as in the day; not in rioting and drunkenness, not in chambering and wantonness, not in strife and envying"* (Romans 13:13): *"Now the works of the flesh are manifest, which are these; Adultery, fornication, uncleanness, lasciviousness, idolatry, witchcraft, hatred, variance, emulations, wrath, strife, seditions, heresies"* (Galatians 5:19-20): *"Let nothing be done through strife or vainglory; but in lowliness of mind let each esteem other better than themselves"* (Philippians 2:3); *"But if ye have bitter envying and strife in your hearts, glory not, and lie not against the truth. This wisdom descendeth not from above, but is earthly, sensual, devilish. For where envying and strife is, there is confusion and every evil work"* (James 3:14-16).

Strife keeps some bad company.

What is it doing in the fellowship of the saints?

Never mind. It is there. What can one do about it?

He can cease from strife. And in so doing, he does an honorable thing in the sight of God.

If you're trying to separate the fools from the honorable men, you can tell them without a scorecard — just notice who refuses to take part in strife!

SAFETY

MEMORY VERSE: *The horse is prepared against the day of battle: but safety is of the LORD* (Proverbs 21:31).

These are perilous times. Dwelling on all the possibilities for death and destruction could make one unable to function.

Fear could keep us from traveling because of the danger of auto accidents. The likelihood of robbery could forbid leaving our homes. The possibility of nuclear war might send us fleeing to some out of the way place to live. The tornado season could drive us to our basements at the first sign of clouds.

But here is a truth worth remembering: SAFETY IS OF THE LORD.

This does not mean that we should never take precautions. God has given us good sense to use. Having carried out sensible safety acts, however, let us relax in the fact that SAFETY IS OF THE LORD.

David faced Goliath in confidence because SAFETY IS OF THE LORD.

Daniel survived the lion's den because SAFETY IS OF THE LORD.

Three Hebrew young men were not burned in Nebuchadnezzar's furnace because SAFETY IS OF THE LORD.

Gideon's three hundred were victorious because SAFETY IS OF THE LORD.

The disciples saw the stormy Galilee become peaceful and calm because SAFETY IS OF THE LORD.

When we get to heaven and learn about the protection God gave during our sojourn on earth, we'll be amazed at how many times He delivered us from injury or death without our knowing it and we'll know beyond all doubt that SAFETY IS OF THE LORD.

Doesn't that make you feel secure?

BOOZE BLIGHTS

MEMORY VERSE: *Look not thou upon the wine when it is red, when it giveth his colour in the cup, when it moveth itself aright* (Proverbs 23:31).

Many Christians seem to be "rethinking" the booze question. Social drinking is becoming accepted among numbers of believers. What should we do about it?

Solomon's instruction is clear: have nothing to do with fermented beverages!

Why?

Booze is a killer. It brings more grief than any other single cause in the world. Alcohol is America's most serious drug problem.

Rampant crime is closely associated with the use of booze. Forty-three percent of all crimes committed by prisoners in state institutions in America were carried out when they had been drinking. In cases of homicide, the influence of alcohol is even greater. Nearly two-thirds of all murders are alcohol related.

Some quote Paul's instruction to Timothy to use a little wine for his stomach's sake. But that advice is strictly for medicinal purposes and has nothing to do with social drinking for pleasure or sensation.

True, Jesus turned water into wine at the marriage at Cana, but this wine had a sobering effect on those who drank it and evidently acted the opposite of the intoxicating beverage with which we are familiar. It was a miracle product — not available today.

It will never be popular to avoid booze. The world is on a binge and doesn't like to face the facts of its beloved destroyer. Nevertheless, God's Word stands: *"Look not thou upon the wine when it is red..."*

GETTING UP

MEMORY VERSE: *For a just man falleth seven times, and riseth up again: but the wicked shall fall into mischief* (Proverbs 24:16).

Becoming a Christian does not end all trouble. Some are surprised at this discovery. They thought:

> "When I walk that aisle
> I'm through with trial."

But Christians endure tribulations.

However, the Christian's trials are different. He does not face them alone. His Lord accompanies him in every difficulty: *"When thou passest through the waters, I will be with thee; and through the rivers, they shall not overflow thee: when thou walkest through the fire, thou shalt not be burned; neither shall the flame kindle upon thee"* (Isaiah 43:2).

The Christian's trials develop his faith: *"Wherein ye greatly rejoice, though now for a season, if need be, ye are in heaviness through manifold temptations: That the trial of your faith, being much more precious than of gold that perisheth, though it be tried with fire, might be found unto praise and honour and glory at the appearing of Jesus Christ"* (I Peter 1:6-7).

The Christian's trials do not destroy him: *"We are troubled on every side, yet not distressed; we are perplexed, but not in despair: Persecuted, but not forsaken; cast down, but not destroyed"* (II Corinthians 4:8-9).

A ninety-year-old man was cautioned by his daughter not to fall down, after a heavy snow storm. "If I fall down, I'll just get up again," he replied.

Christians don't stay down. Their Lord lifts them up again!

THE SNARE

MEMORY VERSE: *The fear of man bringeth a snare: but whoso putteth his trust in the LORD shall be safe* (Proverbs 29:25).

"I wanted to respond to the invitation," said a young man, "but I just couldn't do it with my friends there watching." The fear of man had kept him from the most important decision in life.

"Your friends may laugh you into hell," said a concerned mother to her son, "but they can never laugh you out of it." She was trying to help him see the folly of fearing men when considering his relationship to God.

Public opinion is a powerful force. It is another name for the fear of man.

· What do you leave out of your conversations with others because of the fear of man?

· What Christian convictions do you compromise because of the fear of man?

· What would you change about your life if it were not for the fear of what others will say... the power of public opinion?

To whatever degree you are held back in your Christian walk by fear of others, you are the loser. God will be the final judge. His verdict about rewards and blessings will be the one that will matter. Why should you allow others to keep you from God's best?

By placing full faith in Him to care for you if you give Him your all, you have His promise of safety: "...*whoso putteth his trust in the LORD shall be safe.*"

So, dare to dedicate your life to Him. Cut loose from fear of criticism. Find His will for your life without fear of the reaction of friends or associates. Stop being ruled by public opinion.

Escape the snare!

THE FATHER UNDERSTANDS

MEMORY VERSE: *For he knoweth our frame; he remembereth that we are dust* (Psalm 103:14).

An old song says:

> "God understands your heartache,
> He sees the falling tear;
> And whispers I am with thee,
> Then falter not nor fear."

The psalmist agrees and points out that God never forgets our human limitations. He remembers that we are made of dust.

We are not iron people and therefore burdens and responsibilities can get too heavy for us. Our emotional cords are sometimes strained to the breaking point. We become weary in the race. Panic, on occasion, grips our hearts. Even when we know better.

Never mind. God understands.

God knows our physical limitations. Sickness may drain our normal vitality, making it hard to do even the routine work of the day. Lack of sleep may rob us of our usual alertness and we may become depressed because we haven't had time to rest. Financial needs may be so pressing that our work hours are lengthened to keep food on the table. The pressure may seem unbearable. Still, God knows the limit of our endurance and offers to compensate for our weakness.

God knows about broken hearts. "Where was God when my son died?" demanded an angry father of his pastor. "The same place He was when His own Son died," said the wise man of God. Our Lord knows about grief and tears. He made the human body with the ability to release tension through weeping and designed our emotions to cooperate.

The old song ends: "Then let Him bear your burden; He understands and cares." What good news for needy people!

THE ANT

MEMORY VERSE: *Go to the ant, thou sluggard; consider her ways, and be wise* (Proverbs 6:6).

"If you have a task to be done, find a busy person to do it." This bit of wisdom has endured through the years. And it must be the plan God follows in choosing His servants.

- Moses was busy with his flocks when God called him to serve.

- Gideon was busy threshing wheat by the wine press.

- Elisha was busy plowing with twelve yoke of oxen.

- David was busy caring for his father's sheep.

- Peter and Andrew were busy casting a net into the sea.

- James and John were busy mending their nets.

- Matthew was busy collecting customs.

It is a mistake to wait around for God to open some special door of service. Some people fail to recognize opportunity because it so often comes to them in overalls and looks like work. God intends that we get busy where we are. When we are faithful in the place He has assigned us, He can open doors to greater service.

Phillips Brooks wrote: "Oh, do not pray for easy lives. Pray to be strong men and women. Do not pray for tasks equal to your powers. Pray for powers equal to your tasks. Then the doing of your work will be no miracle; but you shall be a miracle. Every day you shall wonder at yourself, at the richness of life which has come to you by the grace of God."

Finally, do all your work to the glory of God: *"And whatsoever ye do, do it heartily, as to the Lord, and not unto men; Knowing that of the Lord ye shall receive the reward of the inheritance: for ye serve the Lord Christ"* (Colossians 3:23-24).

HIS SON'S NAME

MEMORY VERSE: *Who hath ascended up into heaven, or descended? who hath gathered the wind in his fists? who hath bound the waters in a garment? who hath established all the ends of the earth? what is his name, and what is his son's name, if thou canst tell?* (Proverbs 30:4).

Here is a verse that awaited the coming of the New Testament for its answers. Knowing the answers to each of the questions asked in this cry for information, makes the Christian want to shout: "HOW GREAT THOU ART!"

He has descended to earth, coming to die for us. He ascended to heaven. He holds the wind in His fists. He controls the waters of the earth and calmed the troubled Galilee during a storm that threatened the lives of His disciples. He has established the ends of the earth and created it by His Word. Everything is in His hands. All power belongs to Him.

And what is His Son's name?

It is the name that is above every name. It is the name that angels announced. It is the name that frightened demons. It is the name that declared forgiveness of sins. It is the name proclaimed as the only name under heaven in which is salvation: *"Neither is there salvation in any other: for there is none other name under heaven given among men, whereby we must be saved"* (Acts 4:12).

But hear this: It is the name at which every knee shall bow in a time yet to come: *"Wherefore God also hath highly exalted him, and given him a name which is above every name: That at the name of Jesus every knee should bow, of things in heaven, and things in earth, and things under the earth; And that every tongue should confess that Jesus Christ is Lord, to the glory of God the Father"* (Philippians 2:9-11).

Jesus... there's something about His name!

SHE SHALL BE PRAISED

MEMORY VERSE: *Favour is deceitful, and beauty is vain: but a woman that feareth the LORD, she shall be praised* (Proverbs 31:30).

Dwight L. Moody wrote of his boyhood:

"Dad died when mother was forty-one. What a struggle she had with us; six besides myself, and then the twins were born after father's death. Only three books in the place, and yet they were enough — the family Bible, the catechism, and a book of family devotions. How the spruce log fire sparkled as we sat on the mat on the cold Sunday nights when church was impossible."

"I can hear mother now, solemnly adjuring us to walk in the ways of God, as she read from the big Bible to us. After father died, mother wept herself to sleep every night, sister said, and yet we younger ones who slept soundly in our blissful innocence, knew it not. She was always cheerful to us. Brave old mum! Her motto was, 'Give others the sunshine, tell Jesus the rest.' "

Thankfully, there are millions of Christian women who, like Moody's mother, share God's Word with their children and faithfully pray for them. Not all produce D. L. Moodys who shake continents for God, but their influence is felt throughout the land. They would not make the Hollywood glamour magazines, but their goals are higher. They want to do the will of God as wives and mothers. And there is no higher calling nor worthier goal.

"Who can find a virtuous woman?" the king asked.

Many have. And I am thankful to be among those fortunate men. If you have also, don't let the day close without telling her of your love and appreciation. It's Biblical... SHE SHALL BE PRAISED!

November

GIVE US THIS DAY
OUR DAILY BREAD

Let us come before

his presence with

thanksgiving, and

make a joyful

noise unto him

with psalms.

Psalms 95:2

BITTER WATERS

MEMORY VERSE: *And the people murmured against Moses, saying, What shall we drink?* (Exodus 15:24).

After passing safely through the Red Sea, the children of Israel burst into song. Here is one of their verses of praise:

"The LORD is my strength and song, and he is become my salvation: he is my God, and I will prepare him an habitation; my father's God, and I will exalt him" (15:2).

Only three days later, they had forgotten the parting of the water of the Red Sea because they were out of water and were thirsty. Their song had turned sour. They were murmuring (complaining) against Moses, the man chosen of God to be their leader.

There was water at Marah but it was bitter and undrinkable. Having been delivered from slavery, they had expected smooth sailing throughout their journey. Not so. Here they were with parched throats and nothing but bitter water, the sight of which teased their thirst.

Interestingly, the bitter waters of Marah were encountered directly in the path of God's leading. Some think that trouble always indicates being out of the will of God but that simply is not true. There are some bitter waters along the way in this wilderness journey and God's people are not always detoured around them: *"In the world ye shall have tribulation..."* (John 16:33).

Never mind.

Bitter waters are not serious unless they make us bitter.

The remedy for the bitter waters of Marah was found in a tree. Moses cast the tree into the waters and they were made sweet. This miracle speaks of the power of the message of the cross to sweeten the bitter waters of life. The Christ of the cross will make your song return.

AN ANGRY GOD

MEMORY VERSE: *And when the people complained, it displeased the LORD: and the LORD heard it: and his anger was kindled; and the fire of the LORD burnt among them, and consumed them that were in the uttermost parts of the camp* (Numbers 11:1).

Complaining is considered a "respectable" sin.

Preachers wax eloquent about all kinds of worldliness and receive hearty "amens" from their congregations. But little is said about the unlovely habit of grumbling and complaining.

Why? Because it strikes too close to home.

When a speaker zeroes in on negative attitudes and tongues given to griping, he has quit preaching and gone to meddling. Consequently, we wink at complaining leadership, making no rigid requirements about those holding offices in the church as to whether they are given to pouting or praising. No wonder the work of Christ moves at a snail's pace in so many areas.

According to the Bible, complaining displeases the Lord.

In our text, complaining resulted in God's anger being kindled.

That's serious business.

Complaining among the children of Israel seems strange when one considers the miraculous working of God to free them from Egypt and deliver them from slavery. Having experienced such blessings, it would seem that praise and thanksgiving would have been the order of the day.

Still, Christians in America have been showered with God's blessings, and yet are often given to grumbling. Never have so many had so much and appreciated it so little. Our hearts ought to be overflowing with His praise.

Do you appreciate God's blessings? Does it show?

HE'S LISTENING

MEMORY VERSE: *How long shall I bear with this evil congregation, which murmur against me? I have heard the murmurings of the children of Israel, which they murmur against me* (Numbers 14:27).

Caleb and Joshua were headed for the promised land. None of their associates would make it. Why would this tiny minority out of the entire nation be able to claim their inheritance and possess their property while all the rest would die in the wilderness? There is only one answer: faith.

Apart from these two, the children of Israel had chosen to grumble instead of going ahead. They should have been marching. Instead, they were murmuring. And here lies the difference between success and failure; victory and defeat.

God heard the complaining of that generation of Israelites and rewarded them according to their faith. They claimed to be unable to advance for fear that their little ones would be lost in the battle and so God prevented them from entering the land. When that generation passed off the scene, He gave the land to their children... the very ones who had been used as an excuse for the lack of faith of their parents.

An old song says: "He hears all you say; He sees all you do; My Lord is writin' all the time, All the time."

Jesus warned that words spoken in the closet would be shouted from the housetops. Nothing is kept secret from the One who sees and hears all that we do and say,

Let Him hear words of faith... declarations of confidence, not murmuring and complaining. Blessings come the faith route. Talk about your faith in Christ today.

GOD'S WAY

MEMORY VERSE: *Not by might, nor by power, but by my spirit, saith the LORD of hosts* (Zechariah 4:6).

This is the day of gimmicks and promotions. Products are palmed off on the public through slick advertising methods. Candidates buy their way into office with expensive election campaigns. The American dream of going from a log cabin to the White House is in danger. Because of the fallen nature of man, these things are not surprising but it is sad when Christians adopt this faithless way in doing God's work.

Recently someone estimated that 90 percent of present-day Christian work would continue as is even if the Holy Spirit did not exist. One hopes that guess is wrong, but it is safe to say that a lot of religious machinery runs on the energy of the flesh. And this is not altogether in apostate or unbelieving circles. The time has come to return to spiritual methods of doing spiritual work.

The Holy Spirit works in answer to prayer. Dr. D. L. Moody said: "Every great work of God can be traced to a kneeling figure." I wonder what would happen in America if church boards began spending as much time in prayer during their meetings as they do in tossing around promotional ideas. Can you imagine the spiritual impact of multitudes in prayer for pastors and all aspects of the ministry of the church?

Four men arrived early at Spurgeon's church on Sunday morning and were given a tour of the building. Opening one door, they saw fifteen hundred people on their knees. "That is the heating plant," said their guide.

Start heating up your church through prayer. You'll end the spiritual energy crisis!

GOD'S SERVANT VINDICATED

MEMORY VERSE: *And it shall come to pass, that a man's rod, whom I shall choose, shall blossom: and I will make to cease from me the murmurings of the children of Israel, whereby they murmur against you* (Numbers 17:5).

C. H. Spurgeon once said that he had one blind eye and one deaf ear and that they were the best ear and eye that he had. He meant that we are far better off not to pay any attention to the complainers. And in the case of a servant of the Lord, God's protection and vindication is promised: *"No weapon that is formed against thee shall prosper; and every tongue that shall rise against thee in judgment thou shalt condemn. This is the heritage of the servants of the LORD, and their righteousness is of me, saith the LORD"*. (Isaiah 54:17).

Travelers in the northern lane of ocean traffic have frequently observed icebergs traveling in one direction in spite of the fact that strong winds are blowing the opposite way. The icebergs often move against the wind. The explanation is that the great bergs, with eight-ninths of their hulk under the waters, are caught in the grip of mighty currents that carry them forward no matter which way the winds blow.

So the dedicated Christian leader has the greater part of his being thrust down into the will of God. The currents of God's will move him toward righteousness no matter how the winds of passing opinion blow.

When you know you are in God's will, pay no heed to the detractors. Keep moving ahead. Shrug off the criticism. God's work must be done and there is not time to be diverted from the task by the small ones who grumble and complain.

Keep on for Jesus.

He will vindicate His own.

EXERCISE FOR COMPLAINERS

MEMORY VERSE: *I remembered God, and was troubled: I complained, and my spirit was overwhelmed.* (Psalm 77:3).

The Psalmist was troubled: overwhelmed by his problems. Focusing on his burdens, he complained, wondering why God didn't do something about his situation. Finally, he realized that the problem was not with God but with him: *"And I said, This is my infirmity"* (Psalm 77:10).

From that point on his heart was filled with praise.

The reason?

He had turned his attention from his problems to the faithfulness of God. And that is a good exercise for all complainers.

Has God ever answered prayer for you?

Has God ever provided for you when there was no human way to meet a need?

Has God honored your faith in the past?

Have there been times when you were filled with anxiety only to have your Lord move circumstances and deliver you from your anticipated tragedy? Have you worried in vain?

And what about God's goodness to our nation? The Psalmist reviewed God's care of His people: His many blessings to Israel. As Americans, we also have manifold blessings for which to thank our God. Has He not protected us and guided us through difficult days? As an American and a Christian, you have much for which to thank the Lord. Put your cares to the memory test. And thank God for His faithfulness.

Now about those complaints.

What were they?

Or have you forgotten them in the light of God's wonderful care in the past and His continuing goodness today?

Remember... He cares.

NEW BIRTH

MEMORY VERSE: *Not by works of righteousness which we have done, but according to his mercy he saved us, by the washing of regeneration, and renewing of the Holy Ghost* (Titus 3:5).

"Your religionists came to visit me," the man stormed. He was angry about what he considered an invasion of his privacy. I listened calmly and thought about his words. If he had been right about the visitors being but religionists, he would have had a legitimate complaint. The world does not need any more religion.

A missionary once said: "You have the same problem here in America as on the mission field — religion." He was right. Religion can be a serious barrier that keeps people from salvation. Trusting in their ceremonies and rituals, they often miss the wonderful simplicity of faith in Christ.

Nicodemus was a religious man, a ruler of the Jews. No one would have guessed the emptiness of his heart. Yet, when he came to Jesus, the Lord saw through his religious exterior and informed him that he needed to be born again. Poor confused Nicodemus asked a logical question: *"How can a man be born when he is old? can he enter the second time into his mother's womb, and be born?"* (John 3:4). Jesus then explained that this needed new birth was a birth of the Spirit.

The new birth is a mystery. Jesus said: *"The wind bloweth where it listeth, and thou hearest the sound thereof, but canst not tell whence it cometh, and whither it goeth: so is every one that is born of the Spirit"* (John 3:8). Still, we know how the new birth can be ours: *"For God so loved the world, that he gave his only begotten Son, that whosoever believeth in him should not perish, but have everlasting life"* (John 3:16).

HIS TEMPLE

MEMORY VERSE: *What? know ye not that your body is the temple of the Holy Ghost which is in you, which ye have of God, and ye are not your own? For ye are bought with a price: therefore glorify God in your body, and in your spirit, which are God's* (1 Corinthians 6:19-20).

Your body is important.

Consider the creation.

Everything in the universe, except the human frame, was simply spoken into existence. *"And God said, Let the earth bring forth the living creature after his kind, cattle, and creeping thing, and the beast of the earth after his kind: and it was so"* (Genesis 1:24).

Not so the body of man. *"And God said, Let us make man in our image, after our likeness; and let them have dominion over the fish of the sea, and over the fowl of the air, and over the cattle, and over all the earth, and over every creeping thing that creepeth upon the earth"* (Genesis 1:26). *"And the LORD God formed man of the dust of the ground, and breathed into his nostrils the breath of life; and man became a living soul"* (Genesis 2:7).

When Christ came to earth, He was made in the likeness of men and referred to His body as His temple. He said the resurrection of His body would be the proof of His deity (see John 2:18-22).

The coming resurrection reveals divine regard for our bodies. Christ was resurrected bodily from the grave, just as we shall be at His coming.

The most exciting fact about the Christian's body is that it is the temple of God. This amazing truth should temper every thought and activity. Are you careful about your conduct inside the church building? You should be equally careful at all times. Your body is the dwelling place of God.

STOP COMPLAINING

MEMORY VERSE: *Jesus therefore answered and said unto them, Murmur not among yourselves* (John 6:43).

Complaining is contagious.

Some are always looking for things to complain about. The late T. DeWitt Talmage wrote of such people, "Away with the horrors! they distill poison; they dig graves; and if they could climb so high, they would drown the rejoicings of Heaven with sobs and wailing."

Christians are either power conscious or problem conscious. Churches have been built and blessed by those who focused on the power of Christ and have gone ahead in His service without fear, The work of the Lord has suffered through the centuries because of those who continually dwell on what they conclude is wrong.

The pastor is wrong.

The choir director is wrong.

The church board is wrong.

The program is wrong.

Mentioning money from the pulpit is wrong.

Busing children to Sunday School is wrong.

Contests are wrong.

Evangelistic meetings are wrong.

Humor on the platform is wrong.

And if there be any other method of reaching people and communicating the Gospel to them that calls for sacrifice and involvement of the complainer that is also wrong.

Especially wrong.

Stop being the hold-back in your church.

Break up your griping group and get busy for Christ.

Murmur not among yourselves.

STOP GRIEVING THE SPIRIT

MEMORY VERSE: *And grieve not the holy Spirit of God, whereby ye are sealed unto the day of redemption* (Ephesians 4:30).

You may be surprised to learn that God can experience grief. Yet, there are a number of Bible texts that reveal this.

Moses wrote that God was grieved over the wickedness that was on the earth before the flood. David declared that God had been grieved with the Children of Israel because of their complaining in the wilderness; after their escape from Egypt. Isaiah prophesied that Jesus would be a "man of sorrows" and said that He would be acquainted with grief.

What grieves the Holy Spirit?

The context of today's verse reveals a number of things that grieve Him: *"Let all bitterness, and wrath, and anger, and clamour, and evil speaking, be put away from you, with all malice"* (Ephesians 4:31).

Notice that all these sins have to do with your attitude toward others. You cannot be bitter toward others without grieving the Holy Spirit. You cannot gossip about others without grieving the Holy Spirit. You cannot carry malice in your heart without grieving the Holy Spirit.

To keep from grieving the Holy Spirit, we must be demonstrating the fruit of the Spirit as shown in Ephesians 4:32: *"And be ye kind one to another, tenderhearted, forgiving one another, even as God for Christ's sake hath forgiven you."* Examine your life for attitudes and actions that grieve the Holy Spirit. As they come to mind, confess them to Christ immediately and accept His forgiveness. Enjoy the sweet release that comes from being sure that all is right between you and your Lord.

Grieve not the Spirit.

CRITICIZING JESUS

MEMORY VERSE: *And there was much murmuring among the people concerning him: for some said, He is a good man: others said, Nay; but he deceiveth the people* (John 7:12).

Perhaps you are enduring undeserved criticism.

Never mind.

They criticized Jesus.

Dr. Henry Clay Trumbull and Dr. Charles G. Trumbull, editors of *"The Sunday School Times"* from 1875 to 1941 gave the following advice to those being criticized by others:

1. Commit the matter instantly to God, asking him to remove all resentment or counter-criticism on our part, and teach us needed lessons.

2. *"Consider him that endured such contradiction of sinners against himself, lest ye be wearied and faint in your minds,"* (Hebrews 12:3), remembering that we ourselves are very great sinners, and that the one who has criticized us does not actually know the worst.

3. Take account of the personal bias of the speaker or writer.

4. Remember that *"a soft answer turneth away wrath: but grievous words stir up anger"* (Proverbs 15:1).

5. If the criticism is true, and we have made a mistake or committed a sin, let us humbly and frankly, confess our sin to Him, and to anyone whom we may have injured.

6. Learn afresh that we are fallible, and that we need His grace and wisdom moment by moment to keep us in the straight path.

7. Then, — and not until then — *"forgetting those things which are behind, and reaching forth unto those things which are before... press toward the mark for the prize of the high calling of God in Christ Jesus"* (Philippians 3:13-14).

START WALKING

MEMORY VERSE: *This I say then, Walk in the Spirit, and ye shall not fulfill the lust of the flesh* (Galatians 5:16).

Walking demonstrates faith.

Jesus told the man who had been sick of the palsy that he was to take up his bed and walk. That demanded faith. He had not been able to walk. The fact that he did get up and walk gave living evidence of his confidence in the power of Christ (see Matthew 9:2-7).

Peter walked on the water to go to Jesus. That was a walk of faith. When Peter's faith faltered he began to sink (see Matthew 14:28-31). Faith made the miracle possible.

The person who walks in the Spirit has taken the filling of the Spirit by faith. As he moves through the day, he expects the Holy Spirit to control him. And control is what the Spirit-filled life is all about. Does the Holy Spirit control your life? If not, you are controlled by your sinful nature...the old nature...the old man.

It is time to discover who sits on the throne of your life. Who is King? Lord? Master? The Bible teaches that either God rules over that kingdom called your life, or you live under sin's dominion. It's as simple as that. See how Paul explained this struggle to the Christians at Rome: *"Let not sin therefore reign in your mortal body, that ye should obey it in the lusts thereof. Neither yield ye your members as instruments of unrighteousness unto sin: but yield yourselves unto God, as those that are alive from the dead, and your members as instruments of righteousness unto God. For sin shall not have dominion over you: for ye are not under the law, but under grace"* (Romans 6:12-14).

Walk in the Spirit!

STOP QUENCHING THE SPIRIT

MEMORY VERSE: *Quench not the Spirit* (1 Thessalonians 5:19).

If we quench a fire, we stop it in its path. If we quench the Holy Spirit, we halt His work in us. We stifle or suppress Him. When you quench the Holy Spirit, you exalt your will above the will of God. To quench the Holy Spirit is to resist Him. It is going your own way when His leading is clear.

Quenching the Holy Spirit is like changing channels on your television set. It is like turning off the radio to avoid its message. It is turning your mind away from the things you know the Lord wants you to do or say.

When you stop quenching the Holy Spirit, you will find some wonderful things happening. Your day will unfold as a part of His plan. You will see opportunities that you would otherwise have missed. His calming voice will comfort you when everything seems to be falling apart. Life's irritations will be recognized as experiences that enable you to be patient and longsuffering. The needs of others will be brought to your attention and you will be refreshed in ministering to them. Having your own way will become less important. Allowing Christ to have His way in your life will receive priority.

So, stop tuning out that still small voice that always gives the right direction. Lend an obedient ear to the Lord. Be quick to do His bidding. Look for opportunities to follow His leading this very day. Don't be afraid to be an obedient child.

Remember, the Lord always gives His best to those who follow Him completely.

THE CRITICS

MEMORY VERSE: *And Jesus said, Let her alone; why trouble ye her? she hath wrought a good work on me* (Mark 14:6).

John Wesley tells of a man whom he thought of contemptuously as being covetous. One day when he contributed a gift to one of Wesley's charities that seemed to the fiery preacher to be too small, Wesley's indignation knew no bounds and he criticized him with blistering condemnation.

Wesley says in his diary that the man quietly replied, "I know a man who at each week's beginning goes to market and buys a penny's worth of parsnips and takes them home to boil in water, and all that week he has parsnips for his food and water for his drink; and food and drink alike cost him a penny a week."

The target of Wesley's criticism was broken. He had been skimping in order to pay off debts contracted before his conversion. Wesley was ashamed. He had criticized a brother in Christ without knowing all the facts. Many follow Wesley's poor example (Matthew 7:1).

Those who sacrifice for Jesus must expect criticism: *"Yea, and all that will live godly in Christ Jesus shall suffer persecution"* (II Timothy 3:12). Many will claim to know better uses for money and talents invested in the work of Christ.

Why?

Because their values are based on the temporary things of this earth. Coveted toys here mean more than souls or riches laid up in heaven. Sometimes their choices may seem to be best.

But a day of reckoning is coming.

Live for that day.

MONOPOLY

MEMORY VERSE: *Likewise reckon ye also yourselves to be dead indeed unto sin, but alive unto God through Jesus Christ our Lord* (Romans 6:11).

A group of ministers were discussing whether or not they ought to invite Dwight L. Moody to their city. The success of the famed evangelist was brought to the attention of the men as a reason for inviting him.

One unimpressed minister commented, "Does Mr. Moody have a monopoly on the Holy Ghost?"

Another quietly replied, "No, but the Holy Ghost seems to have a monopoly on Mr. Moody."

Search for the spiritual secret of all great servants of God and you will find it to be total surrender. To Moody, life was the great adventure of finding out what God would do with one who was totally and completely yielded to Him. William Booth saw as his reason for success the fact that God had all there was of him. F. B. Meyer looked back to a time when he gave the keys to every room in his heart to Christ. Paul urged the Christians at Rome to yield their members as instruments of righteousness. In other words, he was calling for the yielding of every hand and heart to the service of Christ and the glory of God. He summed it up with this moving challenge: *"I beseech you therefore, brethren, by the mercies of God, that ye present your bodies a living sacrifice, holy, acceptable unto God, which is your reasonable service"* (Romans 12:1).

We have been furnished with some wonderful examples of all-out dedication in both the Scriptures and in history. What about your personal surrender to the will of God? Are you really willing to do what He wants you to do this very day?

HE RECEIVES SINNERS

MEMORY VERSE: *And the Pharisees and scribes murmured, saying, This man receiveth sinners, and eateth with them* (Luke 15:2).

The enemies of Jesus thought they had found a weakness on which to build their case: He welcomed sinners and ate with them.

But what if Jesus had not cared for sinners?

There would be no hope for any, for all have sinned: *"As it is written, There is none righteous, no, not one... For all have sinned, and come short of the glory of God"* (Romans 3:10, 23).

Commenting on this text, Dr. H. A. Ironside says: "Our Lord Jesus Christ was always interested in sinners. He came down from the glory of His Father's house to save sinners. These legalists could not understand it. We are told here that a great company of publicans and sinners drew near to Jesus, but the self-righteous and haughty scribes and Pharisees looked on with contempt, for they could not comprehend why Jesus did not withdraw Himself from these wretched and wicked people, and why He did not rather seek out such respectable individuals as they thought themselves to be. They murmured among themselves, saying, 'This man receiveth sinners, and eateth with them.' They did not know they were declaring a wonderful truth when they said that. Jesus receives sinners, and takes them into fellowship and communion with Himself. Thank God, this has been true all through the centuries since. Is it not wonderful grace that He receives all who will come, and He delivers them from their sins?"

Do you think yourself too guilty to be saved?

Christ will receive you the moment you come to Him in faith.

Don't delay. Come to Christ... right now!

DON'T BE BITTER

MEMORY VERSE: *Husbands, love your wives, and be not bitter against them* (Colossians 3:19).

Bitterness keeps bad company. Note some of its associates: *"Let all bitterness, and wrath, and anger, and clamor, and evil speaking, be put away from you, with all malice"* (Ephesians 4:31).

Bitterness is destructive anywhere, but especially in the home; clouding love's looks and turning them into icy stares. Words spoken in bitterness cut deeply.

Husbands who harbor bitter feelings toward their wives are losers. They waste valuable time that could be used for showing love. And time is swiftly passing on its way.

Bitter husbands are disobedient to God's command. No man can walk closely with God and still remain bitter toward the woman he has promised to love as Christ loves the church.

Bitterness may surface through nagging. C. H. Spurgeon says of nagging mates:

> "What she proposes,
> Be it good or bad,
> He still opposes,
> Till he drives her mad."

While nagging and criticism are common fruits of bitterness, they may also be the cause. Some husbands carry bitter feelings for years over some harsh comment made by a wife early in the marriage.

What a waste!

And how inconsistent with Christian living. We who have been forgiven must always be quick to forgive.

Banish bitterness.

Build love instead.

ALL THINGS?

MEMORY VERSE: *Do all things without murmurings and disputings* (Philippians 2:14).

A long time ago I received a letter with a tract enclosed. I have forgotten the message of that leaflet, but its title *"What Made You Cross?"* has stayed with me. It is a good question.

If we are honest, I suspect most of us would admit that we are ashamed that trifles touch off our tempers and disturb our dispositions.

J. Hudson Taylor wrote: "It is not so much the greatness of our troubles, as the littleness of our spirit, which makes us complain."

It doesn't take a theologian to discover the characteristic joy of early Christians. Under the toughest of circumstances they were triumphant! Even in prison they sang praises to God.

The disturbing dimension to this comparison is the thought that most present-day Christians might really cave in if persecution came. If we are edgy in affluence, what might we do in oppression: *"If thou hast run with the footmen, and they have wearied thee, then how canst thou contend with horses? And if in the land of peace, wherein thou trustedst, they wearied thee, then how wilt thou do in the swelling of Jordan?"* (Jeremiah 12;5).

The need of dealing with this problem may be far more urgent than we realize. We do not know what the future holds. At any rate, there is sure to be great profit for hearts and homes if we stop exploding to gain our "rights," and start yielding to the Holy Spirit in all things. It is only then that we will be able to *"do all things without murmurings and disputings."* And others will know that our Lord controls "all things" in our lives.

CONVICTION

MEMORY VERSE: *And when he is come, he will reprove the world of sin, and of righteousness, and of judgment* (John 16:8).

An evangelist is preaching in a large crusade. Next to the aisle in the fourth row from the front sits a man who appears to be the classic picture of boredom. His wife coaxed him to come to the meeting and he finally yielded to please her. His mind moves from business deals to the golf course. He keeps glancing at his watch, anticipating the final prayer so that he can get on with more important things.

Suddenly a statement from the speaker strikes home. The man who seemed so distant and untouchable fixes his attention on the evangelist and hangs on every word. Though still captured by the message, he becomes uneasy, shifting his weight a number of times and folding and unfolding his arms. Occasionally he wipes his brow.

When the evangelist gives the public invitation, the man who had come to the service so reluctantly steps out into the aisle and makes his way toward the preacher. He wants to be born again.

What happened to change his attitude and melt his heart?

The conviction of the Holy Spirit.

The work of the Holy Spirit is to bring conviction of sin to the world. The human conscience cannot be trusted to recognize the seriousness of sin. Influenced by falling standards, people are able to rationalize immorality and borderline honesty. When under conviction, however, true standards of holiness and sin are brought into focus.

No wonder you have been uncomfortable in your sin!

MONEY FAILS

MEMORY VERSE: *He that loveth silver shall not be satisfied with silver; nor he that loveth abundance with increase: this is also vanity* (Ecclesiastes 5:10).

Money may make three different sorts of speeches.

It may say: "Hold me and I will dry out the foundations of sympathy and benevolence in your soul and leave you barren and destitute. Grasp me tightly and I will change your eyes that they will care to look upon nothing that does not contain my image, and so transform your ears that my soft metallic ring will sound louder than the cries of widows and orphans and the wail of perishing multitudes. Keep me, clutch me and I will destroy your concern for souls and your love and reverence for God."

Or it may say: "Spend me for self-indulgence and I will make you indifferent to all except your own pleasure. I will become your master and you will think that I only am all powerful."

Or it may say: "Give me away for the benefit of others and I will return in streams of spiritual revenue to your soul. I will bless the receiver and the giver. I will supply food for the hungry, raiment for the naked, medicine for the sick and homes for the homeless. My most exciting task is in carrying the Gospel of Christ to the ends of the earth. Invest me in this important cause and I will bring eternal dividends; blessings now and rewards at the Judgment Seat of Christ."

Money fails to satisfy if kept or wasted on the toys of earth. But when it is given to reach the souls of men it performs a vital work.

Thank God for material blessings.

Invest them in His work.

Lay up eternal wealth.

THE PERFECT STATE

MEMORY VERSE: *Not that I speak in respect of want: for I have learned, in whatsoever state I am, therewith to be content* (Philippians 4:11).

Millions seek contentment.

Paul had found it.

Matthew Henry says: "The apostle was often in bonds, imprisonments, and necessities; but in all, he learned to be content, to bring his mind to his condition, and make the best of it. Pride, unbelief, vain hankering after something we have not got, and fickle disrelish of present things, make men discontented even under favorable circumstances. Let us pray for patient submission and hope when we are abased; for humility and a heavenly mind when exalted. It is a special grace to have an equal temper of mind always."

Nor is Paul dependent on a certain amount of money received for contentment. Boldly, he declares his independence; announcing that his sufficiency is of God. He is pleased with gifts sent to him but wants it made clear that he can make it through without handouts from anybody. He is God's servant and is content to take each day from his Father's hand.

We have become very dependent people. We are dependent on the utility companies for power to heat our homes and run our appliances. We are dependent on other nations for energy to operate our factories and businesses. We are dependent on a chain of workers and businesses to bring food to our tables.

But for contentment our source can be the same as Paul's. God is unchanged. Trusting in Him and believing His promises still brings independence. We are complete in Him.

And that is the perfect state... safe in His hands.

THE CLOAK DOESN'T FIT

MEMORY VERSE: *For neither at any time used we flattering words, as ye know, nor a cloak of covetousness; God is witness* (1 Thessalonians 2:5).

To covet is "to desire eagerly; to long for; especially to desire something belonging to another."

Covetousness is as old as sin and first affected man in the Garden of Eden. Eve coveted the fruit that God had forbidden, resulting in the fall with all of its attendant sorrows.

The first evidence of covetousness in Israel's new land is recorded in Joshua 7:21 and has to do with the sin of Achan, whose thievery and disobedience halted the victorious march of his people and their conquest of the land of Canaan.

The early church was shocked by the coveting couple: Ananias and Sapphira, who lied to God and lost their lives as a result of their sin.

Another moving Bible example of covetousness is the account of King Ahab and his confiscation of Naboth's vineyard. This good man refused to sell his property to the wicked king and became the victim of Queen Jezebel's wrath. See I Kings 21.

Covetousness opens the door to all sin.

Covetousness has no place in a Christian's life.

It isn't fitting.

Not Christlike.

What do you want that you should not have? Are you willing to trample on others to get it? Beware of the sin of covetousness.

Victory over covetousness comes through setting one's affections on things above rather than on things of earth. When our goals are within the will of God, covetousness is conquered.

WHAT DO YOU HAVE?

MEMORY VERSE: *Let your conversation be without covetousness; and be content with such things as ye have: for he hath said, I will never leave thee, nor forsake thee* (Hebrews 13:5).

How easy it is to overlook blessings already ours! The late T. DeWitt Talmage demanded an inventory of present possessions, writing: "It is high time you began to thank God for present blessing. Thank Him for your children, happy, buoyant, and bounding. Praise Him for your home, with its fountain of song and laughter. Adore Him for morning light and evening shadow. Praise Him for fresh, cool water, bubbling from the rock, leaping in the cascade, soaring in the mist, falling in the shower, dashing against the rock, and clapping its hands in the tempest. Love Him for the grass that cushions the earth, and the clouds that curtain the sky, and the foliage that waves in the forest. Thank Him for a Bible to read, and a cross to gaze upon and a Saviour to deliver."

William R. Newell says of our text, "but mark that great word 'content,' that God uses to describe that state of heart pleasing to Him in His people. *'Content with such things as ye have.'* Would that these words described all Christians!"

What do you have?

Do you have health?

Do you have food enough for today?

Do you have shelter... a home?

Do you have a Bible? A home church?

Do you have friends? Family members who love you?

Lift your heart in praise for what you have.

And remember that God is the giver.

GREAT GAIN

MEMORY VERSE: *But godliness with contentment is great gain* (1 Timothy 6:6).

The Pulpit Commentary says of this text: "the godly man is content with what he possesses; submits meekly to God's will, and bears patiently the adverse dispensations of his providence. The godly heart is freed from the thirst for perishing treasures, because it possesses treasures of a higher and more enduring character."

It adds: "Men are rich in what they can do without... Let us study, not so much what we may secure, as what we are able to enjoy existence without. Men multiply their cares often as they multiply their means; and some men, with competency in a cottage, have not been sorry that they lost a palace. 'Contentment is great gain;' it sets the mind free from anxious care; it prevents straining after false effect; it has more time to enjoy the flowers at its feet, instead of straining to secure the meadows of the far-away estate."

The less you need, the more freedom you enjoy.

And here is the heart of Paul's argument: *"for we brought nothing into this world, and it is certain we can carry nothing out."* Materially speaking, we live in a segment of time between two nothings. What few things we accumulate during threescore and ten (possibly) must all be left behind at the end of life. Not one knows when that end will come, or if Christ may come before death ends man's earthly journey. Therefore, the sensible thing is to live for Christ daily, laying up riches above while enjoying this pilgrimage through consecrated Christian living.

While others strive for added earthly treasures, let us appreciate God's daily blessings and be content with them.

Now you know the ultimate in success.

Godliness with contentment is great gain.

BE THANKFUL

MEMORY VERSE: *Continue in prayer, and watch in the same with thanksgiving* (Colossians 4:2).

Sergeant Vernon W. Entrekin relates how he recited the 145th Psalm while dangling by his left foot from a parachute after bailing out of a C-47 transport plane during a swirling snowstorm. Entrekin was one of six aboard the plane when the pilot lost control above Dwight, Nebraska. It was his first parachute leap. He had been reading the 145th Psalm just before starting out on the flight. He found himself saying: *"The Lord upholdeth all that fall, and raiseth up all those that be bowed down... The Lord is nigh unto all that call upon him, to all that call upon him in truth."*

Entrekin asked for strength to climb back into the parachute harness which he had failed to fasten securely. Gasping for breath in the icy air, and summoning the last ounce of his energy, he doubled his body, and caught hold of the harness above his foot. Slowly he was able to climb back to a sitting position while dropping swiftly through the air. Finally he landed with a jolt and unbuckled his parachute harness.

"Thank you, Lord," he said.

And who wouldn't be thankful under those circumstances?

Still God has called us to be thankful all the time: *"In everything give thanks: for this is the will of God in Christ Jesus concerning you"* (I Thessalonians 5:18).

Our circumstances would make millions thankful. Food enough to survive should call forth as much thanksgiving in this good land as in one where many die of starvation.

Be thankful... continually.

THANKSGIVING WITH JESUS

MEMORY VERSE: *It is a good thing to give thanks unto the LORD, and to sing praises unto thy name, O most High* (Psalm 92:1).

At this time of year suggestions abound about the priorities of thanksgiving. Family, friends, home and country are contenders for the most important places on our list as we thank God for His blessings. But what would Jesus do? His example is the best to follow.

Jesus gave thanks for the simplicity of the Gospel. *"Jesus answered and said, I thank thee, O Father, Lord of Heaven and earth, because thou hast hid these things from the wise and prudent, and hast revealed them unto babes"* (Matthew 11:25). Aren't you thankful that His salvation is available to you on the basis of simple faith? Tell Him of your gratefulness. Thank Him!

Jesus also gave thanks for daily food. When feeding five thousand with a few loaves and fishes, John says that Jesus took the loaves and *"when he had given thanks, he distributed to the disciples"* (John 6:11). You may not take time to give thanks for your food, but Jesus did. He held the loaves made from grain that He had brought into existence, and gave thanks.

Jesus even gave thanks for His cross. His most difficult act of thanksgiving must have been at the first communion table. Paul wrote: *"And when he had given thanks, he broke it, and said, Take, eat: this is my body, which is broken for you: this do in remembrance of me"* (I Corinthians 11:24). That broken bread symbolized His coming death, yet He gave thanks. Anyone can be thankful for sunshine and success, but what about the crosses and losses?

At this Thanksgiving, let us follow our Lord. *"In everything give thanks"* (I Thessalonians 5:18).

THANKSGIVING

MEMORY VERSE: *Bless the LORD, O my soul, and forget not all his benefits* (Psalm 103:2).

Your holiday plans have probably been in place for a long time. You're anticipating a special day with loved ones. Thanksgiving is one of America's favorite holidays. And you expect this one to be the best you've ever known.

But, if you aren't careful, it will be a day of everything except giving thanks. Activities that have attached themselves to the tradition of Thanksgiving often crowd out the real purpose of this holiday. The purpose is THANKS- GIVING.

So, take time to be thankful.

Thank God for another day to live. Our breath is in His hands. I wonder how many times He has spared your life during the past year. We live in a hostile world of disease and violence. Accidents could have claimed our lives. Yet, here we are. Alive. Thank God.

Thank God for friends and family. How important it is to love and to be loved! Look about you! Give thanks for that wife, or husband, and those children. Lift your heart to Him in thanksgiving for friends who care for you and would stand with you in need.

Thank God for opportunities to serve Him. While multitudes plod through life storing up things on this perishing planet, the Christian knows the blessing of laying up treasures in heaven. Every day brings opportunities for eternal investment.

Thank God for His love. Out of His love His blessings flow. *"Herein is love, not that we loved God, but that he loved us, and sent his Son to be the propitiation for our sins* (I John 4:10).

Thank God.

BREAD AND MEAT

MEMORY VERSE: *The people asked, and he brought quails, and satisfied them with the bread of heaven* (Psalm 105:40).

A wagon train passing through one of the difficult sections of the Oregon Trail seemed to have encountered more than its share of trouble. Water and grass had been scarce for several days and some of the wagons were broken down. A general feeling of depression settled over the train that was unlike the former optimism of the group. In order to get the problems aired and solved, a meeting was scheduled for the next night's stop.

When the emigrants had gathered around the campfire, one of them arose and said, "Before we do anything else, I think we should thank God that we have come this far with no loss of life, with no trouble with the Indians, and that we have enough strength left to finish our journey."

The suggestion was taken and then there was silence. After giving thanks, no one had any complaints. This is the transformation the thankful heart can often make. It enables us to see the real value of many worthwhile things already received that have been taken for granted and in so doing it dispels the gloom that troubles us.

The children of Israel were given both bread and meat; manna and quails as they journeyed in the wilderness. Had they focused on these blessings instead of complaining, their journey would have been a joy.

And how about the bread and meat that God has given to you this week? Is His provision adequate? Thank Him for these blessings. As you cultivate thanksgiving, gloom will disappear.

Remember the order: Thanksgiving first! It makes the journey better. And the difficulties flee.

AN ACCEPTABLE TIME

MEMORY VERSE: *But as for me, my prayer is unto thee, O LORD, in an acceptable time: O God, in the multitude of thy mercy hear me, in the truth of thy salvation* (Psalm 69:13).

Experiencing trouble, the psalmist fills his mouth with expressions of deep feeling: a flood is overwhelming his soul, he is sinking in deep mire, he is crossing a body of water and it is about to cover him, he is tired of crying, his throat is dry, he has difficulty seeing.

Much of David's misery had to do with others. His enemies hated him and they had no reason to be his enemies. Even members of his family had turned on him. People gathered in groups to drink and ridicule him. Some considered him a religious fanatic.

In his sorrow, the psalmist turns to the Lord for help and expresses confidence that the Lord will hear him in an acceptable time. But what is an acceptable time? To whom is this time acceptable?

David is simply expressing the wonderful truth that we can all call upon the Lord when we are having trouble. Some shrink from praying when in difficulties, thinking they will be accused of only coming to God in times of great need. Christians need to remember that they are invited to come to Christ with their burdens at precisely the time of need: *"Let us therefore come boldly unto the throne of grace, that we may obtain mercy, and find grace to help in time of need"* (Hebrews 4:16).

Come then when you feel overwhelmed with problems.

Come when the lump in your throat won't go away.

Come when others have turned against you.

Come when people gather in little groups to talk about you.

Come NOW...it's an acceptable time.

BAD COMPANY

MEMORY VERSE: *These are murmurers, complainers, walking after their own lusts; and their mouth speaketh great swelling words, having men's persons in admiration because of advantage* (Jude 16).

Jude described a crowd bound for judgment. Yet some of their characteristics are copied by those claiming they are headed for heaven.

These ungodly ones are called murmurers... complainers. So those who are given to griping and grumbling are in bad company. Pride and lust are given as some of their many sins. Note again that these serious sins are mentioned in the same verse as are murmuring and complaining.

Perhaps this study has helped you to realize how serious it is to complain... to grumble. You're convicted about your sins in these "respectable" areas. What can you do?

First, you must confess these sins to the Lord: *"If we confess our sins, he is faithful and just to forgive us our sins, and to cleanse us from all unrighteousness"* (I John 1:9). Don't hold back. Be honest with the Lord. Name your sins... the complaining at home, at church, about your neighbors, about the weather, about the pastor.

After confessing your sins, accept the fact that they are forgiven. Don't be troubled about them anymore and don't trouble God about them. They are forgotten... buried.

Now, begin a regular devotional time that includes Bible reading and meditation on portions of the Bible. God's Word is the Divine detergent. It cleans up a life: *"Wherewithal shall a young man cleanse his way? By taking heed thereto according to thy word... Thy word have I hid in mine heart, that I might not sin against thee"* (Psalm 119:9,11).

Memorize Bible verses about joy and praise. You're a child of the King. Stay in character. Praise the Lord!

December

GIVE US THIS DAY
OUR DAILY BREAD

*Thanks be
unto God
for his
unspeakable
gift.*

II Corinthians 9:15.

TOMORROW

MEMORY VERSE: *Boast not thyself of tomorrow; for thou knowest not what a day may bring forth* (Proverbs 27:1).

A leader of a dance band once told me that a number of his friends in the bars had confided to him that they thought they ought to be saved... someday. He agreed and thought he would also come to Christ... someday. To the best of my knowledge, he is still lost.

The Bible calls "today" the day of salvation: *"...Behold, now is the accepted time; behold, now is the day of salvation"* (II Corinthians 6:2).

This very moment God wants to save you: *"Come now, and let us reason together, saith the LORD; though your sins be as scarlet, they shall be as white as snow; though they be red like crimson, they shall be as wool"* (Isaiah 1:18).

James amplified Solomon's warning about tomorrow: *"Go to now, ye that say, Today or tomorrow we will go into such a city, and continue there a year, and buy and sell, and get gain: Whereas ye know not what shall be on the morrow. For what is your life? It is even a vapour, that appeareth for a little time, and then vanisheth away. For that ye ought to say, If the Lord will, we shall live, and do this, or that"* (James 4:13-15).

So, we cannot be sure about tomorrow.

But we have today... right now.

Today to be aware of sin. Today to turn from sin to Christ. Today to believe... to receive Him.

Take Him now... before the vapour vanishes.

Receiving Christ today gives tomorrow its only certainty... salvation!

THE FATHER'S LOVE

MEMORY VERSE: *For the Father himself loveth you, because ye have loved me, and have believed that I came out from God* (John 16:27).

Billy Bray, who was known for his constant Christian joy, once had a very poor crop of potatoes. He said the devil came to taunt him about his small potatoes and to mock him for continually rejoicing in the Lord. But Billy was up to the confrontation, "There you go criticizing my Father again," said Billy. "Why, when I served you, I had not potatoes at all."

Billy had learned that discouraging experiences do not mean that our Heavenly Father loves us less. His love is unchanging. He loves with a Father's love. Paul wrote to his friends in Thessalonica about the comfort of knowing that the Father loves us: *"Now our Lord Jesus Christ himself, and God, even our Father, which hath loved us, and given us everlasting consolation and good hope through grace, comfort your hearts, and stablish you in every good word and work"* (2 Thessalonians 2:16,17).

If we should ever be tempted to doubt the Father's love, we can simply remember that He sent His Son to die for us. Every step of Jesus along the dusty roads of Palestine said: "The Father loves you!" Every lash of the cruel Roman whip in the scourging of Jesus said, "The Father loves you!" The shout of Jesus "It is finished!" as He completed His work of redemption on the cross was really a shout conveying that same wonderful message: "The Father loves you!"

Rest secure in the Father's love.

OUR FATHER

MEMORY VERSE: *Jesus saith unto him, I am the way, the truth, and the life: no man cometh unto the Father, but by me* (John 14:6).

Some teach that God the Father is the spiritual father of all people and that we are all His children. This is known as the Universal Fatherhood of God. It is a false teaching.

Jesus shocked the religious leaders of His day by calling them the children of the devil: *"Ye are of your father the devil, and the lusts of your father ye will do. He was a murderer from the beginning, and abode not in the truth, because there is no truth in him. When he speaketh a lie, he speaketh of his own: for he is a liar, and the father of it"* (John 8:44).

We become the children of the Heavenly Father through faith in His Son, the Lord Jesus Christ: *"But as many as received him, to them gave he power to become the sons of God, even to them that believe on his name"* (John 1: 12). The disciples were taught to pray: "Our Father which art in heaven, Hallowed be thy name."

As a result of the new birth, the Christian is a child of the Father. He has been born into the family of God. And all the family benefits belong to him.

Samuel Zwemer wrote: "I understand the loving fatherhood of God as Jesus taught it because I saw it in my own father." The tender and close relationship of a father to his child enables us to grasp something of the Heavenly Father's closeness to us.

I feel secure with my Father's hand in mine.

BURDENS AND BLESSINGS

MEMORY VERSE: *But the angel said unto him, Fear not, Zacharias: for thy prayer is heard; and thy wife Elisabeth shall bear thee a son, and thou shalt call his name John* (Luke 1:13).

Zacharias and Elisabeth were good people. Their reputations are preserved for us by Luke: *"And they were both righteous before God, walking in all the commandments and ordinances of the Lord blameless."* They must have had a wonderful life together. Still, they had one burden: they had no child because Elisabeth was barren.

We are all familiar with burdens. Some carry loads that are especially heavy. Burdens may concern any area of life. It is important to know what to do with them. Zacharias and Elisabeth prayed about their burden and though the answer was long in coming, their prayer was heard. Their burden drove them to their knees and therefore it became a blessing. Prayer may sometimes seem futile. There were probably times when Zacharias and Elisabeth joined their hearts in prayer for a child and found their faith small. Nevertheless, they kept praying and finally they were rewarded.

Zacharias was going about his regular duty when the angel appeared to let him know that Elisabeth would bear a son. Though he was burdened, he did not allow his concern to cripple him. He kept on working — serving the Lord — performing his daily tasks. We must not forget that God is still on the throne and that we are always to pray and not to faint. Fainting fails, but faith prevails.

The angelic message was difficult to accept. Zacharias was overwhelmed and asked for a sign that this experience was real, therefore he was stricken dumb until the miracle was completed. Remember that God is both faithful and able. Give your burdens to Him today.

THE WORD BECAME FLESH

MEMORY VERSE: *And the Word was made flesh, and dwelt among us (and we beheld his glory, the glory as of the only begotten of the Father) full of grace and truth* (John 1:14).

John the Baptist was the "voice." Jesus Christ is the Word. A word remains long after a voice is silent. It was that way with John and Jesus. John came to announce the coming of the Saviour, His purpose was to decrease as Christ increased. That is a good plan for life — self decreasing. Jesus increasing.

Christ did not have His beginning in Bethlehem's stable. When John began his Gospel by going back to the beginning, the Word was there: *"In the beginning was the Word, and the Word was with God, and the Word was God"* (John 1:1). When Christ returns to end the Battle of Armageddon and set up His Kingdom, He will be called "The Word of God." *"And I saw heaven opened. and behold a white horse; and he that sat upon him was called Faithful and True, and in righteousness he doth judge and make war. His eyes were as a flame of fire, and on his head were many crowns; and he had a name written, that no man knew, but he himself. And he was clothed with a vesture dipped in blood: and his name is called The Word of God"* (Rev. 19: 11-13).

Here, now, is the miracle of love: "The Word became flesh and dwelt among us." This is two-way grace. In His coming to dwell among us we caught a glimpse of His glory. The Father is revealed to us through the Son. Since He has dwelt among us, He knows our needs and understands our infirmities (Hebrews 4:15). In becoming flesh, He shared our sorrows. Because He became flesh, we can one day share His glory. Hallelujah!

YOUR LIFE STORY

MEMORY VERSE: *For we are his workmanship, created in Christ Jesus unto good works, which God hath before ordained that we should walk in them* (Ephesians 2:10).

Dr. Ironside was once approached by a lady who offered to tell his fortune. He replied that he had a book in his pocket that told her past, present, and future. Surprised, she asked what book that might be. He immediately produced a New Testament.

Our text presents the life story of any Christian. We were all dead in trespasses and sins before being born again and at that time lived under bondage to the lusts of the flesh. As Paul puts it, we "were by nature the children of wrath, even as others." Had it not been for the entrance of the love and grace of God, we would have been without hope.

The grace of God flows out of His love and offers completely unmerited favor. We deserve hell, but through His grace we gain heaven. We deserve to be eternally separated from God, but through His grace we will be with Him forever.

As wonderful as the grace of God is, it would be frustrated apart from the death of Christ on the cross as our substitute. Even grace could not provide another way of salvation. The songwriter was correct: "Grace Is Flowing From Calvary."

Those saved by grace are the workmanship of God, ordained to walk in good works. The purpose of our good works is given in Matthew 5:16: *"Let your light so shine before men, that they may see your good works, and glorify your Father which is in heaven."*

LIGHT AND SIGHT

MEMORY VERSE: *Blessed be the Lord God of Israel; for he hath visited and redeemed his people* (Luke 1:68).

A doctor approached an anxious father in the waiting room of a New York City hospital and informed him that his child had lived but two hours after birth. As the sympathetic doctor turned away, the quick-thinking father said, "I read only recently about the need of human eyes for corneal operations. Could my baby's eyes be used to enable someone to see again?"

The next day, two corneal transplants were performed in two different hospitals. In one, sight was restored to a working man with a large family. In the other, sight was given to a mother. A babe who had lived but two hours gave physical sight to two needy people.

Nearly two thousand years ago, a baby was born in a dark stable in Bethlehem. The prophet Isaiah had written of the impact of His birth as that of light and sight coming to a dark world: *"The people that walked in darkness have seen a great light"* (Isaiah 9:2).

Though His life was not long, the child born that night has imparted spiritual sight and insight to millions. The eloquent Phillips Brooks once said: "I am far within the mark when I say that all armies that ever marched, and all the navies that ever were built, and all the parliaments that ever sat, and all the kings that ever reigned, put together, have not affected the life of man upon this earth as powerfully as has that one solitary life — the life of Christ."

In his famous hymn *"O Little Town of Bethlehem,"* Brooks made it personal: "No ear may hear His coming, But in this world of sin, Where meek souls will receive Him still — The dear Christ enters in."

HIS NAME IS JOHN

MEMORY VERSE: *And his mouth was opened immediately, and his tongue loosed, and he spake, and praised God* (Luke 1:64).

John the Baptist was named twice. On the day of his circumcision in the temple he was named Zacharias, after the name of his father. That name could not stand, however, because his Heavenly Father had sent down another name. Elisabeth demanded that his name be John. Confused, those in the temple asked advice on the matter of Zacharias. He had been unable to speak since the angelic appearance in the temple and so he immediately called for a writing table and wrote: *"His name is John."* At that moment he was able to speak again.

Our names are important to God. The names of those who are born again are written in heaven. Jesus spoke of Himself as the good shepherd and said that He calls His own sheep by name. Your name echoed through heaven the day you were converted to Christ. You are special to the Lord.

John had a vital mission to fulfill. And nearly two thousand years following the completion of his ministry, his name continues to be remembered around the world. He was the forerunner of Christ. That is, he came to prepare the way for Jesus. His message was one of repentance and faith. He called sin by its first name and was fearless as a preacher. There were many important people in that day who must have thought they were making a lasting mark on the world. Still, we know very few of them. We remember John because of his association with Jesus and His work for the Lord. When you invest your life for Jesus you don't have to make a name for yourself.

IMMANUEL

MEMORY VERSE: *Therefore the Lord himself shall give you a sign; Behold a virgin shall conceive, and bear a son, and shall call his name Immanuel* (Isaiah 7:14).

Those who doubt the virgin birth of Christ are themselves a contradiction. They wrestle with the sign, yet often claim to accept the Saviour. There is no question but that the virgin birth required God's intervention, but the name Immanuel is given by Isaiah to show that the child to be born would be God robed in flesh. Immanuel means "God with us."

Do you have trouble believing the Bible account of the miracles surrounding the birth of Christ? Do the angelic appearances seem beyond the realm of reality? Do you doubt the experience of the shepherds and their encounter with the heavenly host? Does the journey of the wise men from the East seem too farfetched for you? If so, remember that this is the birth of Immanuel. God was in that stable. All doubts fade in the light of this great truth.

Now let us go a bit deeper. The moment you received Jesus Christ as your Lord and Saviour, you ceased being alone. He came into your life. This means God is with you. And here's good news for the future: He has promised "...I will never leave thee, nor forsake thee" (Hebrews 13:5). Rest on this wonderful promise and live each day in the assurance of His presence and care. You do not have to face any problem alone. "*...If God be for us, who can be against us*" (Romans 8:31).

Immanuel assures the child of God that all is well.

THE COMING KING

MEMORY VERSE: *And there shall come forth a rod out of the stem of Jesse, and a Branch shall grow out of his roots* (Isaiah 11:1).

Some who claim to be Christians do not like to think about the Jewish ancestry of Jesus. Somehow these double minded people are able to blot out the truth that, in His human line, Jesus came from the family of David. Often they blame the Jews for all the ills of the world.

The truth is that when Jesus returns to set up His earthly Kingdom, He will occupy the throne of David. That promise was given to Mary by the angel Gabriel: *"He shall be great, and shall be called the Son of the Highest; and the Lord God shall give onto him the throne of his father, David. And he shall reign over the house of Jacob forever; and of his kingdom there shall be no end"* (Luke 1:32-33).

The return of Christ is necessary to fulfill the prophecies concerning Him. Though the angels rejoiced at His birth in Bethlehem and spoke of peace on earth, the centuries since have been filled with war and wrong. The Prince of Peace was rejected and the world has blundered on in sin and violence. But a better day is coming.

When Christ comes to do on this earth what He now does in individual trusting hearts, the world will know real peace. It will be a great day. Justice and righteousness will cover the earth. The enmity between animals and men will be put away. Men will beat their swords into plowshares and their spears into pruning hooks. The angels' song will be fully realized. Until then, walk with Christ and experience

His peace in your heart.

ALL THINGS POSSIBLE

MEMORY VERSE: *For with God nothing shall be impossible* (Luke 1:37).

The birth of Jesus Christ was a miracle. Any attempt to understand it apart from that perspective is doomed to failure.

Some have tried to come up with a medical explanation of the virgin birth of Christ. These sincere people have searched the centuries for another example of a virgin with child, hoping to make the Christmas message more palatable to doubters. It is an impossible dream. Like the resurrection, the virgin birth of Christ required a miracle.

Others have focused on some bright star that might have been the one that guided the wise men to Bethlehem. But that conclusion disregards the Bible account. Try to get any known star to meet the requirements of Matthew 2:9: *"...and, lo, the star, which they saw in the east, went before them, till it came and stood over where the young child was."* That was a miracle!

We should not be surprised that the incarnation boggles the mind of man. Even Mary struggled with the angelic announcement that she would bear the Christ child. She asked: *"How shall this be, seeing I know not a man?"* Gabriel gave her the only answer that makes sense: *"For with God nothing shall be impossible."*

So, it is a miracle that we celebrate at Christmas — the incarnation of the Son of God. Let that thought capture your mind and warm your heart. It is the greatest love story ever told, the story of God's love for you and me. Those are not just "catchy" lyrics that announce: "JOY TO THE WORLD, THE LORD IS COME."

He has come!

For with God nothing is impossible.

GABRIEL'S MISSION

MEMORY VERSE: *And the angel said unto her, Fear not, Mary: for thou hast found favour with God* (Luke 1:30).

The prophets had foretold the coming of the Saviour and the world had waited. When prophetic voices ceased, some doubted. Suddenly the silence was broken. Angels were sent on missions of earth-shaking importance. John the Baptist would come, Christ would be born.

The angel Gabriel brought the announcement of the coming birth of Jesus to Mary, The first words of this messenger of God were: *"Hail, thou that art highly favoured."* Multitudes seek favor with God. The purpose of most religious ritual is to gain favor with God. Some give large gifts or afflict their bodies to gain favor with God, There is but one route to favor with God and that is the faith route: *"But without faith it is impossible to please him: for he that cometh to God, must believe that he is, and that he is a rewarder of them that diligently seek him"* (Hebrews 11:6).

Gabriel spoke to Mary's fears: *"Fear not, Mary..."* And then followed that assurance of favor again: *"...for thou hast found favour with God."* Fears will not flee unless we understand that in Christ we have favor with God. But once that wonderful position is assured, faith soars and fear can be overcome.

Mary's future was now explained. She would conceive in her womb and give birth to the Son of the Highest. He would sit upon the throne of His Father David. Mary's life would now be on a miracle basis. Her future was as bright as the promises of God. And this is true of all who place their faith in Him of Whom the angel spoke that day.

THE MAGNIFICAT

MEMORY VERSE: *And Mary said, My soul doth magnify the Lord* (Luke 1:46).

In response to Elisabeth's pronouncement of blessing, Mary's full heart overflowed with a song of praise. We have come to know her words as "The Magnificat."

Mary rejoiced that day in her personal Saviour: *"My spirit hath rejoiced in God my Saviour."* This is one of the great miracles in the story of Christ's birth. Often those of high spiritual privilege or of honored position do not realize their personal needs. Paul observed that truth and spoke of it to the Corinthians: *"For ye see your calling, brethren, how that not many wise men after the flesh, not many mighty, not many noble, are called"* (I Corinthians 1:26).

Having recently met with an angel who guaranteed her God's favor, it would have been human to glory in her spiritual attainment. Instead, Mary broke forth into a song of thanksgiving and praise. Only the humble can be truly thankful, and Mary's humility was evident as she poured out her heart before God: *"For he hath regarded the low estate of his handmaiden: for, behold, from henceforth all generations shall call me blessed"* (Luke 1:48). Her feelings toward her Lord were revealed as she praised Him for His might, His mercy, His grace and His goodness.

In concluding the Magnificat, Mary gave praise to God for His Word. She remembered His promises to Abraham and the other patriarchs of Israel. She gloried in the fact that God's Word is dependable. She had undoubtedly heard the promises of the coming Saviour all her life. Now she was assured of the fulfillment of that promise through the One who would be born of her.

The promises of God had become first-hand information: Mary's promises... and yours!

BLESSED BELIEVERS

MEMORY VERSE: *And blessed is she that believed, for there shall be a performance of those things which were told her from the Lord* (Luke 1:45).

Elisabeth, filled with the Holy Spirit, acknowledged Christ as her Lord before He was born. Mary had gone to the hill country of Judah to spend some time with Elisabeth who was there awaiting the birth of John. At Mary's greeting, the babe leaped in Elisabeth's womb and she began to magnify the Lord for what He was doing in Mary and for the coming Saviour. As she concluded her statement of praise she exclaimed: *"Blessed is she that believed."*

God always sends His blessings to believers. Some doubt their beliefs and others believe their doubts, but the blessings of God are for those who believe His Word. This truth was again made clear immediately following the resurrection of Christ. Thomas doubted that the Lord was risen since he missed the Lord's meeting with the disciples. At the next meeting, Thomas was present and Jesus invited him to place his fingers in the nail prints in His hands and to thrust his hand into the wound in His side. Ashamed of his unbelief and sure of the Saviour, Thomas cried, *"My Lord and My God."* Jesus responded, *"...Thomas, because thou hast seen me, thou hast believed: blessed are they that have not seen, and yet have believed"* (John 20:29).

Believers have the promise of answered prayer. Jesus said, *"If thou canst believe, all things are possible to him that believeth"* (Mark 9:23).

The final words of Elisabeth's Spirit-directed declaration have to do with receiving blessings. As a believer, Mary became a receiver. Those who dare to believe God for the impossible still receive His blessings in reward of their faith in Him.

THE FORERUNNER

MEMORY VERSE: The voice of him that crieth in the wilderness, Prepare ye the way of the LORD, make straight in the desert a highway for our God (Isaiah 40:3).

Sometimes we forget that there were two miraculous births. Though John the Baptist was not born of a virgin, his birth was miraculous in that it was a fulfillment of prophecy. John was sent by God to prepare the way of the LORD.

John is called a "voice." And what a voice he was. Multitudes came to hear him. Kings stood in his audience. He was fearless and faithful. His boldness cost him his head. But not until his work was finished.

It is important to notice that John came preparing the way of the LORD. Notice that all the letters in "LORD" are capitalized, showing that John came to prepare the way of Jehovah. Isaiah had no doubts about the deity of the coming Saviour. The Creator was coming to redeem His fallen creation. God would come to earth in flesh and die for sinners. The prophet would later write of Him: *"Surely he hath borne our griefs, and carried our sorrows: yet we did esteem him stricken, smitten of God, and afflicted. But he was wounded for our transgressions, he was bruised for our iniquities: the chastisement of our peace was upon him; and with his stripes we are healed"* (Isaiah 53:4-5).

The courageous "voice in the wilderness" gave his all in preparing hearts for the coming Saviour. Jesus gave His all on the cross for us.

How can we do less than give Him our best? Our lives reach their highest potential when they become "voices" for the LORD.

THE LIGHT OF THE WORLD

MEMORY VERSE: *In him was life; and the life was the light of men* (John 1:4).

An artist once drew a picture of a winter twilight — the trees heavily laden with snow and a dreary dark house, lonely and desolate, in the midst of the storm. It was a sad picture. Then with a quick stroke of yellow paint, he put a light in one window. The effect was magical. The entire scene was transformed into a vision of comfort and cheer. The birth of Christ was just such a light in a dark world.

How long the years of waiting must have seemed. The prophets had said that He would come. "He will be born of a virgin and will be the Prince of Peace," declared Isaiah. "The place of His birth will be Bethlehem," insisted Micah. And all the other inspired spokesmen added their voices until the birth and mission of the Saviour became the hope of the ages. Still, century rolled into century and Christ did not come.

Finally even the prophetic voices were stilled and inspired writing ceased. The voice of God was silent except as it was heard through the words already written. Darkness descended. Israel was ruled by Rome's iron hand. Hope was nearly gone.

Then, suddenly, all was changed. Angels were dispatched with urgent messages. The forerunner of Christ would be born. A virgin would give birth to One who would be called the "Son of the Highest." The Roman Empire became part of the miracle and taxed its citizens, sending Joseph and Mary to Bethlehem to fulfill the prophet's word. The heavenly host raised voices of highest praise. The hour the world had waited for had come. Christ was born.

The light that began shining that night dispels the darkness in every trusting heart. And yet some choose the night.

JOSEPH'S FEAR

MEMORY VERSE: *But while he thought on these things, behold, the angel of the Lord appeared unto him in a dream, saying, Joseph, thou son of David, fear not to take onto thee Mary thy wife: for that which is conceived in her is of the Holy Ghost* (Matthew 1:20).

Only one verse in the Bible is taken to tell about Joseph's discovery that his bride-to-be was with child, but the emotional trauma for this good man must have been devastating. His engagement to lovely Mary had undoubtedly set him to building dreams about their life together. Though a poor man, he was a carpenter and would be able to provide Mary many beautiful items made with his own hands. Then, all his world came crashing in on him. Mary was with child. There was no simple solution in such a case, but Joseph was a just and merciful man and so he decided that he would put her away as quietly as possible.

In Joseph's hour of trouble, an angel was sent to give him guidance. God often meets us in our times of trouble and fear. The angel's message was intensely personal. He called Joseph by name and then immediately went to the heart of his misery. *"Fear not,"* the angel said. Those good words seem always to be in the vocabulary of angels. Explaining the miracle that was happening in Mary, the heavenly agent advised Joseph to go ahead with the marriage and assured him that the child conceived in her was of the Holy Ghost.

What good news this was for Joseph! Beyond his expectations. The opposite of all his fears was true. What he had thought was the end of his dreams as a husband turned out to be the answer to his needs as a man. Joseph laid aside his fears and obeyed the Lord. And this is a good course for each one of us to follow.

THE NAME JESUS

MEMORY VERSE: *And she shall bring forth a son, and thou shalt call his name JESUS: for he shall save his people from their sins* (Matthew 1:21).

While Joseph, the carpenter was still reeling from the revelation that Mary was with child, an angel appeared to him and explained the miraculous coming birth of Christ. Months before, a similar announcement had been made to Mary: *"And, behold, thou shalt conceive in thy womb, and bring forth a son, and shalt call his name JESUS. He shall be great, and shall be called the Son of the Highest..."* (Luke 1:31,32).

There are many names in the Bible and in history that are of great and lasting significance. But none compare with the name JESUS. Moses seems to have originated the name when he changed the name of Oshea to Jehoshua (Joshua), the Hebrew form of the name Jesus meaning "God's salvation." Joshua was a type or picture of Jesus. He succeeded Moses as leader. The Bible says that the law was given by Moses but grace and truth came by Jesus Christ (John 1:17). Joshua led the wandering people from the wilderness to Canaan. Christ is the great deliverer from slavery and leads His own to freedom and purpose. Walls fell before Joshua. Christ has broken down the wall between Jews and Gentiles and all can be saved by faith (Ephesians 2:14). Joshua led his people across the Jordan to the promised land. Christ leads His people to the abundant life and finally to heaven.

That name meant salvation to the shepherds. It meant destruction to demons; cleansing to lepers; resurrections to the dead; and it brought hatred from the hypocrites. The name JESUS brings eternal life to those who trust the Saviour as their own today (Acts 4:12).

THE VIRGIN BIRTH

MEMORY VERSE: *Behold a virgin shall be with child, and shall bring forth a son, and they shall call his name Emmanuel, which being interpreted is, God is with us* (Matthew 1:23).

Belief in the virgin birth of Christ is a must if you accept the Bible as the Word of God. For centuries the prophets had been pointing toward the hour of the incarnation. Isaiah had written that the promised child would be born of a virgin (Isaiah 7:14). The New Testament writers agree. Matthew's quote of Isaiah's prophecy settles the matter.

The virgin birth of Christ is a miracle that must be accepted by faith. Some are always trying to find ways to make miracles understandable. These faithless ones seek for a shallow place in the Red Sea through which the children of Israel could have crossed; a whale that could have swallowed Jonah and kept him alive for three days; a spring beneath a rock for Moses to strike in order to give water to his people and a wooden axe head to float when Elisha need to aid the troubled prophet. Away with such folly! We have a God of miracles. And the virgin birth of Christ is one of those miracles.

The virgin birth of Christ is symbolic of the miracle of new birth that the Saviour will work in you if you come to Him and receive Him by faith. It is not enough to believe that Christ is capable of miracles. You can believe that and be lost. You can believe the historical facts about Jesus and be lost. But you can come to Him as a sinner and receive Him by faith and be saved. Be saved today.

BETHLEHEM

MEMORY VERSE: *But thou, Bethlehem Ephratah, though thou be little among the thousands of Judah, yet out of thee, shall he come forth unto me that is to be ruler in Israel, whose goings forth have been from of old, from everlasting* (Micah 5:2).

Great truths leap from this verse about Bethlehem. Though but a tiny village, Bethlehem would be the birthplace of the Messiah. The One born there would one day rule Israel. The birth in Bethlehem would be the incarnation of the Eternal God.

Why was Bethlehem chosen?

Bethlehem had been the birthplace of the son of sorrows. There Rachel gave birth to Jacob's son and called him "Benoni," meaning "son of my sorrow." Jesus would be the "man of sorrows."

Bethlehem was the home of Boaz, who took Ruth to be his wife. Ruth was widowed, poor, discouraged and broken-hearted. Nevertheless, Boaz loved her and had compassion for her. He redeemed her — paid her debts — and took her for his own. Jesus receives the broken and discouraged. It was said of Him: *"This man receiveth sinners."*

Bethlehem was the place of the anointing of David. As the anointed king, he finally took the kingdom from Saul, who had failed. Jesus will sit upon the throne of His father David and bring peace to the world when man has run his course of bloodshed, violence and failure.

Bethlehem was known as the "place of bread." Jesus said, *"...I am the bread of life: he that cometh to me shall never hunger; and he that believeth on me shall never thirst"* (John 6:35).

Bethlehem had a cool refreshing well. And all who come to Jesus find satisfaction for their thirsty souls.

No wonder Jesus was born in Bethlehem.

HIS MANY NAMES

MEMORY VERSE: *For unto us a child is born, unto us a son is given: and the government shall be upon his shoulder: and his name shall be called Wonderful, Counselor, The Mighty God, The Everlasting Father, The Prince of Peace* (Isaiah 9:6).

There are many names and titles given to Christ by the prophets.

The reason?

The language of man does not contain any one word to describe Him.

Jesus is wonderful. He was wonderful in His birth; in His life; in His death; in His resurrection. He is wonderful in His power to change lives today. He will be wonderful in His return for His own, when He resurrects the Christian dead and catches all the saints up to Himself. He will be wonderful in His kingdom on earth, when all wrongs are made right and all the earth is filled with peace and blessing.

Jesus is the greatest counselor known to man. He knows all about us. No problem is too difficult for Him and no appointment is needed to meet with Him. We can come to Him in every time of need. He has imparted more wisdom, lifted more burdens, dried more tears and shared more sorrows than all earth's counselors and philosophers combined.

Jesus is the Mighty God and the Everlasting Father. He combines omnipotence and compassion in meeting the needs of those who call upon Him. No wonder poets and composers fall short in their efforts to describe Him.

Jesus is the Prince of Peace. Peace — what a good word it is! Yet, millions seek it in vain at the bottom of a bottle, at the end of a needle, or in the accumulation of money and property. Peace is received through faith in the Prince of Peace. And that makes it available to you today.

HE HUMBLED HIMSELF

MEMORY VERSE: *And being found in fashion as a man, he humbled himself, and became obedient unto death, even the death of the cross* (Philippians 2:8).

Jesus humbled himself.

If we are to be like Him we will have to forsake the way of pride and choose humility.

He chose a stable instead of a palace.

He chose swaddling clothes instead of costly garments.

He chose a poor family instead of royalty.

He chose shepherds as His first visitors instead of princes.

He chose humble men to be his disciples instead of an honor guard.

He washed the feet of His disciples when they were arguing over who should be the greatest in the kingdom.

He chose the cross in order to purchase salvation for all who believe.

D. L. Moody said: "A man can counterfeit love, he can counterfeit faith, he can counterfeit hope and all the other graces, but it is very difficult to counterfeit humility. You soon detect mock humility. There is an old saying that as the tares and the wheat grow they show which God has blessed. The ears that God has blessed bow their heads and acknowledge every grain, and the more fruitful they are the lower their heads are bowed. The tares lift up their heads erect, high above the wheat, but they are only fruitful of evil. If we can get down low enough, God will use us to His glory."

Andrew Murray wrote: "Just as water seeks to fill the lowest places, so God fills you with His glory and power when He finds you empty and abased."

Let us get low enough for God to bless.

SIMEON'S SECRET

MEMORY VERSE: *And it was revealed unto him by the Holy Ghost, that he should not see death, before he had seen the Lord's Christ* (Luke 2:26).

Simeon had a secret. It was just between him and the Lord. The Holy Spirit had revealed something to him and he didn't tell a soul. He knew that he would not die until he had seen the Saviour.

When Joseph and Mary brought Jesus to the temple, Simeon knew that the promise of the ages had been fulfilled. Taking the babe in his arms, he blessed the Lord and said: *"Lord, now lettest they servant depart in peace, according to thy word: For mine eyes have seen thy salvation"* (Luke 2:29-30).

Some sacred secrets are locked away with God forever. No one can know the day or the hour of the Lord's second coming. Many have made the mistake of thinking they have figured out the Scriptures enough to pinpoint the hour of the Lord's return — only to be disappointed when that date has come and gone.

There is, however, Bible evidence that God does reveal some of His secrets to those who will walk close enough to Him. *"The secret of the LORD is with them that fear him; and he will show them his convenant"* (Psalm 25:14). The prophet Daniel said: *"But there is a God in heaven that revealeth secrets... "* (Daniel 2:28).

The information that we have about Simeon lets us know that he was *"...just and devout, waiting for the consolation of Israel: and the Holy Ghost was upon him"* (Luke 2:25). In other words, he was a man of faith and totally dedicated to the Lord. Those are requirements for receiving God's best. And that's no secret.

GLORY TO GOD IN THE HIGHEST

MEMORY VERSE: *Glory to God in the highest, and on earth peace, good will toward men* (Luke 2:14).

When Jesus came out of the ivory palaces into this world of woe, the world witnessed a miracle of grace and humility. And what great grace it was! The condescension of Christ defies understanding. The voice of the One Who had spoken the worlds into existence would now be limited to the vocal chords of an infant. The hands that had thrown planets into orbit would appear as a child's palms. The mind that contains all the wisdom of the universe would be packed into the brain of a human skull. And here we only touch the surface of salvation's story.

On the night of Christ's birth, the angelic message was given to shepherds who were urged to go and see the newborn Saviour. As soon as that first birth announcement was given, heaven's host began to praise God and say: *"Glory to God in the highest."*

"Glory to God" was not a new expression for the heavenly host. According to Job, the angels shouted God's praise in creation. But now there is a new dimension to this heavenly hallelujah: "GLORY TO GOD IN THE HIGHEST!" When God came down from heaven to save men, earth was introduced to heaven's highest glory. Higher in goodness God could not go. What lessons are here for us! Spurgeon said: "We must learn from this, that if salvation glorifies God, glorifies Him in the highest degree, then that doctrine which glorifies man in salvation cannot be the GOSPEL... for salvation glorifies God. Some preachers may delight to preach a gospel that glorifies man, but in their gospel the angels have not delight."

We glorify God most in sharing the message of salvation with others.

SINGING SHEPHERDS

MEMORY VERSE: *And the shepherds returned, glorifying and praising God for all the things that they had heard and seen, as it was told unto them* (Luke 2:20).

The shepherds who were notified of Christ's birth by the angelic messenger and who witnessed the heavenly concert of praise, lost no time in going to Bethlehem to see the Saviour for themselves. As a result of that journey, they became the first human missionaries: *"And when they had seen it, they made known abroad the saying which was told them concerning the child"* (Luke 2:17).

From that moment they became men on the move. Our last look at them finds them going out and returning giving praise to God for sending His Son into the world. Tending sheep would never be quite enough again. They had been entrusted with the most important message ever given to man and they were determined to share it.

The moving force in their lives is now the fact that Christ has come and that He is all that was promised. They have found enough in Him to fill their hearts. And that truth is vital if we are to be effective witnesses. No one can be a convincing representative for the Saviour until he finds Him sufficient for his own needs. If we give ourselves to complaining and griping over our lot in life and in our everyday experiences, we will be of little influence on others. Faultfinding Christians are poor ambassadors of the King. Sour citizens of heaven have little impact on citizens of earth.

The Lord has come! This is a day for rejoicing, a time to glorify and praise God as did the shepherds so long ago. And better still, a day to start a life of praise that lasts throughout the year.

ANNA'S ADORATION

MEMORY VERSE: *And she coming in that instant gave thanks likewise onto the Lord, and spake of him all them that looked for redemption in Jerusalem* (Luke 2:38).

God has many wonderful old people. Anna the prophetess was a widow and well up in years. She gave all her time to serving the Lord. Prayers ascended from her heart to God night and day. Only eternity will reveal the value of fervent prayer. James has written that it "avails much" and so it is likely that many surprises await us when we discover how much of the work of God has been accomplished through prayer. The church is fortunate that has senior citizens who have gone far in the college of prayer, The pastor who is upheld in the closets of older saints will be sure to be a blessing in his church.

Anna recognized Jesus as the Saviour the moment she saw Him, though He was but a babe. That very instant she began to thank God for His goodness in sending her Lord. Not only that, she began to witness. Knowing many who were concerned about the Redeemer, she set out to let them know that He had come.

When some reach the age of Anna, they settle back and wait for life to end. A searching of the Scriptures will reveal that God has often made the later years of people their most productive. Moses was eighty years old when he was called by God to serve. Caleb and Joshua were older men when conquering Canaan. Whatever your age you have today to live and be a blessing. That may be as much as others much younger. Get busy for the Lord this very day.

WISE MEN STILL SEEK HIM

MEMORY VERSE: *Now when Jesus was born in Bethlehem of Judaea in the days of Herod the king, behold, there came wise men from the east to Jerusalem* (Matthew 2:1).

The wise men who came from the east to worship Jesus are the most mysterious of all the characters connected with the Christmas account. We know little about them.

We do not know how many wise men there were. Though tradition calls for three wise men because of their gifts of gold, frankincense, and myrrh, the Bible simply says: *"There came wise men from the east to Jerusalem. "*

No one knows exactly when the wise men began their journey. It may have been as long as two years before their arrival in Jerusalem. A clue is found in Herod's slaughter of all children under two years of age, an action that was prompted by his conversation with the wise men. Neither do we know when they arrived in Bethlehem, though it was not while Jesus was in the stable. Matthew says they came into the *house*.

Where did they come from? Nobody knows. We are only sure that it was east of Jerusalem. Perhaps the most interesting idea is the one that locates the home of the wise men in the area once occupied by the ancient Babylonian empire where the prophet, Daniel, had once been in captivity. This view has the wise men coming to find the King of the Jews as a result of studying the writings of Daniel, who had been held in high esteem there.

Were they kings? Probably not. At least there is no Bible support for that theory.

Beyond all the speculation one fact remains. Wise men still seek Him!

GUIDANCE AND GIFTS

MEMORY VERSE: *And when they were come into the house, they saw the young child with Mary his mother, and fell down, and worshipped him: and when they had opened their treasures, they presented unto him gifts; gold, and frankincense, and myrrh* (Matthew 2:11).

The star that guided the wise men on their journey is one of the great miracles surrounding the birth of Christ. There is no question but that this was a one-time, supernatural heavenly light that led the wise men on their long journey. Only once did they get off the path to their destination and that was when they trusted tradition instead of the guidance of God. Arriving in the general area, they went to the king's palace instead of continuing on their guided way. They evidently expected the King to be at the home of the king and therefore abandoned the heavenly light. We're all prone to that trap — trusting our own judgment instead of the guidance of God. It was their Bible that finally set them straight and brought them back to the star and finally to Jesus.

When the wise men reached the Saviour, they humbly worshipped Him and opened their treasures to Him. Their gifts were fitting. Gold would speak to future generations of His royalty; frankincense would typify His priestly work as an intercessor; and myrrh would remind the world of His suffering on the cross. The Gospel is found in the gifts of the wise men.

Jesus is deserving of our treasures. We will do well to give Him our best. In the light of eternity, it's the only wise thing to do.

THE WARNINGS OF GOD

MEMORY VERSE: *And being warned of God in a dream that they should not return to Herod, they departed into their own country another way* (Matthew 2:12).

In describing Herod's effort to destroy Jesus, DeWitt Talmadge wrote: "In a sense it was the narrowest and most wonderful escape of the ages that the child was not slain before he had taken his first step or spoken his first word. Herod could not afford to have him born. The great oppressions and abominations of the world could not afford to have him born. 'Put him to death!' was the order all up and down Palestine," BUT THAT ORDER WAS NEVER CARRIED OUT, though hundreds of infants died in Herod's wicked slaughter. Both the wise men and Joseph were warned by God of danger to the child and their action caused Herod's plan to fail. God often warns us through His Word today.

God's warnings are to change the direction of our lives. The wise men departed into their own country another way. That move of obedience likely spared their lives as well as that of Jesus. If God has warned you about sin or disobedience through the reading of His Word, change the direction of your life.

God's warnings are to deliver us from the destroyer. Herod was but the human instrument. Satan is the destroyer. It was his plan that Jesus came to thwart. He is the killer who stalks the human race, the enemy of God and man. Heed the warnings of God's Word and enjoy abundant life instead of yielding to the tempter, the destroyer.

God's warnings are to bring our lives into the design of His Word. Joseph and Mary took Jesus as directed to fulfill the Scriptures. Obey the warnings of God so that your life will be blessed, conformed to the design of His Word.

HERBS AND LOVE

MEMORY VERSE: *Better is a dinner of herbs where love is, than a stalled ox and hatred therewith* (Proverbs 15:17).

When the choice is love or money... take love.

The Bible gives a wonderful pattern for the home. A loving husband cares for his responsive wife and they together picture the walk that Christ has with His church. The picture is distorted when love is not present. When hatred replaces love, everything is out of focus.

Sometimes love is lost in the mad race for success and worldly possessions. Solomon warns that a stalled ox, ready for steaks or the plow, is no substitute for love. Love with herbs is better than steak with hate.

Love ought to be expressed with regularity. But how does one express love? Here's the Bible way: *"Charity suffereth long, and is kind; charity envieth not; charity vaunteth not itself, is not puffed up, doth not behave itself unseemly, seeketh not her own, is not easily provoked, thinketh no evil; rejoiceth not in iniquity, but rejoiceth in the truth; beareth all things, believeth all things, hopeth all things, endureth all things"* (I Corinthians 13:4-7).

The building of love in a home ought to receive more effort than earning a living. Fat paychecks can contribute to a bankrupt home if earnings have priority over time together.

Opportunities for expressing affection must be seized when they appear. How many escaped yesterday?

And there are many ways to say "I love you."

How long has it been since you communicated your love?

Do so today. It's the Bible way to live!

ALMOST

MEMORY VERSE: *Then Agrippa said unto Paul, Almost thou persuadest me to be a Christian* (Acts 26:28).

Paul was in bonds.

King Agrippa was in bondage.

Paul was a prisoner of Rome.

King Agrippa was a prisoner of sin.

Paul was innocent before the earthly judge.

King Agrippa was guilty before the Judge of all the earth.

Paul was certain about salvation.

King Agrippa came close but retreated into unbelief.

Paul offered the king eternal life.

King Agrippa declined.

Paul left his meeting with King Agrippa unharmed.

King Agrippa left his meeting with Paul unhelped.

All the world is divided as were Paul and King Agrippa that day. Some are sure of heaven and are building their lives around eternal things...laying up treasures in heaven where they shall go when their journey is over. Others are so taken with the passing honors and treasures of this world that they are blind to the issues of life that really matter.

Paul or King Agrippa...which are you?

Are you almost a Christian?

Almost being a Christian is like almost being alive.

Come to Christ and receive Him by faith.

Be an altogether Christian.

It's the only way to get life all together.